THE EVOLUTION OF MODERN GRAND STRATEGIC THOUGHT

The Evolution of Modern Grand Strategic Thought

LUKAS MILEVSKI

OXFORD
UNIVERSITY PRESS

OXFORD
UNIVERSITY PRESS

Great Clarendon Street, Oxford, OX2 6DP,
United Kingdom

Oxford University Press is a department of the University of Oxford.
It furthers the University's objective of excellence in research, scholarship,
and education by publishing worldwide. Oxford is a registered trade mark of
Oxford University Press in the UK and in certain other countries

© Lukas Milevski 2016

The moral rights of the author have been asserted

First Edition published in 2016

Impression: 2

All rights reserved. No part of this publication may be reproduced, stored in
a retrieval system, or transmitted, in any form or by any means, without the
prior permission in writing of Oxford University Press, or as expressly permitted
by law, by licence or under terms agreed with the appropriate reprographics
rights organization. Enquiries concerning reproduction outside the scope of the
above should be sent to the Rights Department, Oxford University Press, at the
address above

You must not circulate this work in any other form
and you must impose this same condition on any acquirer

Published in the United States of America by Oxford University Press
198 Madison Avenue, New York, NY 10016, United States of America

British Library Cataloguing in Publication Data

Data available

Library of Congress Control Number: 2015956033

ISBN 978-0-19-877977-3

Printed in Great Britain by
Clays Ltd, St Ives plc

Links to third party websites are provided by Oxford in good faith and
for information only. Oxford disclaims any responsibility for the materials
contained in any third party website referenced in this work.

Maniem vecākiem,
Sandrai Milevskai un Robertam Milevskim

Preface

This history of the evolution of grand strategic thought began as my PhD dissertation, which I started researching in 2011 at the University of Reading. I began the project believing I knew what grand strategy was and how I would use the concept. By March 2012, I had come to the realization that there were simply too many distinct and even mutually contradictory definitions of grand strategy simply to 'use' grand strategy as a conceptual basis for analysis. I would have needed not only to explain why I chose whichever definition I might prefer, but also why I did *not* choose all the others. As I gradually saw the anticipated portion of my PhD which dealt with other definitions increase relative to my own use of the concept, I abandoned that latter section as an academic bridge too far. After all, how could one use grand strategy in a productive manner if one's choice of definition among the many in use was, ultimately, nearly entirely arbitrary? I began asking myself how strategic studies had reached a point where grand strategy had attained so many different meanings and thereby lost all real meaning. Thus was born the dissertation which I completed, submitted, and defended in 2014 and which, with substantial revisions, is now in the reader's hands.

Researching and writing a book—especially a first book—is an expensive undertaking. I would like to thank the University of Reading, whose three-year Social Sciences Research Studentship provided the greatest support in this regard. The John F. Kennedy Library Foundation was kind enough to extend a Research Grant to me, allowing me to conduct research at the Kennedy Library. The IJ Group, publisher of *Infinity Journal* and the *Journal of Military Operations*, also supported my archival research at a crucial early stage. I must also thank the Latvian Embassy in Washington, DC, for providing me with accommodation as I conducted research in that city.

I am also grateful to the archives and special collections whose material I have cited—the John F. Kennedy Presidential Library in Boston, MA; the Richard M. Nixon Presidential Library in Yorba Linda, CA; the Department of Special Collections of the Charles E. Young Research Library at the University of California, Los Angeles; the Caird Archive and Library at the National Maritime Museum in London; the Seeley G. Mudd Manuscript Library at Princeton University; the Liddell Hart Centre for Military Archives at King's College London; the Manuscript Division at the Library of Congress; and finally the National Archives and Records Administration in both Washington, DC, and College Park, MD—as well as to the hospitality of those libraries whose material did not ultimately make it into this final product—including special collections at the Alexander Library at Rutgers University in New Brunswick, NJ, special collections at the Sheridan Library at Johns Hopkins University in Baltimore, MD, and the library at the US Army Heritage and Educational Center in Carlisle, PA. My usage of archival material mostly falls under fair use or is in the public domain, but the Trustees of the Liddell Hart Centre for Military Archives kindly allowed me to use material from their holdings.

Three years provide a lot of time for a young researcher to stray off the path of the sensible and the realistic. I must therefore thank my supervisors, Colin S. Gray and Patrick H. Porter, for benignly watching over and occasionally correcting the research avenues I was treading. I also would like to thank Beatrice Heuser for the initial impetus of inviting me to return to the University of Reading to commence my doctoral work, an invitation which ultimately resulted in this book. My comrade in studies Peter Randall often provided useful insight and even the odd but eye-opening bit of historical evidence, usually accidentally discovered. Birte Julia Gippert contributed significantly to my social life during this project despite my nearly monomaniacal focus on research, thereby instilling some slight balance to my life. Last but not least, my parents, Sandra and Robert Milevski, were wholly supportive throughout my work and provided vital moral and occasionally logistical support throughout the whole endeavour as I became the first holder of a Ph.D. in my family.

Lukas Milevski

Oxford, Great Britain
September 2015

Contents

Introduction: Or the Incomplete History of Grand Strategic Thought   1

Part I: Early Grand Strategic Thought (1805–1945)

1. Pre-Modern Grand Strategic Thought   15
2. The Maritime Origins of Modern Grand Strategic Thought   27
3. Grand Strategy in British Reactions to the World Wars   45
4. Grand Strategy in American Reactions to the World Wars   61

Part II: The Fall and Rise of Grand Strategy (1945–2015)

5. Cold War Strategic Thought and Grand Strategy   83
6. Grand Strategic Thought Eclipsed   97
7. The Re-emergence of Grand Strategic Thought   108
8. Post-Cold War Grand Strategic Thought   127
    Conclusion: Or Thinking Theoretically about Grand Strategy   143

Bibliography   155
Index   171

Introduction

Or the Incomplete History of Grand Strategic Thought

In both strategic studies and international relations grand strategy is a staple concept, long considered to have merit or even to be vital. Unfortunately, its promise does not seem to have been borne out. The modern literature on grand strategy, emanating from multiple disciplines, does not adhere to a single overarching understanding of the term, which is frequently invoked without any definition at all. The result is discussions which 'muddle or obscure more than they illuminate'.[1] This is of particular concern within strategic studies, whose interdisciplinary character enables confusion among competing and sometimes mutually exclusive notions of grand strategy. This situation contrasts with the military-focused strategic studies understanding of strategy, whose differing definitions offer only disparate perspectives on a single phenomenon, rather than incompatible or unique phenomena altogether.

The major modern interpretations of grand strategy to which scholars most frequently refer include those of an assortment of historians, strategists, and political scientists—Paul Kennedy, John Lewis Gaddis, Edward Luttwak, Barry Posen, and Robert Art. A sixth interpretation of grand strategy effectively views it as the ideology fuelling state action. These definitions determine the situation today; display a wide range of meaning, of conceptual purpose, and of theoretical function; and differ not only among disciplines but also within single disciplines.

Art's offering is the narrowest of all, as he states that grand strategy 'concentrates on how the military instrument can best be used to support foreign policy goals'.[2] Posen describes grand strategy as 'a political-military, means-end chain, a state's theory about how it can best "cause" security for

---

[1] Hal Brands, *The Promise and Pitfalls of Grand Strategy* (Carlisle: Strategic Studies Institute, 2012), 1.
[2] Robert J. Art, *America's Grand Strategy and World Politics* (London: Routledge, 2009), 1.

itself'.[3] Gaddis posits that grand strategy 'is the calculated relationship of means to large ends'.[4] Luttwak asserts that grand strategy is at 'the level of final results. This is also the everyday form of strategy, because the dynamic workings of the paradoxical logic are constantly present in international politics, even when war in any form is only a highly theoretical possibility.'[5] Kennedy has suggested that grand strategy is 'about the evolution and integration of policies that should operate for decades, or even centuries'.[6] One common final interpretation stipulates that grand strategy acts as a framework for foreign policy or at the level of fundamental assumptions: 'Without the guidance of a unified grand strategy, the state's policies will, by necessity, manifest ad hoc behaviours when policymakers respond to various threats.'[7]

These modern definitions are certainly not equivalent in meaning and may even be contradictory; for example, security today may require mortgaging the future in a manner which an analysis focused on surviving the end of the century might not imagine or accept. They do not even describe a single level of analysis, as the enormous range of levels of activity between what is effectively military strategy at one end and ideological assumptions at the other attests.

A more important question is whether any of these definitions is actually strategic while also usefully distinct from either military strategy or policy. Hew Strachan has argued that the twentieth-century development of grand strategy, particularly during the Cold War, contributed to diluting the meaning of strategy, an unfortunate result given that '[s]trategy is about war and its conduct, and if we abandon it we surrender the tool that helps us to define war, to shape it and to understand it'.[8] The question of whether grand strategy actually is or is not strategic has significant import as war and armed conflict are generally inevitable. Much of grand strategic thinking today, particularly in the United States, now tends to be ideological rather than strategic.[9] The literature focuses on how the United States should interact with the rest of the world, to be neo-isolationist, or primacist, or to engage selectively, or to

---

[3] Barry R. Posen, *The Sources of Military Doctrine: France, Britain, and Germany between the World Wars* (Ithaca, NY: Cornell UP, 1984), 13.

[4] John Lewis Gaddis, 'What is Grand Strategy?' American Grand Strategy After War (26 Feb. 2009, Triangle Institute for Security Studies and Duke University Program on American Grand Strategy, unpublished), 7.

[5] Edward N. Luttwak, *Strategy: The Logic of War and Peace* (Cambridge, MA: Belknap Press of Harvard UP, 2001), 207.

[6] Paul Kennedy, 'Grand Strategy in War and Peace: Toward a Broader Definition', in Paul M. Kennedy (ed.), *Grand Strategies in War and Peace* (New Haven: Yale UP, 1991), 4.

[7] William C. Martel, 'Grand Strategy of "Restrainment"', *Orbis*, 54/3 (Summer 2010), 358.

[8] Hew Strachan, 'The Lost Meaning of Strategy', *Survival*, 47/3 (July 2005), 48.

[9] Adam Elkus, 'Must American Strategy Be Grand?', *Infinity Journal*, 3/1 (Winter 2012), 24–8.

cooperate internationally for security.[10] Yet this is all without reference to any particular end to be achieved. Much of what presently passes for grand strategic thought concerns doctrine and modes of engagement for their own sake.

As a result certain authors have described grand strategy not only as unimportant, but even as a publicity exercise for academics.[11] Other commentators have actually celebrated grand strategy's lack of definition. One review essayist argued of a recent book on grand strategy that '[p]art of the beauty of the book is that Hill never defines precisely the concept of "grand strategy"'.[12] How an analytical tool can have any worth without actual definition is not explained. Still other academics consider the idea of grand strategy itself, or at least certain interpretations of it, unhelpful. Marc Trachtenberg has suggested that

> one of the main problems with the idea of grand strategy is that it places a premium on a certain kind of intellectualizing. It is never enough just to call for a particular course of action; one has to justify the strategy by rooting it in a certain theory about what is at the bottom of international politics, or at least what is at the heart of the situation one is trying to deal with. Since the strategy needs to be simple and all-encompassing, there is a tendency for the theory to be framed in rather grandiose terms—that is, for the theory to overdefine or to misdefine the problem, and in any case to misdirect attention away from the real issues that policy should focus on.[13]

It is apparent that grand strategy is a contentious idea at all levels, from theoretical meaning to its actual utility as a concept and analytical tool. The current scattershot state of grand strategic thought violates the fundamental purposes of theory—clarification and communication.[14] Modern grand strategy has achieved the opposite, given that the same term may be used to describe significantly different activities, considerations, or attitudes and that some authors even feel that definition is counterproductive. A concept lacking definition cannot logically be a useful analytical instrument. 'Words convey concepts: if they are not defined, the thinking about them cannot be clear, and there is also danger that one person's military strategy is another's policy, just as one person's naval strategy is another person's maritime strategy.'[15] Or, in

---

[10] One early review of the literature is Barry R. Posen and Andrew L. Ross, 'Competing Visions for U.S. Grand Strategy', *International Security*, 21/3 (Winter 1996–7), 5–53.

[11] Daniel W. Drezner, 'Does Obama Have a Grand Strategy? Why We Need Doctrines in Uncertain Times', *Foreign Affairs*, 90/4 (July/Aug. 2011), 59–61.

[12] Braz Baracuhy, 'The Art of Grand Strategy', *Survival*, 53/1 (Feb.–Mar. 2011), 151.

[13] Marc Trachtenberg, 'Making Grand Strategy: The Early Cold War Experience in Retrospect', *SAIS Review*, 19/1 (Winter/Spring 1999), 36.

[14] See Carl von Clausewitz, *On War*, ed. and tr. Michael Howard and Peter Paret (Princeton: Princeton UP, 1984), 132; also Julian S. Corbett, *Some Principles of Maritime Strategy* (Annapolis, MD: Naval Institute Press, 1988), 4.

[15] Hew Strachan, *The Direction of War: Contemporary Strategy in Historical Perspective* (Cambridge: CUP, 2013), 151.

the case of grand strategy, one person's grand strategy is not another's, nor yet another's.

THE INCOMPLETE HISTORY OF GRAND STRATEGIC THOUGHT

The current confusing state of the grand strategic literature has necessarily evolved out of the grand strategic literature of the past, in combination with other strategic (and, in some cases, international relations) literature. This evolution is historically verifiable, yet the history of grand strategic thought has been incomplete and unstudied. The current state of our understanding of the history of grand strategic thought draws on three strands of received belief about that history: first, that grand strategy was a concept invented by Basil Liddell Hart; second, that Liddell Hart developed the *modern* interpretation of grand strategy; and third, that grand strategy as presently understood is a recent invention.

The notion that Liddell Hart invented grand strategy is a simple and popular one. It is generally assumed that no concept of grand strategy existed prior to Liddell Hart's discussion of it in 1929 in *The Decisive Wars of History*. That is factually incorrect. At this point, it suffices to indicate that John Frederick Charles Fuller was developing his own interpretation of the concept as early as 1923, in *The Reformation of War*, where he dedicated an entire chapter to it and defined it as 'the utilization of the national energies for purposes of war'.[16] Moreover, some contemporaries of both Fuller and Liddell Hart seemed to discount, or were unaware of, their ideas on grand strategy. Halford Mackinder, for instance, considered it to be an American idea.[17]

This leads directly to a second presumed strand, that Liddell Hart, although he did not invent the concept itself, was the first to develop it in a recognizable modern form. According to this belief, Liddell Hart's contribution, together with Edward Mead Earle, was to shape decisively the trajectory that the further evolution of grand strategy would take. Some scholars have pointed to Earle as a more important figure for the development of grand strategic thought than Liddell Hart.[18] The individual or combined contributions of Liddell Hart and Earle, however, are commonly considered to have defined what grand strategy

---

[16] J. F. C. Fuller, *The Reformation of War* (London: Hutchinson & Co., 1923), 68.

[17] Halford J. Mackinder, 'The Round World and the Winning of the Peace', *Foreign Affairs*, 21/4 (July 1943), 603.

[18] Williamson Murray, 'Thoughts on Grand Strategy', in Williamson Murray, Richard Hart Sinnreich, and James Lacey (eds), *The Shaping of Grand Strategy: Policy, Diplomacy, and War* (Cambridge: CUP, 2011), 7.

ought to be and, indeed, they are the only two theorists ever mentioned in standard historic overviews of grand strategic thought.

The validity of this strand is arguable, for it depends on what one considers the defining features of modern grand strategic thought to be. There are differing interpretations. Colin Gray suggests that '[i]f the concept of grand strategy is to have intellectual integrity it has to admit a necessary connection to military force as a, not the only, defining characteristic'.[19] Yet if this suggestion is accepted, neither Liddell Hart nor Earle, nor even Fuller, founded the modern concept of grand strategy, but rather Julian Corbett, who seems to have been the first to define grand strategy in a manner that accounted for non-military instruments. Fuller was the first to define grand strategy as a peacetime activity, and exclusively so.[20] Earle was apparently the first to elevate grand strategy above the level of policy.[21] Thus the second strand may have some truth to it, but only according to one's own interpretation of the necessarily modern features of grand strategic thought, which the incomplete history currently oversimplifies.

The final presumed strand is that the present interpretation of grand strategy is a product of recent scholarship. Kennedy's explicit aim in 1990 was, of course, to provide a new, and broader, definition of grand strategy.[22] As with the second strand, however, the veracity of the third strand depends on what one considers to be the defining features of present grand strategic thought. Grand strategy as a framework for foreign policy, as ideological assumptions, is certainly a development largely enabled by the Cold War. Yet the definitions of grand strategy most frequently drawn upon by current scholars of grand strategy to underpin their own idiosyncratic interpretations were propounded before the advent of the Cold War.

These conclusions are based on three factors, the first being incomplete research. Only two historical theorists of grand strategy are highlighted in the literature, and one of them only sporadically. These two are the British interwar strategic theorist Basil Liddell Hart and the American wartime theorist Edward Mead Earle, the latter of whom is mentioned only occasionally. This scanty historical perspective ignores the writings of Julian Corbett, who was the first to use grand strategy seriously in a manner which is identifiably modern, as well as the writings of J. F. C. Fuller, Liddell Hart's older contemporary who had a large influence on him. Considerable portions of the actual history of grand strategic thought have universally tended to be obscure, but Corbett and Fuller at least should have been noticed. The research

---

[19] Colin S. Gray, *The Strategy Bridge: Theory for Practice* (Oxford: OUP, 2010), 114.
[20] Fuller, *Reformation of War*, 220.
[21] Edward Mead Earle, 'Introduction', in Edward Mead Earle (ed.), *Makers of Modern Strategy: Military Thought from Machiavelli to Hitler* (New York: Atheneum 1966), p. viii.
[22] Kennedy, 'Toward a Broader Definition', 1–7.

is incomplete in part because no one has previously studied the actual history of grand strategic thought in its full depth. Existing studies may also misrepresent the history of grand strategic thought by assuming a particular definition of grand strategy and then cherry-picking writers to convey that interpretation. This may lead to anachronistic reliance on authoritative historical figures who could never have had any knowledge of grand strategy, such as the political philosophers Thomas Hobbes, John Locke, and Immanuel Kant.[23]

The second major factor is the false assumption that there is only one historical tradition of grand strategic thought into which both Liddell Hart and Earle fit. This is hardly the case. They wrote about grand strategy at slightly different times (1925–9 versus 1941–2), but in significantly different geopolitical, strategic, and historical contexts from which each drew differing lessons. Once one includes Corbett and Fuller, as well as a number of other authors on grand strategy including the modern theorists, the impact of context in all its forms becomes apparent. Geopolitical and strategic concerns, history and its identified lessons, and the intellectual landscape itself of strategic studies have all significantly influenced theorists' personal interpretations of grand strategy, of its purpose, its ideational content, and its conceptual limits. There exists not one evolving tradition of grand strategic thought, but numerous ones.

The third factor is a product of the first two. There is an implicit teleological assumption that the conceptual state and theoretical location of grand strategic thought is correct for the concept. Liddell Hart and Earle are emphasized because they allegedly contributed to the expansion of the meaning of grand strategy, which is assumed to be appropriate. Not only is this assumption unexamined, but it may lead to faulty history. The majority of historical grand strategic thought is not only neglected, but other factors which contributed to the current state of grand strategy (such as its geopolitical context or other concepts within strategic studies) are neglected as well. This teleological assumption ignores how conceptual and contextual contingency shaped the meaning of the term. The expansion of grand strategy was as much, if not more, an accident of history as it was a deliberate attempt by numerous theorists, most of whom were modern rather than historical theorists, to broaden the concept purely for the sake of breadth. By implication, this teleological assumption also pretends that basic equivalence exists in current usages of grand strategy, which is hardly the case.

Thus the basic understanding of the history of grand strategic thought that underpins the current grand strategic literature actually misrepresents that history. By designating Liddell Hart the beginning of (modern) grand strategic

---

[23] The notable example is William C. Martel, *Grand Strategy in Theory and Practice: The Need for an Effective American Foreign Policy* (New York: CUP, 2015), chs 3–6.

thought, scholars of grand strategy have avoided a number of hard questions concerning the content of the idea of grand strategy, both currently and historically. These questions concern the unexamined assumptions that make up not just modern grand strategic thought, but also the evolution of the idea in its entirety.

The meaning of modern grand strategy consists of a number of specific building blocks, and each to some extent may be identified with the particular theorist who first introduced it. Yet, although each addition is comprehensible with regards to the given geopolitical context, the new building blocks were never justified theoretically. Each individual theorist merely assumed that his expansion of the idea was legitimate and useful, leaving the assumption unexamined. By eschewing most of the actual history of grand strategic thought, these individual contributions are misrepresented not only as all being developed by only Liddell Hart or Earle, but also as being fundamental to the very idea of grand strategy rather than being in fact significant deviations from previously or concurrently understood concepts of grand strategy in their own right.

Does the current jumble of ideas called grand strategy require reconsideration? Arguably yes. Existing grand strategic theory does not clarify it, nor is it easily communicable. Theory means little unless it informs practice, but an unclear mass of somewhat incommunicable ideas stands a lower chance of exerting influence. There will always be discrepancies among fundamental definitions, yet they can surely be reduced to emphasizing different facets of one topic rather than designating entirely different phenomena as grand strategy.

Exploring the full history of grand strategy, both in its concepts and in its history of practice (i.e. practice as if influenced by those concepts), is a necessarily multi-stage endeavour which is beyond the scope of a single work. The first stage is simply to uncover the actual evolution of grand strategic thought, and the complexity and variety of views, definitions, and interpretations therein. It is a chronicle of the changes in the meaning of grand strategy over time. Bernard Brodie rightly noted that

> if we examine the history of ideas contained in these convictions, we usually find they have evolved in a definitely traceable way, often as the result of the contributions of gifted persons who addressed themselves to the needs of their own times on the basis of the experience available to them. Our own needs and experience being different, we are enabled by our study to glimpse the arbitrariness of views which we previously regarded as laws of nature and our freedom to alter our thinking is thereby expanded. Where new circumstances require fundamental adjustments to our thinking, such aids to adjustment may be useful.[24]

---

[24] Bernard Brodie, *Strategy in the Missile Age* (Princeton: Princeton UP, 1959), 19.

The approach required for this endeavour is conceptual history, a methodology developed, amongst others, by Reinhart Koselleck.[25] Conceptual history traces the semiological or semantic evolution of terms over time, with regard to their specific—usually social—historical context. Rather than social history, the backdrop for this study of 'grand strategy' will be strategic history, the history of war and other defence concerns to which theorists hoped to apply their grand strategic ideas. The successive concepts of grand strategy themselves are explored, their functions mapped, and their ideational limits delineated—they each occupy a certain conceptual space in strategic studies.

Koselleck perceived in semantic history the phenomenon of diachronity—that '[s]ocial history and conceptual history have different speeds of transformation and are based in distinguishable structures of repetition'.[26] This premise assumes that society and concept are each unitary. This is not the case with grand strategy in either concept or context. For example, because during the interwar period grand strategy meant different things in Great Britain and the United States, the semantic study of grand strategy requires studying at least two, if not more, sets of diachronic concept–context relations. Grand strategic interpretations evolve at different speeds towards different meanings in different historical and strategic contexts, as developed by different authors who applied their idea of grand strategy to different tasks and problems.

This semantic approach to grand strategic thought differs significantly from most, if not all, other studies of the history of (non-grand) strategic thought, such as Heuser's history of strategy of 2010 or Freedman's of 2013.[27] These studies are onomasiological in character, emphasizing the core function of strategy and examining how it has been described and discussed over time. The purpose of taking the opposite, semantic or semiological, approach is to illustrate how 'grand strategy' never referred to a single concept or even necessarily described a single function. Thus an onomasiological examination of grand strategy is actually impossible without making semi-arbitrary assumptions about the true meaning of the concept, and then either ignoring inconvenient diverging usages of grand strategy or somehow fitting them into one's own meaning.

However, the approach cannot be exclusively semantic/semiological, as this would lead to an incomplete history of the evolution of grand strategic thought. Specifically, while it would be apparent how grand strategy as a concept evolved, there would be certain major points where it would be unclear *why* it evolved. Grand strategy was but one of many concepts in the

---

[25] Reinhart Koselleck, *The Practice of Conceptual History: Timing History, Spacing Concepts*, tr. Todd Samuel Presner (Stanford, CA: Stanford UP, 2002).
[26] Ibid. 37.
[27] Beatrice Heuser, *The Evolution of Strategy: Thinking War from Antiquity to the Present.* (Cambridge: CUP, 2010); Lawrence Freedman, *Strategy: A History* (Oxford: OUP, 2013).

ongoing study of strategy, and other ideas or considerations have periodically usurped functions that specific interpretations of grand strategy have had at particular times. For instance, the idea of air power threatened the very utility of grand strategy, and nuclear strategy eclipsed it for the first half of the Cold War. Thus, in some ways grand strategy had no onomasiological coherence over the course of its existence, due to the context of the fast-moving intellectual and practical discipline of strategic studies within which it developed.

STRUCTURE AND CONTENT

This is the first book-length historical overview of the evolution of grand strategic thought to be undertaken. It examines only the Anglophone literature of grand strategy, a unified whole within its common language which by itself covers over two hundred years of ideational history. Besides the introduction and conclusion, the book comprises eight substantive chapters organized into two parts. Each part is dedicated to one segment of the historical narrative of the evolution of grand strategic thought: its pre-modern and early modern development; and its eclipse and subsequent re-emergence.

Chapter 1 examines concepts of grand strategy during the nineteenth century. It presents the greatest concentration of new, largely unknown historical material and includes the first known use of 'grand strategy' as an actual term in English, in 1834. The term derives from French, 'la grande stratégie', of which the English were aware as early as 1805. The chapter speculates that the English usage of the term was perhaps originally synonymous with Napoleonic strategy, and examines the major interpretations of grand strategy during the nineteenth century. This chapter uncovers previously unknown usage and meanings of grand strategy; establishes that 'grand strategy' began as a solely military concept; and identifies certain themes that recur often in much later iterations of grand strategic thought.

Chapter 2 examines the work of maritime strategists Alfred Thayer Mahan and Julian Stafford Corbett. These two theorists developed concepts of strategy or explicitly of grand strategy which marked the first transformation of the concept into an idea larger than solely military strategy, primarily by associating non-military instruments with grand strategy. This sea change in the meaning of grand strategy derived from their consideration of maritime as opposed to military strategy. Their work also marks the first major theories of grand strategy, allowing for full exploration of the limits of how they considered the idea and how they theorized its practice and implementation. This change of meaning which Mahan and Corbett initiated forms the basis of most modern definitions of grand strategy.

Chapter 3 explores the grand strategic thought of the interwar British theorists J. F. C. Fuller and Basil Liddell Hart, the two giants of British strategic thought during that time, as well as a far less known work by two obscure British authors, which actually was the first dedicated book-length treatment of grand strategy. This chapter examines the continuing development of what might be called the 'British school' of grand strategic thought begun by the maritime theorists. Notable differences abound, however, due to the impact of the First World War on the thinking of Fuller and Liddell Hart. Both were prolific writers, allowing for full exploration of their thoughts on grand strategy with reference to their idealized limits of the concept and how it should be practised. The obscure work by Henry Sargeaunt and Geoffrey West, written and published in 1941, is an excellent example of the influence of context upon grand strategic thought, being significantly different in purpose and scope from the theories propounded by the 'British school'.

Chapter 4 examines the grand strategic thought of the interwar United States. Unlike Britain, there was no dominant theory or theorist during this time in the United States, which allowed a plethora of implicit or explicit interpretations of grand strategy to flourish. These concepts varied significantly from those being developed in Britain during the same period, as the geopolitical context differed considerably, as also did the lessons drawn from the experience of the First World War. Interestingly, the various concepts of, or attitudes towards, grand strategy diverged within the United States as well. Thus although Edward Mead Earle is the best known of the American interwar and civilian wartime strategic theorists, his work may not be considered representative of American grand strategic thought of that time. The air power theorists held a far different attitude toward grand strategy, and actual war planners in the War Department implicitly considered one of the then-identified functions of grand strategy to be situational in its utility.

Chapter 5 delves into the early Cold War concepts of nuclear strategy and limited war theory, which together overshadowed most major concepts of grand strategy and usurped their functions during the first half of the Cold War. This chapter examines how these emerging theories sought to explain concerns which previous interpretations of grand strategy had once claimed as their own.

Chapter 6 surveys what little usage of grand strategy persisted during its eclipse by theories of nuclear strategy and limited war theory. Grand strategy and even its more popular synonym, national strategy, were largely neglected by academia during this time. Despite this, they gained popularity among certain government institutions, including the United States Armed Forces—particularly the Navy—and the US Congress. Nevertheless, no significant new thoughts on grand strategy emerged during this period, almost no one studied it with any degree of seriousness, and few associated themselves with it in practice. Its persistence did, however, guarantee a basic awareness of the term which proved to be the foundation for its re-emergence after the Vietnam War.

Chapter 7 explores the defence debates after the Vietnam War. Strategists during this period began turning again to the big questions, away from the technical and tactical details of nuclear war and limited war. A renewed interest in grand strategy coincided with the revitalization of geopolitical analysis, and the introduction of strategic culture. Many well-known historians and strategists introduced their own concepts of grand strategy during this period, including Edward Luttwak, Paul Kennedy, Barry Posen, and John Lewis Gaddis. As during the interwar period, interpretations of grand strategy differed fundamentally, particularly as scholars addressed various issues during the defence debates. The result was that each interpretation was unique, reflective more of the author's particular interests and concerns than of any potential theoretical core of the concept.

Chapter 8 brings the evolution of grand strategy to the present day through examination of post-Cold War concepts of grand strategy. It also scrutinizes the interpretations established during the last decades of the Cold War, which remain in use to this day despite their potential lack of utility in the new strategic and geopolitical context.

The Conclusion attempts to judge theoretically the history of grand strategic thought and weighs in on such questions as whether or not there is an actual grand strategic function, and whether or not it has any real place in the general theory of strategy. In this context, it also reflects on the themes, first established during the nineteenth century, which frequently recur in the grand strategic literature despite the continually changing purpose, scope, and even nature of the concept. The Conclusion also dwells upon the role of context in indelibly shaping the many interpretations of grand strategy.

Part I

Early Grand Strategic Thought (1805–1945)

Most scholarship identifies the early twentieth century with the birth of 'grand strategy' and highlights Basil Liddell Hart and/or Edward Mead Earle as its prime progenitors. Yet by the time these men were writing, the term had already existed for more than a century. It had already been employed by strategic theorists equal in stature to Liddell Hart or Earle, including Julian Stafford Corbett and John Frederick Charles Fuller. As grand strategy passed through myriad hands over the course of its first century and a half, its meaning continuously changed, casting doubt on the notion that *any* theorist's ideas on grand strategy could be definitive. Grand strategic thought has an as yet undiscovered historical depth, which continues to have implications for the meaning and development of the concept of grand strategy.

In four chapters, the first one hundred and forty years of the evolution of grand strategic thought will be examined. The first chapter deals with the pre-modern grand strategic thought of the nineteenth century, which contains the roots of many themes which continually resurface throughout its later evolution. The first changes which turned grand strategy into a recognizably modern concept stemmed from theories of maritime strategy, covered in Chapter 2. Chapter 3 examines British developments in grand strategic thought resulting from the experience of the First World War. The United States drew different lessons for grand strategy from the World Wars than did Britain, resulting in notably different strands of thought, which are the subject of Chapter 4.

1

Pre-Modern Grand Strategic Thought

The roots of the word *strategy* are well known, deriving from the Greek *strategos*, or general. The Byzantine Emperor Leo (866–912) wrote about *strategike*, 'not in the sense of stratagem or ruse, but as the art and the skills that a general must have: tactics, knowledge about architecture (fortifications), logistics, history, philosophy, medicine, geography, and so on'. The modern neologism *strategie* emerged in Europe in the 1770s as a Frenchman and an Austrian simultaneously translated Leo's work *Taktika* into their respective languages.[1] The word only entered into English discourse around 1800, and the *Oxford English Dictionary* first featured it from 1810.[2]

The term and initial idea of 'grand' strategy originally derived from French military thought. The British were aware of it as early as 1805, at the height of Napoleon's continental successes. One military encyclopedia of the time noted that

> [s]trategy, or the knowledge of commanding armies, may be divided into two parts; one comprehending the higher, and the other embracing the lower branches of the art. The first comprehends all that a commander in chief, and all that his subordinate generals, should be acquainted with; and the second (which may also be called *la petite guerre*, being the diminutive of the first,) appertains to the staff, and to a certain proportion of subaltern officers.[3]

Regarding the general's education in the first type, the encyclopedia noted that '[h]e will peruse what related to the first branch or *la grande Strategie*, in the following works', citing works or memoirs by Montecuculi, Puisegur, de Saxe, Mezeroy, and Guibert, among others.[4] In this instance grand strategy was

---

[1] Beatrice Heuser, 'Strategy Before the Word: Ancient Wisdom for the Modern World', *RUSI Journal* 155/1 (Feb./Mar. 2010), 36.

[2] Jeremy Black, 'Strategic Culture and the Seven Years' War', in Williamson Murray, Richard Hart Sinnreich, and James Lacey (eds). *The Shaping of Grand Strategy: Policy, Diplomacy, and War* (Cambridge: CUP, 2011), 64.

[3] Charles James, *A New and Enlarged Military Dictionary, or, Alphabetical Explanation of Technical Terms*. (London: The Military Library 1805), 862–3.

[4] Ibid. 863.

perceived as a subset of strategy, an inversion of the relationship as typically understood today.

Following this early awareness of grand strategy as a distinct term in the military thought of other countries, the first recorded use yet found of 'grand strategy' as a meaningful term in English dates from 1834. An anonymous American writer employed the term while commenting on a furore over the US Military Academy at West Point caused by two states' submissions to Congress to close the Academy down as incompatible with the ideals and virtues of the nascent American republic. Discussing the Academy syllabus in some detail, year by year, the author complains that courses in rhetoric, moral philosophy, constitutional law, civil and military engineering, artillery, and grand strategy were compressed into the last year of study, to the detriment of efforts to teach and learn these topics. He suggested a higher standard of preparation for students enrolling into West Point, or a fifth year to allow time sufficient for teaching the indicated subjects.[5] The author did not define grand strategy. This implies that the term already had some currency in public and military debate, further buttressed by his lament that there was hardly time to teach it at the Academy.

The exact definition which this author from 1834 was using, but not divulging, may be less important than the revelation that the term grand strategy appeared so quickly in the English language. Strategy itself had only been introduced a generation prior at most, yet there was already an apparent need for another strategic concept. The salient question, probably unanswerable on any definitive level, is: why? Ideas and the terms to describe them are developed for a reason, to address particular issues or concerns or to solve specific problems. What were the reasons for introducing a grand strategic concept, what issues or problems was it originally meant to address?

These questions cannot yet be answered definitively. The historical trail leading back to the French distinction between grand strategy and small wars appears strongly indicative of the structure of strategic theory at that early time and of grand strategy's place within it. Its usage by the American author from 1834 implies only limited currency. The House Committee for Military Affairs' written response to the two complainant states does not itself use the term. This report's author, committee chairman Richard Mentor Johnson, discussed the importance of learning French and German to the education of cadets at the Academy, which reinforces the French origin of grand strategy. 'The French language and, next to that, the German are the great repositories of military learning; and he who would become an accomplished officer must

---

[5] Wesley C. Mitchell et al., 'Academy at West Point', *American Quarterly Review* 16/32 (Dec. 1834), 371.

be able to read intelligently and with profit the text books in at least the first of these languages.'[6]

Given the importance of French for reading about military strategy, early grand strategy for English speakers was likely heavily influenced by Napoleon's campaigns and career. If so, researchers should see uses and definitions of grand strategy during the nineteenth century similar to those put forward by Napoleon's students, including his two greatest interpreters, Baron Antoine-Henri de Jomini and Carl von Clausewitz. Considerable similarities do in fact exist between Napoleon's interpreters and concurrent apparent meanings of the amorphous concept of grand strategy in English, as will be further detailed.

Some contentious evidence runs counter to this interpretation. It has been alleged that the American naval figure John Paul Jones wielded the term grand strategy as early as 1791, in a letter to the Frenchman Armand-Guy-Simon de Coetnempren, comte de Kersaint.[7] One of Jones's biographers, Augustus C. Buell, reproduced the letter to Kersaint in full. Such usage ten years prior to the estimated introduction of the word 'strategy' into English could be significant for understanding the early history of strategy as a concept. Buell's sources for the letter, however, do not exist. Moreover, Jones has been a particular favourite target for fabrications. 'Authors of Jones biographies, particularly Augustus C. Buell, invented Jones documents.'[8] The letter to Kersaint was fabricated—Kersaint does not appear at all in the *Guide to the Microfilm Edition of the Papers of John Paul Jones*. The evidence is false.

A POORLY DEFINED CONCEPT

The meaning of grand strategy is difficult to trace prior to the American Civil War as the term appears so rarely. Besides the anonymous author of 1834, another early use dates from 1859, but again in a manner that implies currency. 'The Manual uses the term "strategy" in the restricted sense, which denotes operations, plans, or manoeuvres in an immediate action, with an enemy in sight. Sir Howard uses it in the sense of what is usually and more properly called "grand strategy," denoting the great combinations of a campaign beyond

---

[6] Richard Mentor Johnson, 'Statement of the History and Importance of the Military Academy at West Point, New York, and Reasons Why It Should Not Be Abolished', *American State Papers, 1789–1838*, Military Affairs vol. 5, 1832–1836, 351.

[7] Augustus C. Buell, *Paul Jones: Founder of the American Navy* (New York: Charles Scribner's Sons, 1900), ii. 298–9; see also Holloway H. Frost. 'Our Heritage from Paul Jones', *Naval Institute Proceedings* 44/188 (Oct. 1918), 2292–3.

[8] James C. Bradford, *Guide to the Microfilm Edition of the Papers of John Paul Jones, 1747–1792* (Cambridge: Chadwyck-Healey, 1986), 5.

vision.'[9] Already in 1859, authors could not agree on where grand strategy fit. Reinforcing this sense of confusion, a Colonel Hamilton placed grand strategy conceptually in a very different place. In commenting upon a particular lecture, he suggested that 'this paper may, without paradox, be called the Grand Strategy of Town Attack'.[10]

Of all the early authors mentioning grand strategy, General William Tecumseh Sherman may have been most interested in contextualizing and finding a clearly defined role for it, apparently the only person to have done so. He was aware of the concept during the American Civil War, and referred to it in his official wartime correspondence.[11] At an address Sherman gave to the Society of the Army of the Tennessee in 1887, he suggested that '[t]he science of war is not modern; it is as old as time, and like most sciences has resolved itself into three parts: logistics, grand strategy and combat, each essential to success'.[12] He did not enlarge upon this trinity within the science of war, and it is difficult to extrapolate further from his other writings as he did not keep this formulation for long.

Even by the next year, Sherman had decided to endorse a systematization of the field of strategy developed by the British author Lieutenant-Colonel France J. Soady. It comprised statesmanship, strategy 'or the art of properly directing masses upon the theatre of war', grand tactics, logistics, engineering, and minor tactics.[13] Grand strategy has no apparent place in such an organization unless it was a specific type or subset of strategy, perhaps defined by a multitude of geographical theatres or a number of successive campaigns in time, which might fit a definition of grand strategy heavily influenced by the American Civil War. Sherman did not define grand strategy in that article, although a British author did so for him at a later date. 'The "grand strategy" of which General Sherman speaks covered the whole field of war'.[14] This definition does not clarify the question of whether or not grand strategy is strategy conducted within a particular geographical or temporal context, and, being provided by someone other than Sherman, may not accurately reflect his views

[9] James H. Ward, *A Manual of Naval Tactics: Together with a Brief Critical Analysis of the Principal Modern Naval Battles* (New York: D. Appleton & Co., 1859), 153.

[10] General E. L. Molineux, 'Riots in Cities and their Suppression', *Journal of the Military Service Institution of the United States* 4 (Mar.–Dec. 1883), 369.

[11] In letters to General Grant on 10 Mar. 1864 and to Major General McPherson on 14 Mar. 1864. *Supplemental Report of the Joint Committee on the Conduct of the War, in Two Volumes.* (Washington, DC: Government Printing Office 1866), i. 15, 19.

[12] William T. Sherman, 'Address of General W. T. Sherman to the Society of the Army of the Tennessee', in *Report of the Proceedings of the Society of the Army of the Tennessee at the Twentieth Meeting, held at Detroit, Mich., September 14th and 15th, 1887* (Cincinnati: Press of F. W. Freeman, 1888), 57.

[13] William T. Sherman, 'The Grand Strategy of the War of the Rebellion', *The Century* 35/4 (Feb. 1888), 583.

[14] K. P. Wolseley, 'An English View of the Civil War, VI', *North American Review* 149/396 (Nov. 1889), 599.

at all. Even later an American author assumed that Sherman's usage of grand strategy referred to the longevity of strategy during the war.[15]

Grand strategy in the nineteenth century was not a well-anchored concept, exacerbated by the American Civil War's explosion in the use of the term. It was, however, certainly a concept with currency throughout the period, despite (or perhaps because of) its breadth of meaning. General George Gordon Meade, commander of the Army of the Potomac from 1863 until the end of the war, noted in his journal that 'I see one of the newspaper men is puzzled to know what share we each have in the work, and settles it by saying Grant does the grand strategy, and I the grand tactics.'[16] Even journalists employed the term and so relayed it to the wider newspaper-reading public. By the end of the century there might have been four basic definitions for grand strategy, three of them plausibly Napoleonic in character and one a probable child of the experience of the American Civil War.

GRAND STRATEGY AS NAPOLEONIC STRATEGY

If grand strategy truly originated from Napoleonic strategy, one would expect to see parallels between nineteenth-century uses of grand strategy and the strategic writings and theories of Napoleon's interpreters, particularly Jomini and Clausewitz. Three nineteenth-century definitions of grand strategy do in fact parallel ideas put forward by either theorist.

The most common of these defines grand strategy largely synonymously with strategy itself, but usually with an emphasis on manoeuvre. Thus might one author suggest that 'Grand Strategy "secures those combinations which will assure the highest possible advantage in the employment of military force. It deals with the theatre of war, its character, resources, topographical features, inter-communication, and all substantial difficulties to be overcome in the way of success."'[17] Sherman, in an address to the graduating class of the Michigan Military Academy in 1879, defined grand strategy similarly.[18]

This parallels Jomini's definition of strategy as 'the art of properly directing masses upon the theatre of war, either for defence or for invasion', or later in his work *The Art of War* as 'the art of making war upon the map, and

---

[15] James S. Pettit, *Elements of Military Science: For the Use of Students in Colleges and Universities* (New Haven: The Tuttle, Morehouse & Taylor Press, 1895), 161.

[16] Journal entry for 19 May 1864, George Gordon Meade, *The Life and Letters of George Gordon Meade* (New York: Charles Scribner's Sons, 1913), ii. 197.

[17] Henry B. Carrington, *Battle Maps and Charts of the American Revolution with Explanatory Notes and School History References.* (New York: A. S. Barnes & Co., 1881), 4.

[18] William T. Sherman, 'Address to the Graduating Class of the Michigan Military Academy', Michigan Military Academy, Orchard Lake, Michigan, 19 June 1879, 8.

comprehends the whole theatre of operations'.[19] To make war on a map is to manoeuvre, an action requiring a geographical area, rather than to fight, which in the nineteenth century still represented but a single point on a map. Grand strategy was concerned with manoeuvre rather than with combat. Sherman makes this point as well, commenting about the battle of the Wilderness that Grant 'knew that a certain amount of fighting, "killing," had to be done to accomplish his end, and also to pay the penalty of former failures. In the "wilderness" there was no room for grand strategy, or even minor tactics; but the fighting was desperate.'[20] Sherman's aforementioned division of the science of war into logistics, combat, and grand strategy reinforces this point. Some wartime authors even appear to have taken grand strategy to Liddell Hart's later extreme concerning the conduct of strategy as obviating the need for battle altogether.[21]

This understanding of grand strategy, as manoeuvre in lieu of combat, seeped beyond military and strategic studies into general public usage as well. One author, discussing how to make New Orleans more attractive as a commercial port, suggested in the context of blockade that '[w]e must substitute grand strategy for grand tactics. We must flank the blockade, instead of trying to raise it by direct assault.'[22] This perception of grand strategy was fundamentally tied up with the idea of manoeuvre as opposed to combat.

One interesting implication of this emphasis on manoeuvre, particularly if truly inspired by Napoleon, is how it largely predated the rediscovery of Napoleon in late nineteenth-century France. Azar Gat identified a coterie of French strategic theorists who criticized Clausewitz's writings for interpreting Napoleonic strategy only crudely as focused on directly engaging in decisive battle and noted 'the many instances of Napoleon's *manoeuvre sur les derrières*, the manoeuvre against the enemy's rear, one of the most fundamental patterns of Napoleonic strategy'.[23] Jomini, although recognizing the importance to Napoleonic strategy of manoeuvring outside of battle, still considered combat more important.[24]

The second definition of grand strategy that bears similarity to facets of both Jominian and Clausewitzian thought does not correspond to either's definition of strategy, but rather to a particular skill that strategists ought to have, or feature which good strategies do have. Grand strategy was thus

---

[19] Baron de Jomini, *The Art of War*, tr. G. H. Mendell and W. P. Craighill (Westport: Greenwood Press, 1862), 11, 62.

[20] Sherman, 'Grand Strategy of the War of the Rebellion', 591.

[21] George Ward Nichols, *The Story of the Great March: From the Diary of a Staff Officer* (New York: Harper & Brothers, 1865), 268–71.

[22] Durant Dapont, 'New Orleans and Ship Island Ship Canal', *Debow's Review, Agricultural, Commercial, Industrial Progress and Resources* 6/1 (Jan. 1869), 22–3.

[23] Azar Gat, *A History of Military Thought* (Oxford: OUP, 2001), 395.

[24] Jomini, *Art of War*, 63.

defined as 'the correct recognition of the point at which it was imperative to strike'.[25] The imperative, or decisive, point was not necessarily one which caused the most harm to the enemy. It might also be a point which was weakly defended, or one which threatened multiple important objectives and so forced the enemy to split his forces. It was on this latter basis that one author praised Sherman's march to the sea, which was attended by great success and limited loss because the Confederates could not divine his true intentions.[26] A further possible meaning, as another nineteenth-century author suggested in relation to the Confederate General Pemberton's situation during Grant's Vicksburg campaign of 1863, was 'rising above the letter of war to the spirit of war'.[27]

The main parallel between this concept of grand strategy and ideas presented by Napoleon's major interpreters is Clausewitz's *coup d'oeil*, the intuitive understanding of a situation, and Jomini's idea of attacking at the decisive point. '*Coup d'oeil* therefore refers not alone to the physical but, more commonly, to the inward eye... the concept merely refers to the quick recognition of a truth that the mind would ordinarily miss or would perceive only after long study and reflection.'[28] In a similar sense, Jomini suggested that the first fundamental principle of war was identification of and attack upon the decisive point.[29] In this case, grand strategy is merely *good* strategy, that is, strategy done well. Since Napoleon's campaigns until 1812 consisted primarily of identifying and exploiting decisive points in the local geography or enemy formations, they can be said not only to have been good strategy, but to have been the source for Clausewitz's basic example of *coup d'oeil* and Jomini's first principle of war. Their equivalence with grand strategy appears quite Napoleonic.

The third definition is the most interesting, but also the rarest and most arguable of all the plausibly Napoleonic-inspired usages of grand strategy. As John Allan Wyeth argued of Confederate strategy during the American Civil War,

> [t]his fundamental consideration, that the South could win only by wearing out the North, should have dictated the grand strategy of the Confederacy, and off and on it did. Pretty clearly that strategy was to conserve resources, to avoid

---

[25] Archibald Forbes, 'Abraham Lincoln as a Strategist, Part 1', *North American Review* 155/428 (July 1892), 62.

[26] George Ward Nichols, 'How Fort M'Allister was Taken', *Harper's New Monthly Magazine* 37/219 (Aug. 1868), 368.

[27] William Swinton, *The Twelve Decisive Battles of the War: A History of the Eastern and Western Campaigns, in Relation to the Actions that Decided their Issue* (New York: Dick & Fitzgerald, 1867), 290.

[28] Carl von Clausewitz, *On War*, ed. and tr. Michael Howard and Peter Paret (Princeton: Princeton UP, 1984), 102.

[29] Jomini, *Art of War*, 63.

pitched battles and sieges, to take advantages of a vast terrain, a friendly population, and interior lines of communication; to spread the war as far as possible into the West—even into the trans-Mississippi West; to play for time—and for British intervention which might come with time; to exact a terrible price for every Union advance.[30]

Underpinning this quote lies the idea that grand strategy concerns how best to fight in order to achieve the desired political objective.

This particular usage may also be discernible in one nineteenth-century biography of General George Thomas, whose author suggests that Thomas 'was denied, by his long subordination, the opportunities for grand strategy', but not of implementing his superiors' grand strategies.[31] This may not immediately appear to support the third definition, but Thomas did ultimately command the Army of the Cumberland. Originally under Sherman's overall command, he was semi-detached to defend Tennessee from General Hood as Sherman marched into eastern Georgia. In Tennessee, Thomas was allowed to defend Nashville as he felt proper, albeit subject to frequent exhortations for action from Grant due to his (overly) methodical campaigning style.[32] He thus controlled his own tactics, and by the end of the war had a reasonably autonomous, if not independent, command. The remaining segment of the strategy bridge which Thomas never crossed was campaigning deliberately for political effect, a privilege seemingly reserved for his superiors Sherman and Grant. Additionally, one book review from the mid-1890s, discussing the American Civil War, similarly employed this interpretation of grand strategy.[33] This same reviewer also suggested that grand strategy was a responsibility which could be equally left to the military or the civilian government.[34]

This third interpretation of grand strategy appears similar in character to Clausewitz's definition of strategy as 'the use of the engagement for the purpose of the war'.[35] As a subordinate, despite his autonomy, General Thomas did not consider the entire operational side of war, much less within the explicit framework of attempting to achieve beneficial political effect. He fought battles because others had weighed their political or strategic importance and found it imperative.

---

[30] John Allan Wyeth, *That Devil Forrest: Life of General Nathan Bedford Forrest* (New York: Harper & Brothers 1959 [original 1899]), p. xvi.
[31] Thomas Budd Van Horne, *The Life of Major-General George H. Thomas* (New York: Charles Scribner's Sons, 1882), 462–3.
[32] James M. McPherson, *Battle Cry of Freedom: The Civil War Era* (Oxford: OUP, 1988), 808, 811, 813.
[33] John Hamilton, 'Reviews and Exchanges: The Story of the Civil War', *Journal of the Military Service Institution of the United States* 17 (July–Dec. 1895), 193.
[34] J.H. (John Hamilton?), 'Reviews and Exchanges: History of the Mexican War', *Journal of the Military Service Institution of the United States* 14 (1893), 198.
[35] Clausewitz, *On War*, 177.

Whereas the usage concerning Thomas appears closer to Clausewitz's classic definition of strategy, Wyeth's usage appears almost presciently Neo-Clausewitzian. Rather than focusing merely upon the political impact of giving battle, it considers how best to take advantage of geographical features and how to mitigate the opponent's strengths, within a context of employing force. Anachronistically, this Neo-Clausewitzian perspective on grand strategy may view it as 'the bridge that relates military power to political purpose'.[36] It considers the problem of force and its employment in all of its many dimensions.

A final interesting aspect of this third definition is how it potentially relates to the idea of the American way of war. Russell Weigley, in broaching the topic of the American way of war, suggested that the American military favoured a much narrower definition of strategy as 'the art of bringing forces to the battle in a favourable position'.[37] Such a definition does not connect military means and ways with political ends. In this sense American strategic culture is still frequently considered Jominian. The introduction of this third definition and usage of grand strategy, by Americans, late in the nineteenth century, might take on a whole new meaning in this context of apolitical strategic thought. It may reveal a realization that contemporary definitions of strategy (or grand strategy) were insufficient to understand the entirety of a belligerent's task in war and warfare, particularly in light of the many non-Jominian experiences of the American Civil War. The result is a new concept, higher than strategy, which explicitly links campaigning to achieving the political results desired.

This problem was certainly addressed by some American military thinkers in the late nineteenth century, which indicates that it was an issue of some currency. John Bigelow, although he was aware of the term grand strategy, couched the problem in terms of a two-fold concept he labelled political strategy. 'The one consists in impairing, destroying, or blocking the machinery of the enemy's government; the other in coercing his government, under penalty of dissolution or overthrow.' His formulation gives the impression that political strategy and what he called regular strategy were separate, but he later admitted, in the context of the people as a military objective, that '[p]olitical strategy is often an incident of regular strategy'.[38] Bigelow was perhaps on the cusp of suggesting that 'from day one of a war every belligerent generates strategic effect'.[39] Perhaps one may discern a small group of nineteenth-century authors who felt that conventional ideas of strategy did not suffice either to explain past experience or to guide future strategists.

---

[36] Colin S. Gray, *Modern Strategy* (Oxford: OUP, 1999), 17.
[37] Russell F. Weigley. *The American Way of War: A History of United States Military Strategy and Policy* (Bloomington, IN: Indiana UP, 1973), p. xviii.
[38] John Bigelow, *The Principles of Strategy, Illustrated Mainly from American Campaigns* (Philadelphia: J. B. Lippincott Co., 1894), 224, 228.
[39] Colin S. Gray, *The Strategy Bridge: Theory for Practice* (Oxford: OUP, 2010), 177.

Bigelow's political strategy might be considered one attempt to resolve this problem, and the third usage of grand strategy may have been another.

Three of the four nineteenth-century definitions of grand strategy may thus arguably be considered Napoleonic in origin. With the true original use of grand strategy in any language yet unknown, such connections rely on etymological speculation, comparative textual analysis, and the benefits of historical perspective and anachronism to impose a degree of order on an otherwise undisciplined term and its usage.

GRAND STRATEGY FROM THE AMERICAN CIVIL WAR

The final definition of grand strategy used during the nineteenth century seems primarily inspired by the American Civil War experience. Whereas strategy was simply the handling of military formations outside of battle, grand strategy was a much larger undertaking. It comprised the entire conduct of warfare. It was a unitary phenomenon, as implied by the title (albeit not content) of Sherman's article, 'The Grand Strategy of the War of the Rebellion', as well as by Sherman's foreign interpreters. One late-war author divided Confederate mistakes during the war into two types: operational and grand strategic, the latter of which 'pertain[s] to the management of all the Confederate forces'.[40] Some aspects of this usage overlap with Wyeth's grand strategy, just noted as an exemplar of grand strategy's third interpretation.

This overlap may stem from a geographical understanding of what 'the whole field of war' was. If theatres of war are assumed to only indirectly influence one another, and if strategy is practised across multiple theatres, then any common objectives among them must necessarily be general and perhaps even political—destruction of the Confederate army at the very least, if not subjugation of the Confederate States themselves.

A major emphasis on geography in strategy and theory is a natural consequence of the American Civil War, given its wide geographical expanse, with two major theatres in the east and the west, subsidiary theatres west of the Mississippi, and Union blockade and Confederate commerce raiding in the Atlantic. Managing theatres whose interrelations were only indirect was a necessarily grand task for a strategist of the time.

---

[40] Edward A. Pollard, *Southern History of the War: The Third Year of the War* (New York: Charles B. Richardson, 1865), 132.

CONCLUSION

Grand strategic thought in the nineteenth century was undisciplined, with scattered and disparate definitions of the term. Sufficient similarities existed among the term's many uses to divide them into four basic categories, but other miscellaneous uses still remain beyond the limits of these categories. One, presumably Southern, writer attacked an earlier author for explaining and apparently supporting Sherman's march to the sea, almost snarling that '[w]e have thus seen our author's views of "grand strategy," of negro superiority and of white oppression'.[41] It is unclear from this usage whether grand strategy was used in an ideological manner, related to supposed Negro superiority and white oppression, or whether they were separate offences emanating from the same man. By the same token, in 1899 the historian Charles Oman found the term grand strategy useful as well, particularly in relation to the Crusades. However, what he meant by the term is again unclear; he used it only in the title of a single chapter, 'The Grand Strategy of the Crusades', and did not mention it during the chapter itself.[42] One American officer assigned grand strategy as a responsibility for the general officer, in keeping with the French meaning of the term at the time it was adopted by the English.[43]

The definitive intellectual context for the casual and undisciplined nineteenth-century English usage of grand strategy is likely to be French military literature, from which the term and idea originated. One of the major future next steps in understanding the history of grand strategic thought must be to trace the development of the concept of grand strategy in French military and strategic literature, for such a task will certainly shed light on the context of pre-modern Anglophone grand strategic thought.

What is significant, especially in relation to the entire subsequent history and evolution of grand strategic thought, and what may be said with absolute certainty, is that grand strategy was a fundamentally military concept. No matter which of the four basic interpretations is taken, grand strategy is universally about using military force. Grand strategy may be defined by the way the military is manoeuvred, or whether it is applied to the correct point, or whether it is for political purposes or must be coordinated across multiple theatres. To allow an anachronism, all these uses or definitions of grand strategy would be subsumed into normal definitions of military strategy today. Barring a handful of continuities that have survived until the present

---

[41] John W. Daniel, 'The Great March', *Debow's Review, Agricultural, Commercial, Industrial Progress and Resources* 5/4 (Apr. 1868), 344.

[42] Charles Oman, *A History of the Art of War in the Middle Ages* (London: Meuthen & Co., 1978 [1898]), bk 5, ch. 2.

[43] E. L. Zalinski, 'The Army Organization, Best Adapted to a Republican Form of Government, Which Will Insure an Effective Force', *Journal of the Military Service Institution of the United States* 14 (1893), 931.

day, none of the definitions or usages of grand strategy analysed here would today be considered as remotely grand strategic. Yet, to a significant degree, most definitions of grand strategy which followed this pre-modern usage hewed closely to one class of interpretation or another established during the nineteenth century. Even as meanings of grand strategy evolved and the phenomena they described changed, sometimes radically, the tenor of certain basic concerns has endured.

2

The Maritime Origins of Modern Grand Strategic Thought

The idea of grand strategy, albeit in manifold meanings, was already well-established when the two major theorists of maritime strategy, Alfred Thayer Mahan and Julian Stafford Corbett, began their careers. Yet that idea was military-centric and would not be recognizably grand strategic to most scholars today. If grand strategy was to account for more than military force, it was within a maritime context that it first developed along that identifiably modern trajectory (although a range of instruments is not the only gauge by which to measure modernity in grand strategic thinking). There are two intertwined causes of this marked alteration in the scope of grand strategy with the advent of maritime strategic theory, particularly that of Corbett.

The first is that the breadth of means, military and non-military, of which grand strategy disposes was generally held not to be of much use during war on the European continent. As Julian Corbett argued, not only was there no logical limit to the application of force in such a context, but the nationally organic character of any particular territory was good reason to escalate to prevent its loss.[1] All the other means available to grand strategy tend towards impotence in the face of military force. The aggregate character of the effect achieved by these other means is only to deny control and even that effect is achieved on timescales longer than that of armed force.

Second, most maritime strategy of this period drew its theoretical character directly from the historical epitome of sea power, Great Britain.[2] Maritime strategists turned to Britain, as the most successful and most enduring example of sea power, for historical lessons on geopolitics and particularly on geostrategy. Due to its proximity to the continent, Britain was necessarily

---

[1] Julian S. Corbett, *Some Principles of Maritime Strategy* (Annapolis, MD: Naval Institute Press, 1988), 54–5.

[2] This applied not only to those who favoured Britain such as Mahan and Corbett. Britain's maritime history necessarily dominated the maritime strategic thought of those who would be Britain's enemies, such as the French. See e.g. Arne Røksund. *The Jeune École: The Strategy of the Weak* (Leiden: Brill, 2007).

interested in the great European political questions, yet the English Channel sufficiently isolated it that it was simultaneously aloof from Europe's quotidian political and security concerns. Moreover, with the European discovery of the Americas, Britain became a major portal between two worlds. The new world, across the Atlantic, was a source of wealth or prestige for all European powers which reached it, but which remained at the far end of a long supply line. Due to its peculiar separation from Europe, Britain was able to take greater advantage of its links to the New World than its great power rivals.

Britain's maritime concerns thus touched not only upon the European littoral, but equally upon overseas territories. These territories were external to the continent and to the great powers, which in war were necessarily concerned more with their immediate dangerous neighbours than with the security of their own far-flung dominions of secondary importance. The maintenance and defence of overseas territories were also more expensive and difficult than those of comparable lands in Europe due to difficult logistics, although this was balanced by the smaller absolute numbers of soldiers required. Because of their diminished importance in war, overseas territories may also have been esteemed less in peace. The threshold for acquiring contested territory overseas was correspondingly lower, and distance allowed the other, lesser instruments of grand strategy the time necessary to take effect. Alfred Thayer Mahan proposed such an argument when contrasting naval strategy with military strategy: '[t]he diplomatist, as a rule, only affixes the seal of treaty to the work done by the successful soldier. It is not so with a large proportion of strategic points upon the sea.'[3] Indeed, non-contiguous territories were often traded before competition came to blows because the strong who preyed upon the weak on sea had a broader array of effective instruments at their disposal than merely armed force. Grand strategy in its first modern guise, encompassing all instruments of power, thus grew directly out of maritime strategic theory.

This assessment is supported by some tangential evidence that continental ideas of grand strategy did not develop similar breadth in the same timescale. First, American missionaries in the first two decades of the twentieth century invoked 'what the French speak of as "grand strategy," that which takes in the whole map'.[4] This invokes geographic but not instrumental breadth. Moreover, the interwar French naval theorist Raoul Castex resisted the modern idea of grand strategy, or indeed any expansion of strategy beyond narrowly military and naval considerations.[5] These two pieces of evidence indicate

---

[3] Alfred Thayer Mahan, *Naval Strategy Compared and Contrasted with the Principles and Practice of Military Operations on Land* (London: Sampson Low, Marston & Co., 1911), 123.

[4] John R. Mott, 'Response to the Address of Welcome', *Christian Work in Latin America* 3 (New York: The Missionary Education Movement, 1917), 275.

[5] Raoul Castex, *Strategic Theories*, tr. and ed. Eugenia C. Kiesling (Annapolis, MD: Naval Institute Press, 1994), 15–17.

that peripheral and insular geography as in Britain set particular conditions which encouraged a broadening of grand strategy to include non-military instruments of power and which did not pertain to the great powers of continental Europe, for whom military power had much greater immediate import.

Two naval/maritime theorists may be emphasized in relation to the nascence of this broadened idea of modern grand strategy: Captain Alfred Thayer Mahan (1840–1914) of the United States Navy and two-time president of the US Naval War College; and Sir Julian Stafford Corbett (1854–1922), frequent lecturer at the Royal Navy War College in Greenwich and official naval historian of the Russo-Japanese and the First World Wars.[6] These two men may be highlighted for initially implying and eventually significantly developing grand strategy in a maritime context, and for developing and popularizing a way of thinking which might be considered a 'British school' of grand strategic thought. This school of thought, which never divorced itself from its British maritime roots, drew directly upon the peripheral character of maritime strategy and upon the centrality of commerce and other economic considerations to all action in the maritime sphere. Although the concept of grand strategy existed before either of these two theorists began their careers, the evolutionary path towards a form recognizable to modern scholars began with Mahan and Corbett.

Mahan was not the first to write on sea power, nor even the first American to do so, although he coined the term. He simply became the most famous and influential writer from a wider and older navalist community.[7] Whereas his contemporaries largely lobbied for increases in the naval budget and the laying of modern ships, Mahan strove additionally to create a serious discipline of naval strategy in the United States. His importance lies in implying a concept of grand strategy, hidden within his formulation of naval strategy, and in popularizing a particularly navalist perspective on British strategic history.

---

[6] Much has been written about Mahan. See for instance Philip A. Crowl, 'Alfred Thayer Mahan: The Naval Historian', in Peter Paret (ed.), *Makers of Modern Strategy: From Machiavelli to the Nuclear Age* (Oxford: Clarendon Press, 1986), 444–77; and John B. Hattendorf (ed.), *The Influence of History on Mahan* (Newport, RI: Naval War College Press, 1991). Corbett has received substantially less treatment, although some work exists. See Donald M. Schurman, *Julian S. Corbett, 1854–1922: Historian of British Maritime Policy from Drake to Jellicoe* (London: Royal Historical Society, 1981); James Goldrick and John B. Hattendorf (eds), *Mahan is Not Enough: The Proceedings of a Conference on the Works of Sir Julian Corbett and Admiral Sir Herbert Richmond* (Newport:, RI: Naval War College Press, 1993); and J. J. Widén, *Theorist of Maritime Strategy: Sir Julian Corbett and his Contribution to Military and Naval Thought* (London: Ashgate, 2012).

[7] On this point see Peter Karsen, *The Naval Aristocracy: The Golden Age of Annapolis and the Emergence of Modern American Navalism* (New York: Free Press, 1972) and Benjamin L. Apt, 'Mahan's Forebears: The Debate over Maritime Strategy, 1868–1883', *Naval War College Review* 50/3 (Summer 1997), 86–111.

He may, in retrospect, be considered the unintentional founder of the British school of grand strategic thought.

Corbett, like Mahan, emerged from a tradition of national naval thought older than his own contributions.[8] Although long overshadowed by Mahan—Corbett received a chapter in neither Edward Mead Earle's 1941 nor Peter Paret's 1986 edition of *Makers of Modern Strategy*—he was arguably the superior thinker. His subtlety of thought was controversial both during his lifetime and afterwards for having an allegedly negative influence on the conduct of the naval portion of the First World War. He developed the British school of grand strategic thought out of its primordial Mahanian stage and into a formulation later recognizable in those of his successors.

ALFRED THAYER MAHAN, IMPLYING GRAND STRATEGY

Mahan's first great book, *The Influence of Sea Power upon History, 1660–1783*, neatly encapsulated on its first page his thoughts on grand strategy.

> The history of Sea Power is largely, though by no means solely, a narrative of contests between nations, of mutual rivalries, of violence frequently culminating in war. The profound influence of sea commerce upon the wealth and strength of countries was clearly seen long before the true principles which governed its growth and prosperity were detected. To secure to one's own people a disproportionate share of such benefits, every effort was made to exclude others, either by the peaceful legislative methods of monopoly or prohibitory regulations, or, when these failed, by direct violence.[9]

Mahan's ideas are laid thickly therein and must be unpacked in full to be comprehensively explained. He recognized only one level of (naval) strategy, whose end was 'to found, support, and increase, *as well in peace as in war*, the sea power of a country'.[10] In this formulation, sea power was both a means and an end of strategy. In seeking to reinforce sea power, naval strategy became self-referential and so violated the instrumental nature of strategy by serving only itself. It obscured the division between strategy and the policy to which it must refer, an attribute common also to much of modern grand strategic thought. This was a far cry from Jomini's conception of strategy as 'the art of making war on a map', which limited strategy's role to the manoeuvre of

---

[8] Donald M. Schurman, *The Education of a Navy: The Development of British Naval Strategic Thought, 1867–1914* (London: Cassell, 1965).

[9] Alfred Thayer Mahan, *The Influence of Sea Power upon History 1660–1783* (New York: Hill & Wang 1957 [original edn 1897]), 1.

[10] Mahan, *Naval Strategy*, 123. Also quoted in Mahan, *Influence of Sea Power*, 19.

armed forces outside of battle.[11] Given Jomini's influence on Mahanian thought, this expansion of strategy was clearly deliberate and must have had a purpose.

This purpose stemmed from the intent versus the character of his writing, which threatened to diverge at one point. Mahan's intentions were to instruct and to propagandize, but his writings took on an incompatible determinist bent. The expansion of naval strategy as a concept, and the concurrent implying of grand strategy, occurred to bridge the gap between his intention in, and the character of, his writing, aided and abetted by two coexistent ideas of what sea power actually was.

Mahan's intention in writing was twofold. He was a naval propagandist in a country which had turned its back on the sea to focus on domestic affairs and markets.[12] This was an inclination and task which grew out of his main job as a lecturer. Admiral Stephen B. Luce, founder of the United States Naval War College, had invited Mahan to lecture on naval history and strategy. By force of circumstance, Mahan was given nearly three years to ponder his course before he actually had to teach it, time he spent analysing naval strategy and sea power. Mahan's six conditions of sea power which constrained every polity eventually emerged. 'I. Geographical Position. II. Physical Conformation, including, as connected therewith, natural productions and climate. III. Extent of Territory. IV. Number of Population. V. Character of the People. VI. Character of the Government, including therein the national institutions.'[13]

Most of these principal conditions were external, existing largely out of the purview of men to change them through either policy or strategy. Geographical position, physical conformation, and extent of territory were all physical realities whose influence was difficult to alter without resorting to extraordinary conquest. The number and character of the people might be in flux, but any change could take generations to achieve significant effect. Mahan conceived even the one relatively autonomous factor that contributed to sea power, the character of the government, in a semi-deterministic way by aligning it with the 'natural bias of its people'.[14]

Mahan needed to move away from determinism and towards the potential of human agency. As a navalist in a country he felt was indifferent to naval affairs, Mahan had to address human agency, otherwise the likelihood of favourable change was limited. As a lecturer on naval strategy at the Naval War College, he had to teach the scope of human agency, for his students would eventually be making decisions on naval policy and strategy.

---

[11] Baron de Jomini, *The Art of War*, tr. G. H. Mendell and W. P. Craighill (Westport: Greenwood Press, 1862), 62.
[12] 'The United States Looking Outward', in Alfred Thayer Mahan, *The Interest of America in Sea Power Present and Future* (London: Sampson Low, Marston & Co., 1897), 3–27.
[13] Mahan, *Influence of Sea Power*, 25.   [14] Ibid. 51.

Mahan did not invent grand strategy, for the concept was widely employed by the time he wrote his books, but he was one of the first to advocate an expanded concept of strategy, largely as a response to his dilemma of accommodating theory and agency. Jon Tetsuro Sumida identifies the two main themes of Mahan's writing as the invention of this broadened concept ('naval grand strategy') and teaching the art of command. Sumida ascertains naval grand strategy to be 'the relationships between [sic] naval power, economic development, and international relations'. Naval grand strategy required an expanded formulation of sea power, comprising a tripartite design.[15] One third of the basis of naval grand strategy was largely immutable: the original, deterministic vision of sea power, the context in which the drama of history occurs. One third was human agency specific to war: naval command, relying upon a concept of narrow sea power encompassing only the wartime navy. It on its own, without purpose, was meaningless. The final third of naval grand strategy was human agency in the commercial side of sea power, maritime political economy, and it was the cornerstone of Mahan's entire implicit concept of grand strategy, and of his actual broad understanding of naval strategy. It gave meaning to the physical and cultural context in which grand strategy occurred, and to the wars and battles waged by and for sea power.

Mahan identified the importance of the economic aspect of maritime affairs early in his career and noted that navies usually arose due to the need to defend merchant shipping.[16] Interest in the sea and in sea power began with the mercantile and only took on a military dimension when the commercial stakes were sufficient to warrant the expense. Moreover, the relationships among production, shipping, and colonies were 'the key to much of the history, as well as of the policy, of nations bordering upon the sea'.[17]

Yet Mahan failed to develop economic themes relating to sea power in peace, besides the somewhat facile emphasis on a system of industrial production, merchant shipping, and colonies both as markets for finished products and producers of raw materials. His intention had never been to do so, however, as he envisioned maritime history primarily as a history of war. Economic considerations were the cornerstone of Mahanian naval strategy, by way of the tripartite concept of sea power for naval grand strategy, but although naval strategy worked in both peace and war, the emphasis was on war. A free trader by belief, Mahan did not consider peacetime economic development as much of a problem: it took care of itself. Naval strategy, and the implicit ideas of grand strategy, instead centred on the troubled interaction between war and commerce, which had two dimensions. First was the impact

---

[15] Jon Tetsuro Sumida, *Inventing Grand Strategy and Teaching Command: The Classic Works of Alfred Thayer Mahan Reconsidered* (Washington, DC: Woodrow Wilson Center Press, 1997), 5–6, 27.
[16] Mahan, *Influence of Sea Power*, 23.   [17] Ibid. 25.

of the conduct of war on commerce. Second was the idea that the purpose of naval strategy was the expansion of commerce.

Mahan's first major theme on the impact of the conduct of war on commerce was the relative effectiveness of commerce raiding and destruction versus that of taking control of the sea. The logic of commerce destruction was simple. If an enemy relied upon commerce, there were three broad targets in his system: his industry, his shipping, and his colonies or markets. A weaker naval power could not directly attack the enemy's industry or his colonies across an uncontrolled sea without placing his own army and navy in grave danger of defeat. Given the size of the sea and the resultant ability of raiders to avoid easy detection, attacking the shipping link between industry and colonies was a rational course of action. Mahan's lesson was that it was also the weakest course available.

Incomparably greater was the effect upon commerce of the combination of sea control and the conquest of colonies, which irreparably broke the entire commercial chain rather than harrying only one part of it. During the Seven Years War, the British attacked and captured the two great French sugar-making islands of Guadeloupe and Martinique, 'involving a loss to the trade of France greater than all the depredations of her cruisers on the English commerce'.[18] Commerce raiding could never achieve more than a partial interdiction, whereas the loss of a colony and the associated raw material, market for finished products, and the commerce involved in carrying goods between the home country and the colony, represented a total loss. The British could suffer with confidence the annoyance of French commerce raiding, for raiding could never impose such a catastrophe. Yet Mahan noted that Horatio Nelson believed that the British will to fight during the Napoleonic Wars was contingent on their possession of the islands of the West Indies.[19] The British had the aptitude for sea power, but even they would have had to make peace in the face of the complete collapse of their commercial system.

Mahan's second major theme on the impact of the conduct of war on commerce was intertwined with the adversarial contest of sea power and land power. In such a scenario, neither sea power nor land power could directly assault the other, for each resided in its own bastion. War became a contest of endurance, and endurance was predicated upon economic strength. This was a fact recognized by both Britain and France during the Napoleonic Wars; acting upon it gave them a common arena. The two states fought over where each could trade, Britain denying France overseas markets and France denying Britain continental markets. They disputed the rights of neutral

---

[18] Ibid. 119.
[19] Alfred Thayer Mahan, *The Influence of Sea Power upon the French Revolution and Empire 1793–1812* (London: Sampson Low, Marston & Co., 1892), ii. 160.

carriers to profit from the war by trading with whom they wished, and forced them to choose sides. Recognizing the influence of agency and contingency, Mahan realized that the historical result was not preordained but ultimately depended on 'which of the two would make the first and greatest mistake, and how ready the other party was to profit by his errors'.[20]

A nevertheless inevitable aspect of this economic contest between sea power and land power was the need of land power to expand. The sea power may hold its frontier at the enemy's shore. Little additional effort was required on the part of Great Britain to blockade Europe during the course of the economy-dominated war, particularly after the victory at Trafalgar had removed any potential naval danger. French land power, however, was forced to garrison the entire European coast to prevent otherwise uncooperative local populations from smuggling in desired British goods. This necessary defensive impulse led Napoleon progressively to expand direct French dominion over ever greater lengths of European coastline, and ultimately to invade Russia to enforce the Continental System on her. The consequence was his ultimate defeat, resulting from the invasion of Russia and the subsequent European riposte against France.[21]

The second dimension of Mahan's concept of naval strategy, and implicitly of grand strategy, is that the purpose of strategy is to defend or expand commerce, which would necessarily serve policy. As Mahan admitted, this historically commercial goal was largely achieved through war, but not always. Only during peace could commerce flourish without discrimination, a condition necessary for interactive, interstate economy. The danger of war was that it 'is above all harmful when it cuts a nation off from others and throws it back upon itself'.[22]

Commerce in strategy was thus caught between two competing tendencies. First was the preying upon commerce which occurs during war, either through commerce raiding or through the assault on and collapse of entire commercial systems. Second was the desire to legislate the protection of trade from attack during war. The dilemma was clear: naval strategy had as its goal the defence and expansion of commerce, but war's greatest import on global economy was threat and destruction. Mahan opposed such legislative defence, for two interrelated reasons. First, the fact that war put trade into danger improved the deterrent effect of war, thus decreasing chances of its occurrence. Second, sea power lost much of its utility if commerce were to be untouchable, thus increasing the likelihood of war. Mahan unfortunately never formulated this entire argument in a single work, but the logic is striking.

> Assure the nations and the commercial community that their financial interests will suffer no more than the additional tax for maintaining active hostilities; that

---

[20] Ibid. 201.   [21] Ibid. 400–2.   [22] Mahan, *Influence of Sea Power*, 176.

the operations of maritime commerce, foreign and coastwise, will undergo no hindrance, and you will have removed one of the most efficient preventatives of war.[23]

Commercial vulnerability was only half of the source of deterrent effect, the other half being military and naval preparedness for war, as he advised President Theodore Roosevelt.[24] The navy itself, the armed component of sea power, had to be ready for war, and would lose all purpose should trade be protected by legislation. 'Commercial value cannot be separated from military in sea strategy, for the greatest interest of the sea is commerce.'[25] If commerce were legally invulnerable to attack, then naval strategy exited war altogether, for there was naught it could lawfully achieve. The implicit logical result of such reasoning was that sea power states would remain supreme internationally, for they might blockade continental states nearly at will, ruin their commerce, and so emasculate them, as Mahan held Britain had done with France during the Napoleonic Wars.

This potential power, however, was balanced by the assumed natural tendency of the merchant to prefer peace to war. Peace was a much safer atmosphere for doing business. Moreover, peacetime commerce absorbed all the energies of trading peoples, and distracted them from international affairs, although this also weakened any preference towards preparedness for war.

The purpose of naval strategy was thus to ensure that peace reigned. On one level this was to be achieved through the persistent expansion of mutual commerce, naval preparedness for war, and its threat to commerce. All elements were important for Mahan's implicit vision of grand strategy. Yet Mahan never considered war impossible, another reason why he insisted that commerce remain vulnerable to armed action. He thought the application of sea power not only as more humane, but also as hastening peace and a return to mutual commerce.[26]

Mahan rarely discussed peacetime strategy and policy, except in the context of building and owning a fleet to be prepared for, and so possibly to deter, any new war. Nonetheless, in private correspondence he did touch upon the peacetime economic aspect of grand strategy, with particular reference to Britain's protectionist Navigation Acts, whose utility he acknowledged but nevertheless disapproved of due to his free-trading conviction.[27] Mahan, although placing maritime commerce at the centre of sea power, understood

---

[23] Letter to the Editor of *New York Times*, 15 Nov. 1898, *Letters and Papers of Alfred Thayer Mahan*, ed. Robert Seager II and Doris D. Maguire (Annapolis, MD: Naval Institute Press, 1975), ii. 611.
[24] Letter to Theodore Roosevelt, 6 May 1897, ibid. 507.
[25] Mahan, *Naval Strategy*, 302.
[26] Letter to the Editor of *New York Times*, 2 Nov. 1910, *Letters of Mahan*, ed. Seager and Maguire, iii. 366.
[27] Letter to James R. Thurfield, 22 Jan. 1906, ibid. 154.

that there was a broader context to sea power: politics. Although politics drives and supports economy, economy cannot but be political in nature. Economy entailed more than just the reciprocal exchange of goods and money: *who* benefited the most from that exchange also mattered, which is a political consequence. Sea power was by nature politically purposive, meant to benefit its owner and wielder.

Despite Jomini's influence Mahan adopted an incredibly broad definition of naval strategy. The purpose of this definitional and conceptual expansion was to address the question of human agency in a context largely determined by immutable conditions. The expansion of naval strategy solved this problem through the combined application of ideas on commerce, war, and peace. Commerce was the capstone of his theory of sea power, which flourished in conditions of peace. War was the great challenge to commerce, although it frequently offered notable opportunities for its advancement. That Mahan wrote primarily about war rather than peace is not a contradiction, but merely a reflection of the belief that commerce in peacetime looked after itself, save in particular instances where protectionism was politically necessary to prosper. It was during war that commerce had to be protected most dearly, and when state policy could significantly aid its expansion. What required examination were instead the relationships between commerce and war, and commerce and naval force within war. Although Mahan never used the term grand strategy, the results of his writings would today be conventionally considered grand strategy, as they occupy a place between, and overlapping, standard definitions of strategy and policy.

Mahan's emphasis on naval strategy meant that his theory suited an insular power on the geographic periphery much more than a power in the heart of a continent. Mahan, as a navalist and imperialist, was in this regard somewhat visionary. He tried to break the insular American geostrategic perspective which regarded the United States as the centre of the world, merely to be defended against threats from without.

Admiring Great Britain as he did, Mahan felt that eventually the United States would have to replace Britain as the leading naval power, a transition which would revolutionize American geostrategic thought by positioning the United States as a presence on the periphery of distant continents, rather than at the heart of its own continent. He desired the United States to look into other continents, rather than outward from its own, and so anticipated by sixty years the sea change in American geopolitical analysis brought on by the Second World War and Cold War. Geographically, this position looks into continents from their surrounding seas, ready for American trade. It does not look out from a continental heartland towards potentially hostile oceans whose trade opportunities are beyond reach. Tension between these two geographical outlooks would be one of the main influences on American grand strategic thought during the interwar period which, after being largely suppressed during the Cold War, would be revitalized in the grand strategic debates of the 1990s.

Mahan, writing at a time when naval literature burgeoned on both sides of the Atlantic, was the best known of the American writers on strategy. Many British authors also weighed in on the naval debates of the turn of the century. These included the brothers Colomb, Sir John and Vice-Admiral Phillip; Sir John Knox Laughton; and especially Sir Julian Corbett. All of these writers read each others' works. Despite this interchange of ideas, the strategic and political context which surrounded the British contrasted starkly with that of the Americans. Although their purposes were similar, to influence or aid contemporary policymaking, the content of outwardly similar concepts differed significantly due to the basic contrasts in context. The ideas propounded by Julian Corbett, of all of Mahan's British contemporaries, best reveal this disparity of ideas.

SIR JULIAN STAFFORD CORBETT, DEVELOPING GRAND STRATEGY

Corbett is widely regarded as having presaged the concept of grand strategy with his notion of major strategy, discussed most extensively in the original and revised versions of the Green Pamphlet, a collection of definitions, notes, and strategic relationships which ultimately form the basis for his main theoretical work, *Some Principles of Maritime Strategy*. Yet Corbett's published works clearly display an evolution in the notion of a higher level of strategy, which suggests that Corbett developed his own conception of grand strategy rather than merely anticipating future notions.

As early as 1900 Corbett mentioned 'higher strategy' in *The Successors of Drake*, where it remained undefined and unexplained. The term served merely to contrast English expectations of Spanish actions with actual Spanish plans.[28] However, his undefined use of the term implies some already extant level of reader understanding. His 1904 study of England's maritime role in the Mediterranean continued, and reflected, the lack of definition. He identified higher strategy 'of war', 'of the Mediterranean', and 'of the campaign', but he never resolved the apparent inconsistency between the levels of analysis.[29] Also as early as 1904 Corbett concurrently coined and consistently used another term—grand strategy—in his lectures at the Royal Naval War College in Greenwich. The discussions of grand strategy and its relationship with

---

[28] Julian S. Corbett, *The Successors of Drake*, (London: Longmans, Green & Co., 1916), 147.
[29] Julian S. Corbett, *England in the Mediterranean* (London: Longmans, Green, & Co., 1917), ii. 461, 505, 506.

minor strategy comprised much of his first lecture, where Corbett set out his terms: 'First there is Grand Strategy, dealing with whole theatre of war, with planning the war. It looks on war as a continuation of foreign policy. It regards the object of the war & the means of attaining it. It handles all the national resources together, Navy, Army, Diplomacy & Finance. It is the province of the Council of Defence. Handles Army, Navy, as divisions of one force.'[30] Within two years, he had given up the term grand strategy in favour of major strategy, likely as a more fitting counterpart to minor strategy. Thus by 1906, in the original Green Pamphlet, Corbett had defined major strategy as 'dealing with ulterior objects' and considered the ways and means necessary to achieve those objects.[31]

Corbett defined the purpose of grand, or major, strategy between 1904 and 1906, after having read Clausewitz. Corbett drew much insight from Clausewitz's work, even though the contexts within which they wrote and the purposes of their works differed greatly. Following Clausewitz, he postulated that war had two main classifications. It could be offensive or defensive, and it could be limited or unlimited.[32] The former classification reflected the interest of the particular strategic actor in the war, and whether or not the policy to be fulfilled was positive or negative. The latter, however, was manipulable, and Corbett identified this manipulation as grand strategy's task.[33] The purpose of grand strategy was to establish the boundaries of the war, and thereafter to manipulate them for one's own gain and the enemy's loss. It was possible to expand them beyond the enemy's means, to contract them to limit the enemy's ways, or to match one's ends to one's own limitations in ways or means.

Corbett, as a good student of Clausewitz, recognized the innate tension between limited and unlimited war. It was a product of the interaction between two adversaries, each of whom must try to outdo the other to succeed. Corbett discussed the manipulation of boundaries and the tendency of limited wars to become unlimited in relation to the strategic context of 1759, the midpoint of the Seven Years War, and posited that escalation of effort and aim was an inherent law of war.

Up to the midpoint of the Seven Years War, English grand strategy concerned maximizing its effort in the limited theatre of direct interest, and attempting to minimize action elsewhere as possible. Once the Seven Years War reached an inflection point, marked by the conquest of Canada, the contours of English grand strategy changed. Defeated in Canada, France

---

[30] Julian S. Corbett, *Lectures on Naval Strategy*. CBT/31, Julian Stafford Corbett Papers, National Maritime Museum, 117.
[31] Julian S. Corbett, *Strategical Terms and Definitions used in Lectures on Naval History*, CBT/6/15-16, 1.
[32] Corbett, *Some Principles*, chs 2 and 3.
[33] Corbett, *Lectures on Naval Strategy*, CBT/31, 119.

poured its utmost effort into combating English allies on the continent to salvage a continental victory from a colonial defeat. This parallels Mahan's implicit belief that control of the sea inherently led to escalation in land warfare in Europe. Mahan, however, did not consider the matter any further, being content to limit his discussion to sea power. Corbett, by contrast never divorcing naval thinking from what could ultimately be achieved on land, extended his analysis beyond the first, primarily colonial, phase of the war. Escalation in Europe marked a second phase, defined by a change in English grand strategy to attack France outright and raise the cost of war as high as it could. Corbett extrapolated this logical division between the two phases into a general principle.[34]

The manipulation of the breadth and character of the war might limit as well as escalate the conflict. Corbett fully understood that the unfavourable geostrategic situation of 1776–83 evolved directly from the exorbitant, if justified, desires of the British government, and Pitt the Elder in particular, during the Seven Years War. He warned that 'measures, however plausible, which tend to raise up fresh enemies do not increase the strength of our international position' and 'dreaded our overloading ourselves with colonial possessions, as Spain had done to her ruin'.[35] Limiting the current war as much as possible, particularly in the naval sphere, restricted hostile feeling which might persist until the next war. Corbett believed that war was meant to serve policy. Corbett's counterpart to grand strategy, minor strategy, ensured that manipulation of war's boundaries did indeed serve policy.

Grand strategy and minor strategy were meant to be inseparable, comprising two halves of a whole. Corbett suggested that '[t]his distinction between Grand & Minor Strategy is only another way of saying that every strategical problem must be considered in two separate ways:– 1st from the point of view of its object. 2nd from the point of view of the method, by which that object can be attained.'[36] Grand strategy provided the rationale for action in war, but the details of execution were the concern of minor strategy. By 1906, his purview of grand strategy had expanded, not only to establish the ulterior motive, but also to decide on the means to achieve one's purpose.[37] For Corbett, grand strategy was concerned originally with ends, but by 1906 also with the choice of means, while minor strategy limited itself to ways. Grand strategy and minor strategy together comprised today's well known trinity of ends, ways, and means.

---

[34] Julian S. Corbett, *England in the Seven Years War* (London: Longmans, Green, & Co., 1907), i. 71.
[35] Ibid. 173.
[36] Corbett, *Lectures on Naval Strategy*, 118.
[37] Corbett, *Strategical Terms and Definitions*, CBT/6-15/16, 1.

Corbett wavered on what to include in the possible means for the purpose of manipulating the boundary of war, which reflects the shifting responsibilities he ascribed to grand strategy. In 1904, Corbett believed that grand strategy 'handles all the national resources together, Navy, Army, Diplomacy & Finance'.[38] By 1906, he had backed away from considering diplomacy and finance explicit instruments of grand strategy, although they remained important considerations. Diplomacy and grand strategy were conceptually separate, but practically intertwined: 'To decide a question of grand strategy without consideration of its diplomatic aspect, is to decide on half the factors only.'[39]

Of the two or three instruments—army, navy, and perhaps diplomacy—the army was the most important, '[s]ince men live upon the land and not upon the sea'.[40] The army, however, was not the most useful tool for manipulating the boundary of war, particularly not on the European continent. The geostrategic conditions of Europe denied continental strategists much influence on the limits of war, save in an escalatory fashion. Corbett remarked, in relation to Frederick the Great's conquest of Saxony and von Moltke's conquest of Alsace-Lorraine, that conquering territory organic to another state usually elicited an escalated response.[41] Armies on the continent expanded wars and escalated warfare with ease, but could not effectively limit them because the vital security interests of the great powers coexisted too closely for limitation in warfare not to be self-defeating if unreciprocated.

Navies were different. Vitally, they posed less of a direct threat to the great European powers for they existed physically on the periphery of the continent, yet still remained potent instruments. However, territories beyond the European periphery were not contiguous and so the navy could be used to block transit there from Europe: 'History shows that they can never have the political importance of objects which are organically part of the European system, and it shows further that they can be isolated by naval action sufficiently to set up the conditions of true limited war.'[42] From this basis, Corbett arrived at the conclusion 'that limited war is only permanently possible to island Powers or between Powers which are separated by sea', and specifically to powers which had the wherewithal reliably to interdict the sea lines of communication.[43] Grand strategy, which demanded the ability to wage both limited and unlimited wars, was an activity consistently available only to powerful maritime countries. Only a combination of naval and military power allowed states freely to escalate or deescalate wars as necessary.

---

[38] Corbett, *Lectures on Naval Strategy*, 117.
[39] Corbett, *Strategical Terms and Definitions*, CBT/6/15-16, 1; see also Corbett, *Notes on Strategy*, CBT/6/15-16, 1.
[40] Corbett, *Some Principles*, 16.   [41] Ibid. 54–5.   [42] Ibid. 55.   [43] Ibid. 57.

This power to limit war arbitrarily, as long as one's home territory remained safe, was a potent one. Corbett implicitly identified it with hegemony, particularly of the Mediterranean, 'the waters where the three continents met'. Interestingly, although Corbett's published book would ultimately bear the title *England in the Mediterranean*, the manuscript was named otherwise: 'The Meaning of the Navy'.[44] The meaning of the superior navy was to manipulate the boundaries of war at will, and so to dominate the seas which mattered for global power.

The navy also had another meaning, one less beneficial to its wielder. It could limit war, but limited wars tend to take longer and so are liable 'to raise up fresh enemies for the dominant power in a much higher degree than it does on land, owing to the inevitable exasperation of neutrals'. To be most effective within Corbett's second phase of war, the navy had to bring the pressure of war to bear indiscriminately upon the entire enemy country. This in turn had the potential to escalate the war by drawing in irate neutrals against the naval power. Corbett thus concluded that '[t]he primary and all-absorbing object of a superior naval power is not merely to take the offensive, but to force the enemy to expose himself to a decision as quickly as possible'.[45] Celerity in effect was a mandatory condition of using the navy in order to limit the war. Navies, unlike armies, had the capability both to limit and to expand war.

Corbett recognized that the innately escalatory character of war within Europe posed a strategic difficulty to a maritime state such as Britain, which did not have the means to match its European rivals on the continent. This led Corbett to discern within Britain's strategic history a particular British or maritime way in warfare in Europe which focused on being 'an ancillary to the larger operations of our allies—a method which has usually been open to us because the control of the sea has enabled us to select a theatre in effect truly limited'.[46] This conception of grand strategy assumed an enemy great power with reasonably far-flung overseas domains, where all three instruments of grand strategy worked together. Diplomacy formed coalitions against the European foe to occupy its main forces. The British army campaigned in a distant theatre organic to Europe and there fought the secondary forces of the enemy. The Royal Navy kept the army supplied by sea and protected the flanks of the theatre, and acted against the opponent's colonial possessions elsewhere. It was a way of using force and diplomacy to limit the war for Britain while escalating it for Britain's main foe. All the tools of grand strategy worked together harmoniously to produce the desired circumstance.[47]

---

[44] Corbett, *England in the Mediterranean*, i. 4; see also Julian S. Corbett, *The Meaning of the Navy*, CBT/38, 6–7.

[45] Corbett, *Seven Years War*, ii. 374.   [46] Corbett, *Some Principles*, 66.

[47] For background on the development of Corbett's British Way in Warfare idea, see Andrew Lambert, 'The Naval War Course, *Some Principles of Maritime Strategy* and the Origins of the "British Way in Warfare"', in Keith Neilson and Greg Kennedy (eds), *The British Way in*

This British way in warfare postulated by Corbett has been considered by some a historical fiction, primarily on the charge that 'it was always as a result, not of free choice or atavistic wisdom, but of *force majeure*'.[48] If so, it was a powerful piece of historical imagination which illuminated Corbett's vision of grand strategy. Corbett, unlike Basil Liddell Hart, was unlikely to have considered the British way in warfare a template for action. Instead, he contended that a theory's 'main practical value is that it can assist a capable man to acquire a broad outlook whereby he may be the surer his plans cover all the ground, and whereby he may with greater rapidity and certainty seize all the factors of a sudden situation'.[49] Corbett would likely have considered the British way in warfare the archetype of grand strategy in thought and praxis, but one which informed rather than directed action.

Corbett came to this appreciation of grand strategy because he was a British maritime, rather than narrowly naval, historian writing in a geopolitical context characterized by increasing British self-doubt and concern over their apparently increasing inability to match available financial, naval, and military means to myriad political ends. Joseph Chamberlain, British Colonial Secretary at the beginning of the twentieth century, enunciated this in his famous depiction of the British Empire as a 'weary titan [who] staggers under the too vast orb of his own fate'.[50] As a historian well connected to the Admiralty who taught strategy to future practitioners, Corbett necessarily sought to make history useful to contemporary strategy-making. Working within the intellectual environment of early twentieth-century Whitehall, strategic theory had to emphasize conservation of resources and the limitation of conflict, both in magnitude and in time. This context of relatively waning power was the opposite of the context of ever growing power within which Mahan wrote.

Corbett's concepts of maritime limited war and of grand strategy as regulating the limits of war were historically inspired, but devised for Britain's contemporary geopolitical and strategic context. Britain was being overtaken industrially by Germany and the United States, and France and Russia were catching up as well. It could only continue the two-power standard for its navy by explicitly discounting the burgeoning United States navy. Britain faced the prospect of losing its leading status in international affairs.[51] Corbett was

---

Warfare: Power and the International System, 1856–1956: Essays in Honour of David French (Farnham: Ashgate 2010), 219–56.

[48] 'The British Way in Warfare: A Reappraisal', in Michael Howard, *The Causes of War and Other Essays* (Cambridge, MA: Harvard UP, 1983), 180.

[49] Corbett, *Some Principles*, 4.

[50] See Aaron L. Friedberg, *The Weary Titan: Britain and the Experience of Relative Decline, 1895–1905* (Princeton: Princeton UP, 2010), Chamberlain quote from p. 116. He spoke those words at an imperial conference on burden-sharing in defence in 1902.

[51] John Gooch, 'The Weary Titan: Strategy and Policy in Great Britain, 1890–1918', in Murray et al., *Making of Strategy*, 278–306; Richard Hart Sinnreich. 'About Turn: British

mindful of this reality. He emphasized the classification of war as limited or unlimited and dedicated four chapters to the subject in *Some Principles of Maritime Strategy*. His adaptation of Clausewitz's concepts of limited and unlimited war explicitly addressed Britain's relatively weakening power; the chapter was subtitled 'Development of Clausewitz's and Jomini's Theory of a Limited Territorial Object, and its Application to Modern Imperial Conditions'.[52] It and the Introductory, in which he justified his discussion of theory, were the only chapters in the entirety of *Some Principles of Maritime Strategy* to warrant subtitles, underlining the importance and utility he attached to the ideas contained within those two chapters. Corbett ultimately believed that Britain's best, perhaps only, way of avoiding, or at least slowing, decline was to wage war much as it had done under the tutelage of the Pitts. Britain could best maintain its political status and geostrategic position by limiting the war for itself and delimiting it for whichever adversary awaited. It had to wage war economically, and make the peace it could, which most suited longevity. Corbett's concept of grand strategy thus made a contemporary argument from a historical perspective.

CONCLUSION

Although the concepts of grand strategy drawn from their individual bodies of work differed, Mahan and Corbett together codified the interlocking assumptions which underpinned the British school of grand strategic thought. First, Great Britain was acting as a peripheral, albeit not impotent, power. Directly from this assumption flowed the second, which stipulated that British interest in war, although always political, was typically concerned less with security than with the most economically gainful peace. Such beneficial peaces were necessary because, as a great power interested in keeping European continental politics in balance, another war was inevitable and Britain had to enter it under the most advantageous possible circumstances.

Between them, Captain Alfred Thayer Mahan and Sir Julian Stafford Corbett elaborated their own maritime historical thinking first to imply and later to develop a theoretical concept of grand strategy significantly different from that which had existed before and, along with it, to create a British school of grand strategic thought. This school of thought was to be later adopted and shaped by the major interwar British strategic theorists, John Frederick

---

Strategic Transformation from Salisbury to Grey', in Williamson Murray, Richard Hart Sinnreich, and James Lacey (eds), *The Shaping of Grand Strategy: Policy, Diplomacy, and War* (Cambridge: CUP, 2011), 111–46.

[52] Corbett, *Some Principles*, 52.

Charles Fuller and Basil Liddell Hart, and, in the form of the British way in warfare, remains a topic of scholarly debate to this day. Two defining elements of continuity, from Mahan and Corbett throughout the entire British school of grand strategic thought, were the salience placed upon economic considerations and the undesirability of participating in escalation on land.

Ultimately, the ideas Mahan and Corbett introduced established grand strategy as a concept with important features recognizable to modern scholars, particularly regarding the inclusion of all—not simply military and economic—instruments of political power. Despite this expansion of the concept, Corbett and, to a lesser extent, Mahan focused purely on war, and so their notions of grand strategy were not the theories of all international relations which much later definitions were to become.

3

Grand Strategy in British Reactions to the World Wars

The two giants of British strategic thought, John Frederick Charles Fuller and Basil Liddell Hart, tied the idea of grand strategy to the limits of war, much as their immediate predecessor Julian Stafford Corbett had done. Yet the traumatic influence of the First World War cardinally changed the character of this theme. Rather than a pure Mahanian focus on sea power or a subtle Corbettian appreciation of the malleability of the boundaries of the war, Fuller and Liddell Hart sought only to limit war. Although stemming from the same war, their reasons for prioritizing limitation differed. Fuller anchored his thoughts on grand strategy to the survival of (Western) civilization itself. Liddell Hart's reaction to the First World War was much more emotional, and limiting war became an end in its own right. His entire system of military strategic and grand strategic thought was based upon limiting war for the sake of limitation.

Few other British military and strategic theorists of the interwar period wrote about grand strategy. One exception is a pair of British authors, Henry Antony Sargeaunt and Geoffrey West, who produced the very first book-length treatment of the subject in 1941. Their grasp of grand strategy differed significantly from that of Fuller and Liddell Hart, particularly in that limiting war was not their purpose of grand strategy. They instead emphasized the other prevalent aspect of British grand strategic thought of the time, that it should employ all instruments of power, including economic, psychological, and so on. They rightly understood that this expansion of strategy deepened the relationship between war and society, and so took this premise as the basis for their own thought.

British usage of grand strategy prior to the interwar period and the era's geopolitics set the context in which these four interwar British strategic theorists wrote. The term grand strategy was never as popular in Britain as in the United States during the first two decades of the twentieth century, but it was a concept widely enough known to be used casually. The first British use of grand strategy was K. P. Wolseley's previously mentioned 1889 interpretation of what General William T. Sherman meant by grand strategy, followed by Charles Oman's use of the term in 1898.[1] A South African, commenting on the Second Boer War at the Royal United Services Institute in 1901, spoke of 'the grand strategy of Lord Roberts and the wide and enveloping movements which drove the Boers forward'.[2] James R. Thursfield, a British author of naval history and correspondent of Alfred Thayer Mahan, was unsurprisingly also aware of the term.[3] Herbert Richmond, who corresponded frequently with Corbett, also employed the idea of grand strategy.[4] Even Fuller himself used the term casually during the First World War, employing it in a report written in 1917 titled 'Projected Bases for the Tactical Employment of Tanks in 1918'.[5] Significantly, all of these authors, including Fuller, used it in a highly restricted military or naval sense. It was the First World War which caused Fuller to reconsider and broaden the concept of grand strategy, which in turn influenced the grand strategic thought of Liddell Hart.

THE GEOPOLITICAL CONTEXT

The geopolitical context in which Fuller and Liddell Hart wrote was much the same as that of Corbett, save that the First World War had transpired. Britain ended the First World War deeply, multifariously scarred. Although Britain suffered fewer casualties in absolute terms than any of the other major powers involved for the full duration of the war, it had not been prepared for such a costly effort in lives. The war was also economically grievous, although again Britain suffered less than many other great powers. Finance became a prominent consideration in military policy and strategy making during much of the interwar period. Both of these considerations—the manpower and the financial costs of war—would dominate the grand strategic thought of both Fuller and Liddell Hart. Fuller was influenced primarily by the demands of economy and considered men and women to be economic units who should not be sacrificed in war if at all avoidable lest such sacrifice damage the post-war

---

[1] K. P. Wolseley, 'An English View of the Civil War, VI', *North American Review* 149/396 (Nov. 1889), 599; Charles Oman. *A History of the Art of War in the Middle Ages* (London: Methuen & Co., 1978 [1898]), bk 5, ch. 2.

[2] T. L. Schreiner, 'Some Ideas of a South African about the War', *RUSI Journal* 45/282 (1901), 1093.

[3] James R. Thursfield, *Nelson and Other Naval Studies* (New York: E. P. Dutton & Co., 1920 [1909]), 242, 244.

[4] Herbert W. Richmond, 'Considerations of the War at Sea', *Naval Review* 5 (1917), 8, 10.

[5] J. F. C. Fuller, *Memoirs of an Unconventional Soldier* (London: Ivor Nicholson & Watson, 1936), 122–4.

economy. Considerations of preserving manpower for its own sake, as well as of economy, weighed heavily upon Liddell Hart.

Not so with Sargeaunt and West, however. Their grand strategic thought was entirely a product of the demands and pressures of the Second World War, an ideological conflict involving the mobilization of whole societies in a fight to the finish. Their thinking thus mirrored the demands of that war rather than the trauma of the preceding World War by focusing on the relationship between war and society, and particularly on how societies wage war.

JOHN FREDERICK CHARLES FULLER

Major General J. F. C. Fuller (1878–1966), a veteran of the Boer and First World Wars, was a prolific writer on military and strategic matters. Fuller is more widely known as a military theorist, as a progenitor of operational art, and as a tank proselytizer than as a grand strategist.[6] He has been largely forgotten by the grand strategic literature, yet his use of the term not only predated Liddell Hart but in numerous respects anticipated the latter's own usage. Fuller's shift from a military interpretation of grand strategy to a wider national conception was caused by the extraordinary economic damage wrought by the First World War upon Western Europe. Fuller's grand strategic thought may be viewed as a trifecta comprising grand strategy, civilization, and advocacy of tanks in lieu of mass infantry armies as a limiting factor on warfare. Grand strategy sought to preserve civilization from the ravages of war by replacing infantry with tanks.

That this trifecta is not immediately apparent from his writings stems from the fact that he neglected to draw these three threads explicitly together. Fuller preferred to treat each strand separately, save in his first two books: *The Reformation of War* and *The Foundations of the Science of War*. To explore Fuller's grand strategic thought and forge it into a single whole, his actual definition of grand strategy must be delineated and then must be connected to its purpose of preserving civilization. Finally, his advocacy of armoured-centric warfare must be shown to serve this purpose and so to fulfil the requirements of grand strategy.

Fuller never wavered from his basic interpretation of grand strategy as '[t]he transmission of power in all its forms, in order to maintain policy'.[7] However,

---

[6] See Anthony John Trythall, *'Boney' Fuller: The Intellectual General 1878–1966* (London: Cassell, 1977); Brian Holden Reid, *J. F. C. Fuller: Military Thinker* (London: Macmillan, 1987); and Brian Holden Reid, *Studies in British Military Thought: Debates with Fuller and Liddell Hart* (Lincoln, NE: University of Nebraska Press, 1998).

[7] J. F. C. Fuller, *The Reformation of War* (London: Hutchinson & Co., 1923), 219.

certain details changed over time. His original conception was unique among all definitions of grand strategy by being almost exclusively a peacetime activity. 'Paradoxical as it may seem, the resting time of the grand strategist is during war, for it is during peace that he works and labours. During peace time he not only calculates the resources in men, supplies and moral forces of all possible enemies, but, having weighed them, he, unsuspected by the enemy, undermines them by a plan.'[8] Fuller explicitly argued that grand strategy was planning and activity in the abstract, but that actual implementation belonged to the entirely separate idea of grand tactics. He approved of Clausewitz's dictum that any strategic actor must identify the character of the war embarked upon and linked this act of perception to grand strategy.[9]

By 1926 Fuller had begun shying away from the notion that grand strategy was solely a peacetime concern. This is revealed when Fuller identified an expansion in the skills required by grand strategists over history from being a merely politically sensible soldier to one who 'must also be a psychologist and an economist'.[10] He thus began expanding the responsibilities of grand strategy into wartime, a trend which was continued in his study of the American Civil War. By 1929 he was arguing that '[g]rand strategy secures the political object by directing all warlike resources towards the winning of the war, whilst grand tactics accomplishes action by converging all means of waging war against the forces of the enemy'.[11] He also admitted that 'grand strategy' was not an ideal term, preferring the term 'political strategy'.[12] Fuller did not expand on this statement then or later. It may indicate that he believed that the manipulation of non-military instruments of power, being more integral to the domestic political fabric of any strategic actor, also had greater domestic political effect than use of the military alone could have. Given his assumption that the very purpose of grand strategy was to preserve civilization, particularly economically, this seems reasonable.

The question of civilization must be placed within history. Fuller considered history a semi-teleological force, which necessarily resulted in progress. The only counterforce capable of derailing progress was humanity itself. Thus he bemoaned that man 'cannot see that each epoch in history is but a stepping-stone in the river of life, upon one bank of which capers the ape, and upon the other, we hope, gambols the angel'.[13] Each epoch was defined by a particular characteristic, which determined the congruent character of war for that age.

---

[8] Ibid. 220.
[9] J. F. C. Fuller, *The Foundations of the Science of War* (London: Hutchinson & Co., 1926), 106.
[10] Ibid. 106.
[11] J. F. C. Fuller, *The Generalship of Ulysses S. Grant* (London: John Murray, 1929), 7.
[12] Ibid. 7 n.
[13] J. F. C. Fuller, *The Dragon's Teeth: A Study of War and Peace* (London: Constable & Co., 1932), 8.

Fuller maintained that '[t]he immoralities of war are normally but a continuation of the immoralities of peace'.[14] Indeed, war was in many respects defined by the two periods of peace which sandwiched it, for it connected them. 'If war, as it is so often asserted, is a continuation of peace policy, then war is also a link with the policy which will follow victory.'[15]

Fuller believed that the contemporary age was determined by economics due to the highly interconnected character of international trade, which meant that the wars fought throughout that age were similarly delineated. 'War is not an altruistic but an economic question; it is a continuation of peace policy, and the foundations of peace policy, in the present material age, are economic.' Even more explicitly, he suggested that '[w]ar is a continuation of economic policy in another form'.[16] Wars were not only waged in an economic milieu, which was ever the case, but their most important effects were manifested in the economic sphere. The economic impetus to war was that which specifically pointed strategists in the correct direction for achievement of effect.[17] The effect Fuller identified as necessary and desirable was the continuation of prosperity in the peace succeeding the present war. 'Being a continuation of policy, it logically follows that the termination of a war should be followed by a state of peacefulness in which the policy of the victor is in every way more prosperous economically, ethically and socially than it was the day war was declared.'[18]

The consequence of not connecting economics and war in the manner Fuller indicated was that wars were poorly waged. By Fuller's standards, the First World War represented an obvious failure of policy and strategy for Britain. This was not simply a case of ineffective military strategy but also of grand strategy, of choosing improper tools for the desired overall effect. Fuller particularly and consistently railed against two features of the First World War emblematic of the misguided strategies which failed to connect war and economics beneficially. The first was sheer slaughter. This was not simply the butchery of soldiers of one's own nationality, but extended to the enemy as well. Fuller argued hypothetically that, if Britain had had the opportunity to kill five million German soldiers during the First World War, it should not have taken it. Doing so would ruin the post-war German economy and so weaken British trade.[19] 'Every man killed means a loss of capital.'[20]

The second aspect Fuller opposed was the overuse of economic blockade as an instrument in wartime. He conceded that it was a valid instrument because it could contribute 'to break down the will of the enemy nation'.[21]

---

[14] Fuller, *Reformation of War*, 69.   [15] Ibid. 89.
[16] Fuller, *Dragon's Teeth*, 83.   [17] Fuller, *Foundations of the Science of War*, 64.
[18] J. F. C. Fuller, *On Future Warfare* (London: Sifton Praed & Co., 1928), 164.
[19] Ibid. 166–7.   [20] Fuller, *Foundations of the Science of War*, 76.
[21] J. F. C. Fuller. *Lectures on F.S.R. II* (London: Sifton Praed & Co., 1931), 34.

Nevertheless, it was easy to employ too harshly and with no thought to the connection between war and economics. The result is that '[t]he economic attack is without question the most brutal of all forms of attack, because it does not only kill but cripple, and cripples more than one generation. Turning men, women and children into starving animals, it is a direct blow against what is called civilization.'[22] This direct repudiation of Mahan's assessment of economic blockade as the most humane weapon reveals the sharply differing conclusions on ways and means within the British school of grand strategic thought.

Fuller held so tightly to this connection between war and economics that he associated morality and ethics with the advancement of the global economy. 'In its ultimate form the economic object in war is the national object, namely, survival with profit, which presupposes an ethical outlook, since honesty endows prosperity with its firmest foundation.'[23] The belligerent waging war in a manner which negatively impacts the global economy the least is morally superior and more desirable as a victor.[24] Fuller consequently considered a harsh economic blockade of the enemy to be fundamentally immoral because it directly damaged global prosperity and therefore civilization as a whole.[25]

After the Second World War, he extended his critique to include the bombing campaign as well. In an article titled 'Unstrategic Bombing and World Ruin', Fuller repeated many of the themes already outlined. Critiquing the indiscriminate role of air bombardment, he argued that

> [h]ere we are faced by a dilemma: not only is physical war dependent on industrial power and city life, but our civilization is also dependent upon them. Destroy the factories, and the cities become shells; destroy the cities, and the wheels of industry cease to turn. Destroy both, and civilization reverts back to barbarism and through barbarism back to a purely agricultural civilization.[26]

Fuller, with his highly imaginative and dynamic mind, surely desired eventually to address the difficulties of connecting war and economics. Already planning and writing *Foundations*, Fuller 'had told Liddell Hart as early as 1923 that the book was only the first of ten he wished to write, the others covering such subjects as "The Foundations of the Art of War", "The Foundations of War Training", "The Foundations of Grand Strategy".'[27] Ultimately he never fulfilled these ambitions. His energies during the interwar period were consumed by his advocacy of tanks. This particular interest did not and

---

[22] J. F. C. Fuller, *War and Western Civilization 1832–1932: A Study of War as a Political Instrument and the Expression of Mass Democracy* (London: Duckworth, 1932), 230.
[23] Fuller, *Foundations of the Science of War*, 73.
[24] Ibid. 72–3.   [25] Fuller, *Reformation of War*, 95.
[26] J. F. C. Fuller, 'Unstrategic Bombing and World Ruin', Basil Liddell Hart Papers, Liddell Hart Centre for Military Archives, King's College London, 1/302/687, 94. Permission granted by The Trustees of the Liddell Hart Centre for Military Archives.
[27] Trythall, *'Boney' Fuller*, 110.

could not address entirely the question of connecting war and economics. It did allow him to comment on the issue of slaughter in war, and how to avoid it. This third strand of his extant thought on grand strategy belonged to a separate idea and praxis: grand tactics.

Fuller considered grand tactics to be the implementation of the military aspect of grand strategy.[28] Fuller's use of the term 'strategy' itself is odd when considered in relation to grand tactics: 'Field strategy is grand tactics, or major tactics, set in motion'.[29] He separates grand strategy from its actual practice, and then does the same with grand tactics. Never comfortable with the term, he once remarked to Liddell Hart that 'I admit that I find it most difficult to suggest a suitable definition for "Strategy".'[30] His most consistent use places it as a particular method within grand tactics, a specific way of approaching the battlefield. 'Strategy is the art of moving armies towards the battlefield in such a way that when the battle takes place it will be fought at the greatest advantage... Strategy should aim either at surprising the enemy when the battle takes place, or at concentrating a superior force against a weak point.'[31]

Unlike Liddell Hart, Fuller did not believe that battle could be avoided. For all the utility of manoeuvre and surprise, '[s]trategy is accomplished by battle'.[32] Battle can be given in more or less effective ways, however. Fuller identified two related developments to improve the effectiveness of battle. First, one had to disorganize the enemy by attacking his command systems.[33] This could be achieved by the nascent military technology of his time, tanks and airplanes, whose predominant value was in moral effect which struck directly at the 'nerves of an army, and through its nerves the will of its commander'.[34] New technology allowed battles to be fought efficiently and effectively, minimizing casualties on both sides and increasing the likelihood of a better, more prosperous peace after war's conclusion. This is the full meaning of Fuller's controversial statement that '[t]ools, or weapons, if only the right ones can be discovered, form 99 per cent. of victory'.[35]

Fuller adequately summarized his own system of grand strategic thought by 1926, early in his long authorial career. 'A war, to be economical, must enforce acceptance of the policy under dispute with the least possible harm to commercial prosperity... A military decision, to be economical, must attain more profitable result than the depreciation of capital due to its attainment.'[36]

---

[28] Fuller, *Reformation of War*, 219.
[29] J. F. C. Fuller, *Grant and Lee: A Study in Personality and Generalship* (London: Eyre & Spottiswoode, 1933), 263.
[30] Fuller to Liddell Hart, 8 Jan. 1929, Liddell Hart Papers, 1/302/163.
[31] Fuller, *Lectures on F.S.R. II*, 1.   [32] Ibid. 34.
[33] Fuller, *On Future Warfare*, 94.
[34] J. F. C. Fuller, *Lectures on F.S.R. III* (London: Sifton Praed & Co., 1932), 7.
[35] Fuller, *On Future Warfare*, 153.
[36] Fuller, *Foundations of the Science of War*, 77.

Grand strategy was the lynchpin which tamed war, kept it limited, and so preserved its utility for civilization. Fuller never doubted the natural utility of war for civilization, as opposed to the utility of its particular character at any given moment. 'Until humanity has evolved a more perfect state of peacefulness, wars are likely to be necessary as moral purges.'[37]

BASIL HENRY LIDDELL HART

Captain Basil Henry Liddell Hart (1895–1970) was a veteran of the First World War, a prolific commentator and theorist of military strategy, and wielded some influence with Neville Chamberlain's government in 1937–8. Liddell Hart, like Fuller, is most widely remembered as a progenitor of operational art, as a tank advocate, but also as the proselytizer of the strategy of the indirect approach.[38] Unlike Fuller, his contributions to the field of grand strategy are well recognized. Much like Fuller, he ultimately conceived of grand strategy as a moderating and limiting influence on war due to the experience of the First World War. Indeed, Hew Strachan has noted that he 'belonged to those groups, both in society as a whole and in the army, which suffered disproportionately in the Great War. The middle class, the professions, the public schools, the universities, contributed more men to the forces relative to their aggregate size than did working-class occupations.'[39] Unlike Fuller, he did not tie grand strategy to the idea of progress and civilization, but instead to the idea of post-war deterrence of future aggressors.

Liddell Hart originally broached the subject of grand strategy in his first book *Paris*. Azar Gat suggests that '[s]o profoundly impressed was he [Liddell Hart] with [Fuller's *The Reformation of War*] that he simply plagiarized it almost lock, stock, and barrel in his own first important book, *Paris, or the Future of War* (1925)'.[40] With reference solely to their respective definitions and usages of grand strategy, this analysis appears inapt. Rather than considering grand strategy as the transmission of power in any and all of its forms, and as a primarily peacetime activity, Liddell Hart proffered a very nineteenth-century definition. 'It is the function of grand strategy to discover and exploit the Achilles' heel of the enemy nation; to strike not against its strongest

---

[37] Fuller, *Dragon's Teeth*, 123.
[38] Much has been written on Liddell Hart. See e.g. Alex Danchev, *Alchemist of War: The Life of Basil Liddell Hart* (London: Weidenfeld & Nicolson, 1998); Brian Bond, *Liddell Hart: A Study of his Military Thought* (London: Cassell, 1977); and John J. Mearsheimer, *Liddell Hart and the Weight of History* (Ithaca, NY: Cornell UP, 1988).
[39] Hew Strachan, '"The Real War": Liddell Hart, Cruttwell, and Falls', in Brian Bond (ed.), *The First World War and British Military History* (Oxford: Clarendon Press, 1991), 41–2.
[40] Azar Gat, *A History of Military Thought* (Oxford: OUP, 2001), 665.

bulwark but against its most vulnerable spot.'⁴¹ Grand strategy was merely *good* strategy.

Moreover, this was a conception of grand strategy to which he accorded significant weight. Liddell Hart considered this definition to be one of the salient points raised in *Paris*, as well as one of the book's major contributions to military knowledge.⁴² Despite this early emphasis, Liddell Hart would adopt Fuller's basic idea of grand strategy within a year. '202 B.C.–1919 A.D.! What moderation compared with the conditions of Versailles. Here was true grand strategy—the object a better peace, a peace of security and prosperity.'⁴³ Liddell Hart was not one to change his mind easily, especially on such a serious matter as grand strategy—entire verbatim paragraphs on the subject survived nearly intact for twenty-five years from *The Decisive Wars of History* in 1929 to the second edition of *Strategy* in 1954.

> Furthermore, while the horizon of strategy is bounded by the war, grand strategy looks beyond the war to the subsequent peace. It should not only combine the various instruments, but so regulate their use as to avoid damage to the future state of peacefulness, secure and prosperous. Little wonder that, unlike strategy, the realm of grand strategy is for the most part terra incognita!⁴⁴
>
> Furthermore, while the horizon of strategy is bounded by the war, grand strategy looks beyond the war to the subsequent peace. It should not only combine the various instruments, but so regulate their use as to avoid damage to the future state of peace—for its security and prosperity. The sorry state of peace, for both sides, that has followed most wars can be traced to the fact that, unlike strategy, the realm of grand strategy is for the most part *terra incognita*—still awaiting exploration, and understanding.⁴⁵

There are indications that Liddell Hart considered the definition of grand strategy he had accepted from Fuller to be analogous to his own definition in *Paris*. Besides the quotes just given, Liddell Hart's most widely accepted definition was that '[g]rand strategy should both calculate and develop the economic resources and manpower of the nation in order to sustain the fighting services'.⁴⁶

---

[41] Basil Liddell Hart, *Paris, or the Future of War* (London: Kegan Paul, Trench, Trubner & Co., 1925), 27.
[42] Basil Liddell Hart, 'Salient Points from "PARIS, or THE FUTURE OF WAR"', Liddell Hart Papers, 9/1/2, 3; Liddell Hart, 'References to Passages Which Contribute to Military Knowledge', Liddell Hart Papers, 9/1/3, 1. Permission granted by The Trustees of the Liddell Hart Centre for Military Archives.
[43] Basil Liddell Hart, *A Greater than Napoleon: Scipio Africanus* (London: William Blackwood & Sons, 1926), 194. He quoted Fuller's definition from *Reformation of War* on 256.
[44] Basil Liddell Hart, *The Decisive Wars of History: A Study in Strategy* (London: G. Bell & Sons, 1929), 151.
[45] Basil Liddell Hart, *Strategy* (New York: Meridian, 1991), 322.
[46] Liddell Hart, *Decisive Wars of History*, 151.

In his 1941 revision of *The Decisive Wars of History*, which became *Strategy of the Indirect Approach*, he planned to insert the *Paris* definition into his discussion of grand strategy. 'It should be the aim of grand strategy to discover and pierce the Achilles' heel of the opposing government's power to make war. And strategy, in turn, should seek to penetrate the joint in the harness of the opposing forces.'[47] This insertion did not survive to publication, but it reveals an interesting bias of Liddell Hart's. Because grand strategy was responsible for a wide range of political instruments, assigning a perceptive task to grand strategy implied the possibility that an enemy's Achilles' heel might not be military. It also assumed that Britain was well placed to act against such an Achilles' heel exactly because it was not necessarily military.[48]

Liddell Hart identified the British way in warfare as the reason why Britain was economically so well placed. He suggested that it waged wars economically by refusing to send significant expeditionary forces into the heart of any continental conflict in favour of peripheral operations.[49] As with Corbett's maritime way of warfare, this represented an idealized recounting of history which minimized the enemy's superior force and Britain's proclivity to send armies to the main theatre of war. However, Liddell Hart actually believed the British way in warfare was practicable and should be practised. Liddell Hart, much like Fuller, was obsessed with the prosperity of the post-war peace, but he believed that the ruin of subsequent prosperity stemmed directly from the overzealous pursuit of military victory in war rather than from bad (grand) strategy.[50] Unlike Fuller, however, Liddell Hart did not tie grand strategy or the need for prosperity to the idea of civilization.

Liddell Hart's most theoretically useful, albeit not apparent, anchor for grand strategy and the requirement of peaceful prosperity was deterrence. He wrote little on the subject or the connection. It was also a late addition to his theories, included only in 1931.[51] He preferred to contrast deterrence with the quest for victory in war. 'It is wiser to run risks *of* war for the sake of preserving peace than to run risks of exhaustion *in* war for the sake of finishing with victory.'[52] A prosperous state is a state which is more capable of withstanding the stresses of war. Thus a prosperous state which supports the status quo is not only capable of defending it, but through Liddell Hart's anchor of deterrence, may not have to dedicate many resources to do so 'by convincing him that "the game is not worth the candle"'.[53]

---

[47] Liddell Hart, 'Insertion on Galley 77', Liddell Hart Papers, 9/6/14, 1. Permission granted by The Trustees of the Liddell Hart Centre for Military Archives.
[48] See also, for instance, Basil Liddell Hart, 'Economic Pressure or Continental Victories', *RUSI Journal* 76/503 (Aug. 1931), 486–510.
[49] Basil Liddell Hart, *The British Way in Warfare* (London: Faber & Faber, 1932).
[50] Basil Liddell Hart, *The Strategy of Indirect Approach* (London: Faber & Faber, 1941), 202–3.
[51] Mearsheimer, *Liddell Hart and the Weight of History*, 108–9.
[52] Liddell Hart, *Strategy of Indirect Approach*, 208.   [53] Ibid. 205.

Once a strategic actor had become embroiled in war, Liddell Hart emphasized the utility of the indirect approach in securing the character of the peace he identified as desirable. '[T]he true aim in war is the mind of the hostile rulers, not the bodies of their troops; that the balance between victory and defeat turns on mental impressions and only indirectly on physical blows.'[54] As John Mearsheimer has noted, the 'indirect approach' meant different things to Liddell Hart at different times during his career and, eventually growing overly inclusive, ranged from the bombardment of the enemy's civilian population with airpower, to the naval- and economy-premised British way in warfare, to armoured warfare.[55] The major commonalities of all of Liddell Hart's various conceptions of indirectness were their relative cheapness, financially and in terms of manpower, compared to Britain's experience of its expensive continental-scale army during the First World War.

Liddell Hart tried to transform warfare into battle between the cunning of opposing commanders, rather than between two armies, to be displayed through movement and manoeuvre rather than actual battle.[56] He clearly held that tactics were less important than strategy to a commander, and admonished that 'we concentrate so much on tactics that we are apt to forget that it is [sic] merely the handmaiden of strategy'.[57] Ultimately, movement may be finely controlled. Destruction cannot be, and therefore Liddell Hart's writings eschewed it.

Because deterrence was only a late addition to Liddell Hart's strategic thought, it could not have been the original impetus for his designation of limiting war and warfare as the purpose of grand strategy. Liddell Hart's initial impulse was emotional, based on his experiences as a young man during the First World War.[58] This original emotional basis of Liddell Hart's theory of strategy is reflected in its structure.

The structure of Liddell Hart's entire strategic theory was designed to serve as a straightjacket on military strategy to prevent a repetition of the First World War. He was cognizant of, and dreaded, the ease with which passion and irrationality took hold during wartime. He had relayed a story about the Byzantine general Belisarius, a Liddell Hartian ideal of indirectness, who tried to stem his soldiers' bloodlust. '[H]e tried to point out to them that true victory lay in compelling one's enemy to abandon his purpose, with the least possible loss to oneself.' His troops were not convinced, a battle was fought, his army suffered a sharp defeat, and his troops saw the wisdom of his words.[59]

---

[54] Liddell Hart, *Strategy*, 204.
[55] Mearsheimer, *Liddell Hart and the Weight of History*, 87–93.
[56] Basil Liddell Hart, *Thoughts on War* (London: Faber & Faber, 1944), 230.
[57] Ibid. 48.   [58] Bond, *Liddell Hart*, 51.   [59] Liddell Hart, *Strategy*, 43.

Liddell Hart assumed that, 'while grand strategy should control strategy, its principles often run counter to those which prevail in the field of strategy'.[60] Military strategy thus had to be moderated from above. He defined it as '"the art of distributing and applying military means to fulfil the ends of policy". For strategy is concerned not merely with the movement of forces—as its role is often defined—but with the effect.' Strategy, in this formulation, bridges the chasm between military means and political ends, and so theoretically allows escalation in war to match political requirements. He, however, identified two different kinds of policy: grand strategy, which was 'practically synonymous with the policy which guides the conduct of war...[and] the more fundamental policy which should govern its object'.[61] He did not identify which of the two forms of policy strategy served, but the textual context surrounding his definition indicates that grand strategy, or war policy, is the master of strategy. Thus strategy served the policy which controlled the conduct of war, rather than that which identified its purpose.

The full logic of this claim demands explanation. Liddell Hart assigned both war and grand strategy the same aim: to achieve a better state of peace. Grand strategy thus had to sit between the requirements of fundamental policy, which might demand victory, and a better and more prosperous state of peace, which Liddell Hart basically assumed meant waging limited war. 'Victory in this sense is only possible if a quick result can be gained or if a long effort can be economically proportioned to the national resources.'[62] Grand strategy and war thus were to remain in harmony, despite the contradictory principles of strategy and possibly exorbitant demands from fundamental policy. Even when faced with the Second World War, Liddell Hart never actually accommodated the possibility that fundamental policy might demand total ends. 'He would never concede that "victory" in the Second World War mattered.'[63]

Liddell Hart's assumptions and definitions thus aligned three of four factors to secure the desirable conduct of war: war itself, grand strategy or war policy, and fundamental policy. However, Liddell Hart believed that the principles of the fourth factor, military strategy, encouraged escalation in war and so ran counter to this desirable conduct; thus it became necessary to recast strategy in a manner which made it compatible with the rest of Liddell Hart's strategic thought. The result was the strategy of indirect approach, which stressed avoidance of battle by turning warfare into a conflict between the minds of the commanders. This recalibration of strategy emphasized the particular way in which Liddell Hart hoped war would be fought. '*Its purpose is to diminish the possibility of resistance*, and it seeks to fulfil this purpose by exploiting the

---

[60] Liddell Hart, *Strategy of Indirect Approach*, 202.
[61] Liddell Hart, *Strategy*, 321, 321–2.   [62] Ibid. 357.
[63] Gat, *History of Military Thought*, 803–4.

elements of *movement* and *surprise*.'[64] The purpose of strategy of the indirect approach was no longer to fulfil fundamental policy, but rather to fulfil war policy—that is, grand strategy, which Liddell Hart defined as the entire conduct of war.

Liddell Hart's original emotional response in crafting grand strategy acquired in the early 1930s a cloak of deterrence to complete the theory. His idea of grand strategy thus sought to protect the economic and manpower resources of the nation *in* war to preserve the nation's future peacetime readiness *for* war to deter potential aggressors.

OTHER BRITISH GRAND STRATEGIC THOUGHT

Fuller and Liddell Hart did not hold a duopoly on British grand strategic thought throughout their active careers as strategic theorists and authors. Henry Antony Sargeaunt and Geoffrey West, another pair of British writers, considered the topic in their *Grand Strategy* of 1941. West was a journalist and Sargeaunt was a pseudonym; his true identity is unknown. To that date their book was the only one in the English language dedicated solely to grand strategy. They set themselves the task of understanding what grand strategy actually was, as a universal idea rather than a specific theory for a particular geopolitical actor. Their attempt proved to be of dubious quality, although noteworthy for the topics it emphasized and how it differed from the grand strategic theories of Fuller and Liddell Hart—although they shared Fuller's emphasis on civilization.

Sargeaunt and West approached grand strategy in light of Britain's immediate context: the Second World War, a war more total, more demanding, and more dangerous than the First. They identified grand strategy as dealing 'with the connections between war and the rest of the society or civilization in which war occurs'.[65] The interaction was reciprocal. War moulded society, and societies shaped the conduct of wars fought on their behalf. They did not consider this a process limited to wartime itself, because a considerable portion of a 'modern nation's normal policy is guided by the fact that it must not be manoeuvred into a position where it would be at a disadvantage in war'.[66] Indeed, they subscribed to Heraclitus's view of war: it was the father of all things. The purpose of grand strategy was to understand and master all

---

[64] Liddell Hart, *Strategy*, 323.
[65] Henry Antony Sargeaunt and Geoffrey West, *Grand Strategy* (New York: Thomas Y. Crowell Co., 1941), 1.
[66] Ibid. 1–2.

the social relationships implied within that approach. 'Grand strategy is not merely a military but also a social science.'[67]

The important relationship between war and society became a topic of scholarly significance during the latter half of the Cold War.[68] Sargeaunt and West anticipated by decades this basic scholarly trend in the study of war. Yet strategy—and grand strategy—are practical subjects. To consider the pragmatic aspects of the relationship between war and society, Sargeaunt and West conceived of specific ways of waging war and identified differing patterns of national organization as their main determinant. 'For example, the choice of national organization is undoubtedly one of mankind's major difficulties today. Shall it be the nazi-fascist, the communist-socialist, or the democratic?'[69] They, like Fuller and Liddell Hart, thought that the way war was fought decisively influenced the ensuing peace. '[T]he long-range effects of war depend upon the way it has been fought, and all the agony of victory will be wasted if the possible benefits have been discarded for illusory ones.'[70]

The relationship between war and society determined one's way of war, which in turn was intimately linked to the utility of war for society. Grand strategy was responsible for the entire cycle. The first part is governed by national organization, which Sargeaunt and West linked to the idea of progress and considered in a semi-teleological fashion. In considering future types of national organization after the Second World War, they speculated about '[w]hat grand strategy will emerge and prevail after today's war? So far we have found a series rising to "timed" planning. Will progress stop at this level? There is no cause to think so, and all reason to believe otherwise.'[71] They did not define an endpoint for progress in national organization. What they did believe, however, was that 'each stage of grand strategy must be lived through if the nation was to be sound'.[72] They did not attempt to describe where the evolution of social thought on war was heading, but did require that every society pass through all the historical stages. Nor was there a reason to tarry, as 'the only level which will be effective and will stir the imagination of men [for waging war] is the new and progressive one'.[73]

Sargeaunt and West did not dwell on war and warfare, the other half of the cycle, nearly as much, in part because if national organization were done correctly then the conduct of war would automatically follow. They considered that this second half of the cycle was predicated upon an accurate understanding of how war might benefit society, of its possibilities and limitations as an instrument. Thus 'when people speak of war aims, as often

---

[67] Ibid. 7.
[68] See works such as Alastair Buchan, *War in Modern Society: An Introduction* (London: C. A. Watts & Co., 1966) and Brian Bond, *War and Society in Europe, 1870–1970* (Leicester: Leicester UP, 1983).
[69] Sargeaunt and West, *Grand Strategy*, 8.   [70] Ibid. 10.   [71] Ibid. 159.
[72] Ibid. 129.   [73] Ibid. 185.

as not many of them are asking for results which the human instrument and activity of war cannot give, just as farming cannot produce oil. Such knowledge is all part of modern grand strategy.' Again, 'one of the first tasks of grand strategy is to show in what ways war is an instrument with a limited scope'. Finally, '[g]rand strategy defines the possible range of any particular war in its effect on the rest of society'.[74] This connects to the recurring notion of grand strategy as *coup d'oeil*, of truly understanding war.

Sargeaunt and West assumed war to be a fundamentally progressive force. Grand strategy 'deals with the ever-changing connections between war and the society where war occurs. Moreover, it sets out to find exactly what these progressive connections are.'[75] They comprehended, however, the danger of ethnocentrism and understood that not all types of grand strategy were progressive because not all national organizations were progressive. In contrasting the Nazi-Fascist grand strategy and national organization with that of the Anglo-Saxons, they noted that '[t]he difference is between progress used for war, and war used for progress'.[76]

Sargeaunt and West did not focus grand strategy on a particular task, of limiting war or any other, in the manner that Fuller and Liddell Hart did. However, they accepted many of the same assumptions as both of the better known theorists and focused on exploring them in greater detail. Fuller and Liddell Hart had noted that grand strategy utilized all instruments of power but chose to focus almost exclusively on military strategy. By contrast, Sargeaunt and West realized that this usage of all instruments necessarily narrowed the gap between war and society and used this relationship as the basis for studying grand strategy. Perhaps not advocating any particular style of organization for the armed forces and of strategy led them to consider grand strategy in a manner which was not, ultimately, instrumental for their own purposes. Much of the theory propounded seems superficial or questionable, and was seen to be so at the time.

> This will be a disappointing book to students of military strategy, for it treats this subject only casually. To students of the problems of world organization, it offers only the rather dubious theory that in increased national efficiency (*i.e.*, better grand strategy) on the part of each nation lies the greatest hope for the eventual elimination of war from the world. Somehow the Darwinian process of selection by combat is to be transformed into a process of peaceful competition. Students of history will be struck by its tendency to make simple things complex and complex things simple.[77]

Nevertheless, their theory of grand strategy was universal rather than particular, as have been most other theories of grand strategy both prior to theirs and since.

---

[74] Ibid. 9, 10–11, 11.   [75] Ibid. 9.   [76] Ibid. 24.
[77] John C. Campbell, 'Review of *Grand Strategy*', *Military Affairs* 6/1 (Spring 1942), 40–1.

CONCLUSION

Fuller and Liddell Hart have proven to be the thematic successors in grand strategic thought of Alfred Thayer Mahan and Julian Stafford Corbett. Like the maritime theorists, particularly Corbett, Fuller and Liddell Hart anchored their ideas of grand strategy to limits on war, due to the indelible influence of the First World War. Repeating such an experience was considered unnecessary and undesirable, leading both British interwar theorists to focus purely on limiting war and its impact on society. Fuller and Liddell Hart approached limitation from different perspectives, but with significant agreement on some of the ways for achieving that goal. Another pair of British theorists, Sargeaunt and West, writing under the great strain of the first half of the Second World War, attempted to recalibrate grand strategy to emphasize the relationship between war and society.

Liddell Hart's grand strategic thought remains the only one of the three disparate theories produced in reaction to Britain's great wars of the twentieth century still remembered by the grand strategic literature. This literature, however, mistakenly takes his definition to be universal, rather than as a specific construction whose premise was the trauma of the First World War and the British geopolitical condition thereafter. In adopting Liddell Hart's definition as a standard point of departure for justifications of their own individual interpretations of grand strategy, most modern scholars stray from Liddell Hart's original meaning and purpose.

An important conclusion stemming from the British experience of grand strategic thinking during this period is that it is impossible for grand strategy to avoid the consideration of war. Fuller's interpretation of grand strategy was the only one in the concept's entire evolution which sought originally to be an exclusively peacetime concept. It did not remain so for long—war was, and is, too important not to be encompassed by concepts of grand strategy. War as the ultimate instrument remains at the heart of grand strategy, and in this respect it reflects the original concerns of classical strategic thought and practice.

4

Grand Strategy in American Reactions to the World Wars

American grand strategic thought throughout the interwar era contrasted starkly with that of Britain. The strategic lessons Americans learned from the First World War not only differed from those of the British, but they also varied widely within the United States itself. American grand strategic thought between and during the World Wars had inherited an unruly mosaic of competing and oft-contradictory ideas but subsequently imposed some small order upon that thought. This was due, in part, to less widespread use of the concept, with greater ideational development when used. Edward Mead Earle has sometimes been celebrated in the annals of grand strategic thought, but he was by no means the sole American thinking about grand strategy or advocating ideas which touch upon it. Earle himself seems to have simultaneously held differing ideas of what comprises grand strategy.

Four notable usages or definitions of grand strategy as a concept prevailed in America at this time. Some show continuity with nineteenth-century grand strategic thought, but all were unavoidably greatly influenced by the First World War. The first usage reflects the problems and challenges of waging total war. The second stems from questions not simply of waging war but of avoiding it, if possible. The third is an attitude towards the idea of grand strategy which implicitly questions the worth of the concept. This attitude comes in two shades: that held by actual military practitioners, and that held by the American air power theorists. Finally, there is a minor but still notable definition of grand strategy which is an apparent, even if unintentional, continuation of one particular strand of nineteenth-century grand strategic thought.

(A BRIEF OVERVIEW OF) PRE-FIRST WORLD WAR GRAND STRATEGIC THOUGHT

The first two decades of the twentieth century form an important link in American grand strategic thought between nineteenth-century military-focused types of ideas and the wider or higher level ideas of the interwar period, frequently considered the first modern interpretations of grand strategy. Grand strategy attained greater currency from the turn of the century to the First World War than either during the nineteenth century or, interestingly, during the interwar period. The variety of its usage and interpretation also expanded outward from the prevalent nineteenth-century military centricity, possibly as a result of its wider currency and its appropriation by non-military thinkers and authors.

Most grand strategic thought preceding the interwar period did remain military in character, particularly during the First World War. The war was, as one self-proclaimed amateur strategist suggested, 'a war of the unexpected, not only for the layman, but, it appears, for the expert in grand strategy', his use of grand strategy suggesting an emphasis on manoeuvre.[1] Academic works from these two decades also emphasized the separation of grand strategy from combat. One scholar, writing on the American War for Independence, noted that '[t]he necessities of the American cause called for *Grand Strategy*, and improved *Logistics* rather than *Grand Tactics*' because the Continental Army did not have the grand tactical skill to match Britain in battle.[2] Similarly, a treatment of Sherman's operations in South Carolina not only celebrated the manner in which he manoeuvred his army, but noted that the soldiers were also aware of the advantages of Sherman's formations.[3]

Such usage, as far as it goes, was but a continuation of extant interpretations of the idea of grand strategy, which were nonetheless important, having entered into official governmental discourse. Grand strategy was discussed in Senate hearings during the First World War. One Senator, interviewing an Admiral during a hearing before the Committee on Naval Affairs, questioned him on policy, grand strategy, and fleet strength.[4] The three lines of inquiry broadly parallel the Neo-Clausewitzian understanding of the hierarchy of strategy as the levels of tactics, strategy, and policy. This parallel is reinforced

---

[1] Henry Adams Bellows, 'Notes of an Amateur Strategist', *The Bellman* 23 (1917), 578, 580.
[2] Henry B. Carrington, *Battles of the American Revolution 1775–1781* (New York: A. S. Barnes & Co., 1904), 216.
[3] Henry S. Nourse, 'The Burning of Columbia, S.C., February 17, 1865', *Papers of the Military Historical Society of Massachussets* 9 (1912), 439–40.
[4] US House of Representatives, *Hearings Before the Committee on Naval Affairs of the House of Representatives on Estimates Submitted by the Secretary of the Navy, 1915* (Washington, DC: Government Printing Office, 1915), 999.

when, during another hearing, the responsibility for grand strategy is laid at the feet of the military.[5]

Besides such continuity in interpretation, the wider currency of grand strategy led to non-military usages as well. A reverend, writing on the function of universities, employed the metaphor of tactics, strategy, and grand strategy as they were used by military historians. He suggested that grand strategy particularly was 'something akin to statesmanship. Its greatness is determined by its breadth and sweep, and by its ability to seize upon the essential points that dominate currents of world-travel.' Clashes in grand strategy occurred even 'between holders of differing world-views'.[6] This interesting interpretation fits within the nineteenth-century strand of grand strategy as perceiving the true nature of a phenomenon. Yet it is also a surprisingly modern usage of grand strategy, although proposed in 1902 by an author wholly unconnected to any sort of military studies. Furthermore, it implies that this interpretation had some actual currency among those who did study military history. Similarly, a naval officer, who wrote a prize-winning essay on naval bases in naval policy, equated grand strategy and policy.[7] Walter Lippmann once invoked the term in a similarly broad vein.[8] It has also been argued that when Lippmann discussed 'foreign policy', he actually meant 'grand strategy'.[9]

Such usage at this early stage still represented an anomaly rather than the mainstream of grand strategic thought. Most of the non-military usages of grand strategy relied heavily upon military interpretations. Christian missionaries, concerned that efforts across entire continents be coordinated to best effect, appropriated the idea of grand strategy as coordinating multiple theatres.[10] The language of grand strategy also seeped into business and infrastructural developments. There was discussion of 'the grand strategy of trade'.[11] A translation of a German work on considerations for safeguarding and expanding German commerce after the First World War began with a

---

[5] United States Congress, *Investigation of the War Department: Hearings before the Committee on Military Affairs, United States Senate, Sixty-Fifth Congress, Second Session... 1918* (Washington, DC: Government Printing Office, 1918), 621.

[6] Frank J. McConnell, 'The Function of the University in the Present Intellectual Conflict', *Bostonia* 3/2 (July 1902), 12, 13.

[7] John Hood, 'Naval Policy; as it Relates to the Shore Establishment, and the Maintenance of the Fleet', *Naval Institute Proceedings* 40/2 (Mar.—Apr. 1914), 325.

[8] Walter Lippmann, *The Stakes of Diplomacy* (New York: Henry Holt & Co., 1917), 152–3.

[9] Patrick Porter, 'Beyond the American Century: Walter Lippmann and American Grand Strategy, 1943–1950', *Diplomacy and Statecraft* 22/4 (2011), 557–77.

[10] Cornelius H. Patton, *The Lure of Africa* (New York: Missionary Education Movement of the United States and Canada 1917), 190; John R. Mott, 'Response to the Address of Welcome', *Christian Work in Latin America* 3 (New York: The Missionary Education Movement 1917), 275.

[11] Herbert Quick, 'Inland Waterways', *The Reader: An Illustrated Monthly Magazine* 11/2 (Jan. 1908), 119.

chapter titled 'The Grand Strategy of the German Commercial Offensive'.[12] A separate concept of grand strategy, of any meaning, may have existed in Germany as early as the First World War as well, although this supposition would depend on the translator as much as the original German author. It also indicates that the introduction of grand strategy into non-military fields may have militarized the language used therein, although it could not have been the only source of such expressions. The perceived if not actual totality of the First World War was undoubtedly the largest contributor. Another usage of grand strategy, in relation to the development of infrastructure, implies preference for 'great manoeuvres' rather than 'combat'—or, translated into infrastructural development, for federally funded engineering works rather than local projects.[13]

Grand strategy was also appropriated by some thinkers in social philosophy and evolutionary theory.[14] It had already been applied to American domestic politics prior to the American Civil War, specifically with reference to the Abolitionist aims of the Republican party.[15] It even made the jump from non-fiction to historical fiction.[16]

American grand strategic thought prior to and during the First World War had left the concept increasingly directionless as it was adopted by civilians unrelated to military studies. The First World War significantly refocused grand strategic thought thereafter, although not necessarily in a uniform manner. The established understanding of the interwar period in the United States concluded that entry into the war had been a mistake and that the soundest policy was isolation and neutrality.[17] However, the armed forces certainly did not give up thinking about war and strategy and the First World War served as a lodestone for discussions of future warfare.[18] The United States Army and Navy spent great effort considering how to wage very specific wars. War plans abounded, including against Japan, the United Kingdom, Canada, Mexico, and Cuba.

---

[12] Siegfried Herzog, *The Iron Circle: The Future of German Industrial Exports: Practical Suggestions for Safeguarding the Growth of German Export Activity in the Field of Manufactures After the War*, tr. M. L. Turrentine (London: Hodder & Stoughton, 1918), ch. 1.

[13] Ray Stannard Baker, 'The Valley that Found itself', *The World's Work* 31/6 (Apr. 1916), 685.

[14] William Patten, *The Grand Strategy of Evolution: The Social Philosophy of a Biologist* (Boston: Gorham Press, 1920).

[15] F. J. Herriot, 'The Germans of Iowa and the "Two-Year" Amendment of Massachusetts', *Deutsch-Amerikanische Geschichtsblätter (German-American Historical Review)* 12 (1913), 254.

[16] George Cary Eggleston, *The Master of Warlock: A Virginia War Story* (Boston: Lothrop Publishing Co., 1903), 165.

[17] Gerhard L. Weinberg, 'The Politics of War and Peace in the 1920s and 1930s', in Roger Chickering and Stig Förster (eds), *The Shadows of Total War: Europe, East Asia, and the United States, 1919–1939* (Cambridge: CUP, 2003), 31–2.

[18] Bernd Greiner, '"The Study of the Distant Past is Futile": American Reflections on New Military Frontiers', in Chickering and Förster, *Shadows*, 240.

Two distinct ideas of what grand strategy comprises arose out of this basic schism between isolationism and engagement with the rest of the world. These two disparate approaches were fuelled also by differing understandings of American geography and its significance. By 1918, the United States' only serious potential foes were overseas. The distinctions in American geopolitical thought, which influenced grand strategic thought, are indicated by a cartographical trick, as Nicholas Spykman noted in 1942. The Mercator Projection

> shows that both the Old and the New Worlds have coasts on two oceans and, from a geographic point of view, they can therefore be said to embrace each other. Such a map with the centre along the meridian of 80° east near the top of British India will show the Old World continents surrounded on the east by the west coast of the New World, and on the west by the east coast of the New World. A similar map with the New World in the center along the meridian of 90° west indicates that the Americas are surrounded by the west coast of the Old World on the east and the east coast of the Old World on the west.[19]

Isolationists saw America in the centre, surrounded and besieged by the Old World on all sides. The corresponding idea of grand strategy included responsibilities in both peace and war, over and above military strategy and foreign policy. Its best known proponent was Edward Mead Earle. Yet those who considered American engagement with the rest of the world inevitable, even if not necessarily always beneficial, may have viewed the United States as encircling the Old World. The grand strategic thought analogous to such geopolitical ideas stressed employing all assets of national power in pursuit of victory.

GRAND STRATEGY IN PURSUIT OF VICTORY

The use of all available tools to achieve victory is, for historical reasons, one of grand strategy's stereotypical interpretations. A concept suited to the World Wars, its conception and application remain largely locked into that period of time. Michael Howard, writing volume four of the official history of British grand strategy during the Second World War, offered its quintessential definition. 'Grand strategy in the first half of the twentieth century consisted basically in the mobilisation and deployment of national resources of wealth, manpower and industrial capacity, together with the enlistment of those of allied, and when feasible, of neutral powers, for the purpose of achieving the goals of national policy in wartime.'[20] It was a retrospective definition suited to

---

[19] Nicholas J. Spykman, *America's Strategy in World Politics: The United States and the Balance of Power* (New Brunswick, NJ: Transaction Publishers, 2008), 179.

[20] Michael Howard, *Grand Strategy*, iv. *August 1942–September 1943* (London: Her Majesty's Stationery Office, 1972), 1.

British, indeed Allied, historical experience. Both J. F. C. Fuller and Basil Liddell Hart had incorporated similar notions in their personal definitions throughout the interwar period.

The Americans developed grand strategic thought in a form much closer to Howard's retrospective conception than that provided by Fuller and Liddell Hart. Holloway Halstead Frost, a captain of the US Navy, was one of the first Americans to define grand strategy in this manner in an article published in 1925. Adopting this particular definition was a deliberate choice by Frost, as he had previously endorsed the view of the German General Colmar Von der Goltz. 'Whoever writes on strategy and tactics ought not in his theories to neglect the point of view of his own people; he should give us a national strategy, a national tactics. Only thus will he render a real service to his country.'[21] Frost advocated this interpretation of grand strategy because he believed it was best suited for the United States. This apparently fitting perspective was in fact out of place because the First World War was *not* a total war for the United States, which never experienced the corralling of an entire national effort in pursuit of victory.

However, it did have, to some extent, the will to do so, in the interest of being the most powerful actor during the peace-making.[22] Moreover, the US armed forces were forward-looking and may have anticipated that their next war *would* be a total war.[23] Frost, drawing from European experience and the trajectory of American economic might, may also simply have been anticipating American power for the next war. Finally, he also belonged to the military and naval strategic traditions of Ulysses S. Grant and Alfred Thayer Mahan. The former impelled the pursuit of unconditional surrender, whereas the latter embraced a wide range of non-military or non-naval instruments in achieving policy aims.

Frost thus belonged to a much wider intellectual community when he defined war as 'weighing of our national capacity to exert and resist pressure against that of the enemy nation or nations' and suggested that any war was 'decided when the national strength or the will to conquer of one of the opposing nations or alliances breaks'.[24] Given such assumptions, not all fronts would be geographical or military in character. He grouped the forces a state could deploy into three categories and advocated that each combat its

---

[21] Quoted in Holloway Halstead Frost, 'Our Heritage from Paul Jones', *Naval Institute Proceedings* 44/188 (Oct. 1918), 2276.

[22] Elisabeth Glaser, 'Better Late than Never: The American Economic War Effort, 1917–1918', in Roger Chickering and Stig Förster (eds), *Great War, Total War: Combat and Mobilization on the Western Front, 1914–1918* (Cambridge: CUP, 2000), 395.

[23] J. A. S. Grenville, 'Diplomacy and War Plans in the United States, 1890–1917', in Paul M. Kennedy (ed.), *The War Plans of the Great Powers, 1880–1914* (London: George Allen & Unwin, 1979), 35.

[24] Holloway Halstead Frost, 'National Strategy', *Proceedings* 51/8 (Aug. 1925), 1343.

counterpart in the enemy: armed forces; economic forces; and political forces, which included instruments such as diplomacy, education, and religion.[25]

Although he imbued these categories with universal application, Frost recognized change in the character of war. He considered national strategy to have grown in importance as the apparent effectiveness of armed forces in war fell. Non-military factors thus had to bear greater responsibility than previously for achieving advantageous effect in war. He described three reasons why this evolution, dating from the wars of the French Revolution, had taken place: the diminishing importance of battle; the increasing importance of money; and the waning of autocratic states in favour of democracies or other governments with greater popular interaction.[26]

Such developments had thrown a shadow upon the utility of war to policy. The failure to coordinate and properly to employ Frost's three groups of instruments would result in long, expensive wars even for the victors.[27] The very changes in warfare, both at the front and in all the supporting economies and logistics, had made war slow and expensive. Frost believed that national strategy, properly practised and implemented, could satisfy the necessity for both economy and celerity.[28]

Nevertheless, it is difficult to accept his arguments. Ultimately he himself reconfirmed the primacy of armed force in war.[29] Economic and diplomatic pressures work but slowly upon belligerents. Simultaneously, the First World War had shown that the armed forces, as they then were, faced significant difficulty in attacking and achieving results, even in 1918. Merely improving coordination between military and non-military instruments of power was unlikely to have the impact Frost anticipated unless the character of warfare changed into a more permissive form. Yet in 1925, when Frost published his ideas, Fuller and Liddell Hart had only just begun their crusade for the revolutionary potential of tanks, and the fall of France in 1940 was still fifteen years away. Vital as this interpretation of grand strategy was for the conduct of the Second World War, Frost's grand strategic promise of inexpensive and quick victory was hollow if judged on its own merits, without reference to developments of which Frost could have known little, if anything at all, such as the full impact of tank warfare. He merely assumed that armed force would be more effective than it had been in the First World War, but without explaining how he came to this conclusion.

This basic interpretation of grand strategy and its many instruments persisted nonetheless, although without Frost's promise of cheap and quick victory. One army officer suggested a similar definition for national strategy, and acknowledged the primacy of armed force in war: 'all the economic powers of the nation shall be employed, so as to support effectively the military

[25] Ibid. 1344. [26] Ibid. 1345. [27] Ibid. 1343.
[28] Ibid. 1345–6. [29] Ibid. 1390.

operations'.[30] Later and more significantly, Albert Coady Wedemeyer further developed this same idea of grand strategy. Wedemeyer was a luminary of the War Department war plans division, worked closely with the Joint and Combined Chiefs of Staff during the first half of the Second World War, and was a chief author of the Victory Program, the United States' blueprint for victory during that war. He acknowledged his interwar experience, as a student at the German War College, as his introduction to the idea of grand strategy, which implies a continental understanding of the term.[31] By the Casablanca Conference in January 1943, he had come to believe that narrowly military definitions of strategy were insufficient and 'that a far broader concept of strategy was essential to survival'.[32] Wedemeyer's preferred definition of grand strategy was 'the art and science of employing all of a nation's resources to accomplish objectives defined by national policy'.[33]

Significantly, over time his definition expanded beyond being merely a wartime concept to suggest that the skilful exercise of non-military instruments might fulfil policy aims before the use of armed force was deemed necessary. He believed that the United States had failed to achieve this prior to either World War, resulting in the wars' occurrence.[34] This reveals that, although Wedemeyer had military planning experience based on the assumption that the New World could besiege the Old, his personal attitude was closer to the reverse position. Indeed, Wedemeyer explicitly identified grand strategy with foreign policy and used them interchangeably in advocating establishment of a council responsible for making grand strategy or foreign policy for the United States.[35] This equivalence of grand strategy with foreign policy suited Wedemeyer's final insight, that '[t]he end of a war is not, never has been, and never will be the end of the power struggle'.[36]

GRAND STRATEGY IN PEACE AND WAR

Edward Mead Earle was an American academic who began his career writing about Turkey and the Near East, before rising tensions in Europe during the 1930s led to a shift of focus which eventually brought him to grand strategy. After Basil Liddell Hart, he is the second great figure typically mentioned in the annals of grand strategic thought.[37] Although sometimes left unmentioned

---

[30] Oliver Prescott Robinson, *The Fundamentals of Military Strategy* (Washington, DC: United States Infantry Association, 1928), 167.
[31] Albert C. Wedemeyer, *Wedemeyer Reports!* (New York: Henry Holt & Co., 1958), 52.
[32] Ibid. 81.   [33] Ibid.   [34] Ibid. 85, 93.   [35] Ibid. 437.   [36] Ibid. 439.
[37] For a discussion of some of Earle's contributions to strategic studies, see David Ekbladh, 'Present at the Creation: Edward Mead Earle and the Depression-Era Origins of Security Studies', *International Security* 36/3 (Winter 2011–12), 107–41.

and overshadowed by Liddell Hart's purported role in inventing the idea of grand strategy, some consider Earle's contribution to be greater.[38] Earle famously suggested that '[t]he highest type of strategy—sometimes called grand strategy—is that which so integrates the policies and armaments of the nation that the resort to war is either rendered unnecessary or is undertaken with the maximum chance of victory'.[39]

Earle was not the sole theorist to advocate this understanding of strategy or grand strategy. His work on grand strategy, mostly unpublished, was preceded by that of George Meyers, a US Navy captain and lecturer on strategy at the US Army War College. Meyers argued, similarly to Earle, that '[s]trategy is the provision, preparation, and use of diplomacy and of the nation's armed forces in peace and war to gain the purpose of national policy. Strategy in war is the provision, preparation, and use of diplomacy and of the armed forces to gain the purpose of the war.'[40] Meyers's view of strategy features three major aspects. First, strategy operates both in peace and war. Second, this continuity implicitly betrays a defensive mentality by automatically identifying other political actors as threats. Third, strategy is directed not only against external actors but also has a domestic, developmental component. All three aspects meld together seamlessly in Meyers's strategic thought, particularly the first two.

The continuity of strategy in peace and war was fundamental to Meyers' thinking. Not to incorporate peacetime diplomacy as an instrument of strategy would be inherently contradictory.[41] This idea that strategy was active in both peace and war may stem from two sources. First, Meyers was a US Navy captain. Attributing such breadth to strategy was likely originally inherited from Alfred Thayer Mahan. Meyers noted, much as Mahan had, the power of non-military instruments on the periphery of Europe and European interests.[42]

Second was the experience of the First World War. This war emphasized the salience of peacetime activity to waging war, from the alliance-building which occupied the decade prior to the war to the iron logic of great power mobilization and war plans.[43] Even more significantly from an American perspective, one may be at peace even as one's most important trading partners are fighting—each other—and conspiring to widen the war further, one way or another. Thus Meyers argued that not only '[i]n peace, strategy estimates,

---

[38] Williamson Murray, 'Thoughts on Grand Strategy' in Williamson Murray et al. (eds), *The Shaping of Grand Strategy: Policy, Diplomacy, and War* (Cambridge: CUP, 2011), 7.
[39] Edward Mead Earle, 'Introduction', in Edward Mead Earle (ed.), *Makers of Modern Strategy: Military Thought from Machiavelli to Hitler* (New York: Atheneum 1966), p. viii.
[40] George J. Meyers, *Strategy* (Washington, DC: Byron S. Adams, 1928), p. xiv.
[41] Ibid. 30.   [42] Ibid. 21.
[43] See e.g. Samuel R. Williamson, Jr, *The Politics of Grand Strategy: Britain and France Prepare for War, 1904–1914* (Cambridge, MA: Harvard UP, 1969).

creates war plans, and as far as possible, makes dispositions', but that '[i]t also decides when war shall begin'.[44] Although it had been provoked by belligerent German action, the United States largely enjoyed the relative luxury of determining the timing of its own entrance into the First World War in a manner which the Entente Powers mostly did not have. This belief that strategy was continuous in peace and war linked directly to a defensive mentality in the United States.

The defensive mentality indicates a potentially isolationist perspective on international relations, reflected in the idea that strategy is continuous in peace and war. The rest of the world was a source of danger to the United States, and needed to be kept at arm's length. Scoffing at the notion that the navy was a nation's first line of defence, Meyers identified diplomacy instead.[45] Yet diplomacy was by nature defensive, meant to keep the world at bay rather than extract advantage from global engagement. The First World War spurred such beliefs, for it had threatened to—and ultimately did—draw the United States in despite the best diplomatic efforts to remain aloof and to mediate the conflict.

In discussing Clausewitz and his definition of strategy, Meyers observed that he had neglected the development of the armed forces, which might deter war without recourse to actual violence.[46] This perspective, that strategy also develops national resources in peacetime so that they may be used in wartime, stems from both Mahan's writings and from the major wartime industrial efforts of most of the belligerent states. To those with a Mahanian education and the experience of total war, it seemed logical and natural that strategy should control these activities. Nevertheless, some of Meyer' naval contemporaries from other countries did not necessarily agree. Admiral Raoul Castex argued that '[p]roperly speaking, preparations of this sort constitute naval policy, and their realm borders that of policy as a whole'.[47] The First World War, like all formidable challenges to one's conceptual understanding, did not simply stretch the old boundaries of particular ideas. It also convinced some theorists that concepts had to remain sharply distinct to inculcate and preserve intellectual clarity.

One striking commonality of all three major facets of Meyers' thought is that none of them is explicitly justified. The defensive mentality mirrored societal beliefs of how the United States should—or should not—interact with the rest of the world in the post-First World War environment. The ideas of practising strategy both in peace and war, and of a domestic developmental component as well, were similarly impelled by the experience of the First World War but have precedents in earlier American naval strategic theory. Yet

---

[44] Meyers, *Strategy*, 6.   [45] Ibid. 1.   [46] Ibid. 21.
[47] Raoul Castex, *Strategic Theories*, tr. and ed. Eugenia C. Kiesling (Annapolis, MD: Naval Institute Press, 1994), 17.

Meyers justified none of these facets on a theoretical level. Although he began to do so for both the besieged mentality and for strategy's dual peace and war role, he never explicitly outlined completely his reasoning for why the concept of strategy should be altered in such a way. It appears he believed that the character of events had outpaced the more limited definitions and concepts of strategy.

Edward Mead Earle (1894–1954) noticed this expanding definition of strategy in the late 1930s, and accepted it. In an address to the Academy of Political Science in 1940 he argued that any military-centric definitions of strategy left out '[w]hat has become universal usage of the word'.[48] Indeed, in Earle's undated, probably post-Second World War memorandum regarding the term strategy, only one participant out of twelve argued for a military-focused definition.[49] Earle believed this expansion to be natural and not in need of explicit theoretical justification.

The expansion in the meaning of strategy and grand strategy spilled over the boundaries of war and peace, propelled by the increasing complexity of war. 'Strategy, therefore, is not merely a concept of wartime, but is an inherent element of statecraft at all times.'[50] Strategy—and grand strategy—evolved in reaction to the requirements posed by the actual geopolitical context. Michael Howard has argued that this was an inevitable development, that 'this was a definition that came naturally to an observer of the international scene in the 1940s'.[51] Not only during the Second World War, for Earle was old enough to remember how the United States had become entangled in the First.

Earle found the distinction between war and peace to be insignificant. 'I should say I would not want to sponsor the phrase, short of war, because I think that it is virtually meaningless. It is a phrase impossible to define, because it is impossible to draw a line between peace and war.'[52] Political goals may be worked towards or achieved in either context, the differences among the means employed being a lesser consideration. In such a context, defence was not an activity which could be limited only to the armed forces and in any case Earle preferred the term 'security'.[53] This becomes apparent in his later

---

[48] Edward Mead Earle, 'Political and Military Strategy for the United States', 13 Nov. 1940, Edward Mead Earle Papers; 1894–1954, Public Policy Papers, Department of Rare Books and Special Collections, Princeton University Library, Box 35, Folder 'Post-WW2: Strategy'.

[49] 'Memorandum Regarding the Term "Strategy"', Earle Papers, Box 35, Folder 'Post-WW2: Strategy', 6.

[50] Earle, 'Introduction', p. viii.

[51] Michael Howard, 'Grand Strategy in the Twentieth Century', *Defence Studies* 1/1 (Spring 2001), 2.

[52] Edward Mead Earle in US Congress, Joint Committee on the Conduct of War, 'Discussion: The Bases of an American Defense Policy: Armed Forces', *Proceedings of the Academy of Political Science* 19/2: The Defense of the United States (Jan. 1941), 53–4.

[53] Edward Mead Earle, 'Political and Military Strategy for the United States', *Proceedings of the Academy of Political Science* 19/2: The Defense of the United States (Jan. 1941), 3.

view that the First and Second World Wars merely comprised a single war with an intermediate armistice during which states continued to pursue their goals.[54]

Earle identified continuity of political purpose on the part of numerous actors during and between both wars. In his mind, grand strategy likely required such continuity within and throughout events to achieve desired goals, through war and peace. Whether an actor was at peace or at war was immaterial if he continually advanced towards his consistent policy goals either way. Thus he suggested that with constancy of purpose '[f]or over 300 years or more, the French Government pursued a policy, a grand strategy' of keeping Central Europe weak and maintaining France's borders at natural geographic boundaries.[55]

Hand-in-hand with the notion of grand strategy as equally operable both in war and in peace came the defensive mentality that equated the rest of the world with danger.

> We have been fortunate in having in our early days, and even in our later history, a remarkable group of statesmen who believed that defence or security was not merely a crisis phenomenon, but an obligation of statecraft at all times, and that political as well as military manoeuvres on our part and on the part of other nations in this hemisphere, and indeed in Europe and Asia, must be judged with relevance to their effect upon the security of these United States.[56]

Earle considered the difference between grand strategy and foreign policy to be 'one of emphasis and proportion rather than clearly defined boundaries'.[57] One might question what the variation in emphasis and proportion might be. DeWitt Clinton Poole, a contemporary of Earle's who was involved in developing the memorandum concerning the definition of strategy, suggested that '"[f]oreign policy" is traditionally associated with *civilian political* effort and does not directly connote military effort also, still less industrial, except by very up-to-date interpretation'.[58]

Earle's perspective depended less on who made and enacted the policy than its fundamental defensive or security purpose. Prior to the Second World War, Earle was interested in the influence of war upon policy. 'What I propose: a

---

[54] Earle, 'Lecture on Grand Strategy at Army and Navy Staff College', 15 Sept. 1944, Earle Papers, Box 37, Folder 'Drafts/Transcripts—Lectures-Miscellaneous [1 of 4], 1.

[55] Earle, 'Lecture on Grand Strategy to Army War College', 26 Mar. 1951, Earle Papers, Box 37, Folder 'Drafts/Transcripts-Lectures-Army War Coll. [2 of 4], 4.

[56] Earle, 'Political and Military Strategy for the United States', 5.

[57] Earle, 'Lecture on Grand Strategy to Army War College', 26 Mar. 1951, Earle Papers, Box 37, Folder 'Drafts/Transcripts-Lectures-Army War Coll. [2 of 4], 2.

[58] 'Memorandum Regarding the Term "Strategy"', Earle Papers, Box 35, Folder 'Post-WW2: Strategy', 10.

study of military policy in relation to statecraft. Not war as an instrument of national policy, but national policy as an instrument of war.'[59]

> This is no mere rhetorical device to catch the ear and the eye. It is a statement of fact in the light of which otherwise confusing phenomena become quite intelligible. For example, economic policies which, judged by the accepted criteria of economics, border on the insane become altogether rational if considered as quasi-military measures. Governmental controls of the press, the radio, the church, the school likewise are explicable by reference to the obvious fact that under modern conditions nearly all phases of life must be subordinated to the exigencies of war. The extension of political authority, especially military authority, into virtually every domain of human relations, is of profound significance.[60]

In Earle's mind, grand strategy meant the utilization of policy as an instrument of war—war avoidance if possible, and war-making as necessary. This interest in commandeering policy to serve war needs was not limited to Earle, but was a rather common feature of American grand strategic thought during the Second World War. Colonel Henry L. Stimson, Secretary of War from 1940 to 1945, believed that '[t]he one great overriding objective was total military victory; policy which served that end was good; policy which did not was bad. War was no longer a weapon of policy; policy must become a weapon of war.'[61]

This interpretation of grand strategy has an important thematic continuity, unlikely to be deliberate, with one of the nineteenth-century definitions, that of manoeuvre. Whereas the military-centric nineteenth-century perspective emphasized spatial manoeuvre, as befitting armies, Meyer and Earle proposed instead manoeuvre among various means of achieving the same political goals, that is, among diplomatic, naval, military, and other means as necessary.

GRAND STRATEGY AS A DUBIOUS CONCEPT

Two strands of interwar American strategic thought and practical strategy making implicitly doubted the veracity and worth of grand strategy, at least as a universally applicable concept. Neither explicitly discussed grand strategy, but both commented upon the ideational space occupied by the concept itself.

---

[59] Earle, 'Open Meeting on International Relations at Skytop Club', 15 September 1937, Earle Papers, Box 28, Folder 'Prof. Assoc.—Social Science Research Council'.
[60] Edward Mead Earle, 'American Military Policy and National Security', *Political Science Quarterly* 53/1 (Mar. 1938), 1.
[61] McGeorge Bundy, 'Foreign Affairs and Armed Forces', 1951, McGeorge Bundy Personal Papers, John F. Kennedy Presidential Library, Box 24, Folder 'Foreign Affairs, Armed Forces, 1951', I-12.

The first strand, apparent in the American colour war plans of the era, does not doubt grand strategy so much as consider it relevant only to a specific range of contingencies. This version of grand strategy could not be considered universally applicable even just to waging war, much less to all of foreign policy. The second strand is more extreme in its advocacy of air power as the decisive instrument of war. This leaves little room for other military means, much less the non-military means which by this point had become one of the foundations of grand strategic thought.

The first strand, of grand strategy relevant only to specific contingencies, was dominated by practical military men, designing war plans which could one day be implemented. Most grand strategies, almost regardless of definition, must first be planned and then implemented in operational plans. The concrete war plans of the interwar period show that the forms of grand strategy popular at the time were implicitly considered not universally practicable in every contingency, but rather viable only in particular circumstances. America's war plans during this period were numerous: Special Plan Blue and War Plans Orange, Red, Crimson, Tan, Green, and various combinations thereof. War Plan Orange, against Japan, was ultimately implemented during the Second World War.[62] Being the work of military practitioners, the plans frequently did not refer to ideas or principles of war. Indeed, at times it was frowned upon to do so. One member of the General Staff criticized a paper circulated about Special Plan Blue by noting '[y]our paper is scholarly. In fact, I believe it contains too many references to military principles, and is in consequence too long.'[63] However, the war plans make it clear that the scope with which they considered the problems of waging war against Orange, Red, Tan, etc. included the common grand strategic dimension of non-military instruments, as necessary and when useful.

As necessary and when useful: grand strategy was a situational lens through which to examine the problem of war. A comparison of War Plans Orange (Japan), Red (Great Britain), Tan (Cuba), and Green (Mexico) suffices to indicate the highly situational quality of this idea of grand strategy. Neither Tan nor Green was anything other than a purely military plan. Neither Cuba nor Mexico could provide a military challenge to the United States, belying any need for a breadth of instruments to achieve policy. Both plans limited their discussion of intervention into either country to the purposes, roles, and actions of the navy and the army. Green even imagined special contingencies, including domestic unrest threatening American citizens and property in

---

[62] Edward S. Miller, *War Plan Orange* (Annapolis, MD: Naval Institute Press, 1991).
[63] F. A. Ruggles, 'Memorandum for Major Jenkins, Subject: Special Plan Blue', 1 Sept. 1925, NARA RG165 NM84 Series 282, Box 265, Folder 2230.

Mexico, which would have entailed highly dynamic situations in which non-military tools would have a negligible effect at best.[64]

War Plan Orange, designed against Japan, was a sharp contrast. It emphasized the importance of non-military tools and accorded them high visibility. *'Mission for the Civil Power*: To support the Armed Forces in their operations; to prevent JAPAN from obtaining any means of waging war from Neutral Countries and to destroy JAPANESE credit in order to accomplish the economic exhaustion of JAPAN.'[65] It contained an entire section (XVI) detailing 'Cooperation with Other Government Departments', which contained a high number of necessary actions by the relevant government departments.

2. The subjects which should be studied and for which plans or programs should be formulated include, in addition to any others that may be considered necessary, the following:
   a. The exertion of economic and financial pressure, including preclusive purchase against JAPAN in all parts of the world;
   b. The exertion of pressure upon Neutral Nations to prevent the supply to JAPAN of any means of waging war;
   c. The stoppage of all Japanese-American Trade;
   d. The maintenance of necessary Foreign Trade;
   e. The treatment of enemy merchant vessels in United States Ports upon the outbreak of war;
   f. The regulations for declaration of contraband;
   g. The control of enemy aliens and enemy property in the United States;
   h. The Intelligence Service required throughout the war, including Espionage and Counter-espionage;
   i. The censorship of communications and of the press;
   j. Propaganda measures in support of the war.[66]

Military planners thus saw wide scope for support from civilian instruments of power in prosecuting a war against Japan. Moreover, developing the necessary studies and plans was considered a priority for the planners. As a memo from the Joint Planning Committee to the Joint Board argued, '[i]t is considered that this section is of such importance that there should be as little delay as possible in the appointment of the representative of the various Government Departments'.[67]

---

[64] See Files 'Joint Army and Navy Basic Intervention Plan Tan' and 'Joint Army and Navy Basic War Plan Green', NARA RG165 NM84 Series 284 'Security Classified Correspondence of the Joint Army-Navy Board', Box 13.

[65] 'Joint Army and Navy Basic War Plan—Orange', 17 Apr. 1928, NARA RG165 NM84 Series 282, Box 268, File 368, 3.

[66] 'Joint Army and Navy Basic War Plan—Orange', 28.

[67] The Joint Planning Committee, 'Memo to the Joint Board, Subject: Cooperation with Other Government Departments', 21 June 1928, NARA RG165 NM84 Series 284, Box 12, File 'Cooperation with Other Government Departments Under Joint Army and Navy Basic War Plan Orange'.

War Plan Red provides another major contrast. It considers a potential conflict with Great Britain and its Dominions in grand strategic terms, and explicitly discards the utility of multiple instruments of power.

> The RED financial structure is strong and independent of any BLUE banking interests. BLUE investments in Europe at present have comparatively little effect in neutralizing RED financial influence in that field, and the contingency that they may some time do so, is considered remote. The necessity which many European nations are now under to pay interest on large loans to the BLUE government and to BLUE private banking interests, will probably be utilized by RED to mobilize sentiment in these nations in her favour in a war with BLUE.[68]

These four war plans reveal a nuanced appreciation, however implicit, of the idea of grand strategy, and its specific contemporary foundations using all the instruments of power. War Plans Tan and Green indicate that there are circumstances where grand strategy is not worth practising simply because it is not needed or could have no effect. The army and the navy have the capability to address any problems by themselves. Force is all that may be required. War Plan Orange shows that where civilian instruments of power were considered to be advantageous, their consideration and use were clearly sought. War Plan Red indicates that there are situations where civilian instruments may be sought and rejected due to anticipated ineffectiveness or counter-productiveness. Ultimately, grand strategy could not be a universal activity in war. Grand strategy was instead a form of strategy which required specific contexts to be worthwhile, and outside those situations it was either unnecessary or even futile.

The second attitude which implicitly doubted the efficacy of grand strategy was advocacy of air power by men such as William 'Billy' Mitchell and Alexander de Seversky.[69] Such early promotion, by overpromising the potential of air power, explicitly or implicitly discounted many other ideas. Thus Mitchell claimed that air power was entirely revolutionary, both in war and in peace. It 'has caused a complete rearrangement of the existing systems of national defence, and a new doctrine of peace which eventually will change the relations of nations with each other due to the universal application and rapidity of aerial transport'.[70] Air power as a development would sweep aside any contradictory idea.

---

[68] 'Joint Estimate of the Situation Blue—Red', undated, NARA RG165 NM84 Series 284, Box 12, file 'Joint Army + Navy Basic War Plan Red', 10.

[69] For commentary on the air power advocates see, among other works, Alfred F. Hurley, *Billy Mitchell: Crusader for Air Power* (Bloomington, IN: Indiana UP, 1975); Phillip S. Meilinger, 'Proselytiser and Prophet: Alexander P. de Seversky and American Airpower', in John Gooch (ed.), *Airpower: Theory and Practice* (London: Frank Cass, 1995), 7–35.

[70] William Mitchell, *Winged Defense: The Development and Possibilities of Modern Air Power—Economic and Military* (New York: G. P. Putnam's Sons, 1925), pp. vii–viii.

Both Mitchell and Seversky specifically and incessantly considered air power to be the death knell of naval power.[71] The former would render the latter obsolescent and, in the near future, entirely obsolete. 'I dare to foresee, by the inexorable logic of military progress, the Navy as a separate entity will cease to be. The weapon it represents will have atrophied to the point where it is, at best, a minor auxiliary of air power.'[72] Mitchell's views on the utility also of land power in the age of air power, originally moderate, gradually became more extreme.[73]

At some point, despite his belief in the potency of air power, Mitchell understood that 'everything begins and ends on the ground. A person cannot permanently live out on the sea nor can a person lie up in the air, so that any decision in war is based on what takes place ultimately on the ground.'[74] However, at other times he confidently asserted that 'THE AIRPLANE IS THE FUTURE ARBITER OF THE WORLD'S DESTINY.'[75] He eventually even came to believe that air power would become the prime component of foreign policy, if not replace it entirely. 'If a nation today has sufficient air power, it may make a few preliminary manoeuvres to demonstrate its strength, and a hostile nation will probably capitulate at once.'[76]

The air power advocates never mentioned grand strategy. No concrete evidence has been discovered to indicate that they were even aware of the concept. Nevertheless, the overpromised potential of air power competed for much of the same ideational space as any and all previous and contemporary interpretations of grand strategy. If the promises were true, there would have been no need for a concept of grand strategy. The promises were not true. The balance of ideational competition was further unhinged after the Second World War, however, with the advent of the nuclear, and particularly thermonuclear, age.

A CONTINUITY IN GRAND STRATEGIC THOUGHT

During the nineteenth century one usage of grand strategy (represented by John Allan Wyeth) may be interpreted as Clausewitzian or Neo-Clausewitzian in character, for it may have existed specifically to link military means to political ends. This usage was, depending upon the exact example, either

---

[71] Ibid., p. xvi; Alexander P. de Seversky, *Victory through Air Power* (New York: Simon & Schuster, 1942), 125–8, 155–6.
[72] Seversky, *Victory through Air Power*, 183.
[73] Mitchell, *Winged Defense*, p. xvi. [74] Ibid. 18.
[75] William Mitchell, 'Airplanes in National Defense', undated, Papers of General William Mitchell, Manuscript Division, Library of Congress, Box 28, Folder 'Articles and Addresses', 6.
[76] William Mitchell, 'Aircraft in War', undated, Papers of General William Mitchell, Box 28, Folder 'Articles and Addresses', 7.

analogous to Clausewitz's own definition of strategy or to those of Neo-Clausewitzians such as Colin Gray. During the late interwar period and the Second World War two American scholars also seemed to use the term and the idea of grand strategy in this manner.

The first of these was the lawyer Quincy Wright, author of the monumental work *A Study of War*. His classification identified three levels of analysis: tactics, which win battles; operations, which win campaigns; and grand strategy, which uses campaigns to win wars.[77] This structure is analogous to present-day conceptions of tactics, operations, and strategy. The first two levels, tactics and strategy or operations, are purely military responsibilities. The third level, of grand strategy or strategy, links these military activities to the political requirements and goals which conceived them. Wright noted that 'during periods when dissatisfied powers have, on the whole, gained their ends by a resort to arms, it may be assumed, on the level of grand strategy, that the power of the offensive has been greater. During periods when they have not been able to do so, it may be assumed that the power of the grand strategic defensive has been greater.'[78] This is not merely a commentary on the efficiency and effectiveness of the tactical or strategic/operational defence versus those of attack. It is also commentary upon the durability of the political interests of states or other strategic actors, relative to the forceful blows of the opponent.

The second scholar after Quincy to have employed this interpretation is Edward Mead Earle. Earle's best known and most enduring thoughts on grand strategy stem from *The Makers of Modern Strategy*, previously mentioned. However, he appears to have simultaneously emphasized the necessity of deliberately linking military means to political ends. This aspect of his thinking is revealed in his, unfortunately unsuccessful, attempt to organize a roundtable on grand strategy during the 1942 annual conference of the American Political Science Association (APSA). The context of the Second World War was likely a major catalyst for this emphasis.

As Harold Stokes, the chairman of APSA, wrote to Earle in connection with the roundtable, '[t]here is no doubt but that political science will have to be expanded to include the field of military techniques and activities if it is to remain realistic'.[79] Earle invited Hanson Baldwin, Walter Lippmann, and Edward Warner to speak at the roundtable on military and naval, military strategy or command, and air power questions, respectively.[80] These were not topics which suited Earle's other ideas of grand strategy. Moreover, he was very particular about the speakers. When Baldwin and Lippmann declined, he

---

[77] Quincy Wright, *A Study of War* (Chicago: University of Chicago Press, 1942), i. 291–2.
[78] Ibid. ii. 796–7.
[79] Letter from Stokes to Earle, 20 Oct. 1942, Earle Papers, Box 26, Folder 'Prof. Assoc.—American Pol. Sci. Assoc. [3 of 4]'.
[80] Letter from Earle to Edward Warner, 3 Nov. 1942, Earle Papers, Box 26, Folder 'Prof. Assoc.—American Pol. Sci. Assoc. [3 of 4]'.

cancelled the roundtable rather than invite any second-rate speakers. Writing to a colleague, he suggested that '[a]s you know, the field of military affairs has been, until recently, almost a complete vacuum insofar as the social sciences have been concerned'.[81] He preferred to leave the vacuum rather than fill it with less than top-quality thoughts and ideas, which attests to the importance he attached to them.

Most striking about this roundtable attempt are the assumptions shared by every correspondent that the purpose of the grand strategy roundtable was to bring political science and military activities closer together. The roundtable was to bridge two very different worlds, the ivory tower and the trench. One of the topics suggested for Lippmann, on the political aspects of military strategy, reflects this interest. Moreover, Bernard Brodie (1910–78), who had only just begun his career, had been mooted as a possible chairman for the roundtable.[82] Tellingly, his first book *Seapower in the Machine Age* treats the strategic and political impact of developments in naval technology.[83] This again reflects the purpose of the roundtable of linking two mutually alien disciplines and, by implication of its topic, grand strategy itself.

The idea of grand strategy as bridging military means and political ends was also mooted in a commentary on the Second World War, albeit seven years later and with a unique feature: grand strategy as the result of the interactive pattern of war, rather than the product of any one belligerent.[84] The author Paul Robinett firmly contextualized grand strategy in a setting which was not just adversarial, but actually zero-sum. Grand strategy was the politically purposeful use of military force. However, it was additionally the military pattern of the war. Only those who had the strength to attack, to take, and to hold the initiative, could claim to be practising grand strategy. It also implied that defensive warfare was not politically significant, a perhaps not unfair assessment in the context of an ideologically charged war to conquer completely and then domestically to reform a selection of aggressor states.

CONCLUSION

American grand strategic thought following the First World War represented the first serious, in-depth development of the concept in the United States

---

[81] Letter from Earle to Kenneth Colegrove, 13 Nov. 1942, Earle Papers, Box 26, Folder 'Prof. Assoc.—American Pol. Sci. Assoc. [3 of 4]'.
[82] Letter from Colegrove to Earle, 6 Oct. 1942, Earle Papers, Box 26, Folder 'Prof. Assoc.—American Pol. Sci. Assoc. [3 of 4]'.
[83] Bernard Brodie, *Seapower in the Machine Age* (Princeton: Princeton UP, 1944 [1941]).
[84] Paul M. Robinett, 'Grand Strategy and the American People', *Military Affairs* 16/1 (Spring 1952), 30.

since the idea was implied in the writings of Alfred Thayer Mahan. From an assortment of military-centric interpretations, the purview of grand strategy expanded to include other policy instruments besides armed force and other contexts in which it might be practised besides war alone. Thus Holloway Halstead Frost emphasized the coordination of multiple disparate tools to win wars, and George Meyers and Edward Mead Earle pushed the concept into the realm of peacetime policy and strategy making to deter, even to preclude, the necessity of waging war at all. Each line of inquiry into grand strategy assumed that the concept was universal in some manner. However, there were also counter-currents in American strategic thought which implicitly limited, or even minimized and dismissed, grand strategy as a universal or even useful concept. The American war planners of the 1920s implicitly understood that grand strategic theory was one thing, but not all dangers to American security called for such expansive responses. It was suitable to be practised only in a particular band of contingencies. The air power theorists, on the other hand, were overly caught up in their belief in the potential of air power and implicitly totally rejected the premise of grand strategy regardless of contingency.

One further implication emerges from this mosaic of thought. Wedemeyer's shift from Frost's strand of thinking towards Earle's occurred despite—or perhaps because of—involvement in practical military planning during the Second World War, an activity conceptually closer to Frost than to Earle. Perhaps Meyers had reason to argue, despite his failure to include justification, that (grand) strategy without consideration of peacetime diplomacy and statecraft was inherently contradictory. Just as British interpretations of grand strategy during this period could not avoid consideration of war, so it seems that American interpretations largely could not avoid consideration of peace. This raises the question of whether practical experience encourages more expansive concepts, despite a potential academic impulse to delineate ideas clearly, as well as how different strategic cultures may perceive and nationalize an otherwise general theory of strategy or grand strategy. These questions deserve further consideration, particularly as strategic studies are meant to be a practical academic discipline.

Ultimately, this mosaic of American grand strategic thought would persist only a short time, between the end of the First World War and the end of the Second. Grand strategy would be quickly forgotten as the strategic community grappled with the new and potentially terrifying strategic problem of atomic and then thermonuclear weapons. Nuclear strategy, especially early in the Cold War, was to occupy much the same ideational space as had grand strategy.

Part II

The Fall and Rise of Grand Strategy (1945–2015)

The Second World War ended with the atomic bombing of Hiroshima and Nagasaki, and the immediate rise of a new and pressing concern in strategic studies: nuclear strategy, followed in turn by limited war theory. In this rush of new and revised concepts and theories, the notion of grand strategy was largely forgotten for twenty-odd years. The demands of the Cold War exercised a modifying influence on the meaning of strategy by turning it into a synonym for policy. Once grand strategy returned to mainstream thought, its meanings had inevitably changed, and a new generation of scholars adapted it for their own individual purposes.

In the next four chapters, the past seventy years of the evolution of grand strategic thought will be examined. The fifth chapter gives an overview of the concepts of nuclear strategy and limited war theory to explain why and how they overrode notions of grand strategy. Yet grand strategy was not entirely stamped out; its few invocations during the first half of the Cold War are the subject of Chapter 6. Chapter 7 describes the re-emergence of grand strategy into mainstream American strategic and international relations thinking and the numerous definitions it acquired in the 1970s and 1980s. The end of the Cold War and the emergence of a world without a peer competitor to inspire cohesion in strategic and political thought triggered further developments in grand strategic thinking. This post-Cold War grand strategic thought is the subject of Chapter 8.

5

Cold War Strategic Thought and Grand Strategy

Grand strategy lost much of its conceptual attractiveness with the conclusion of the Second World War, due to the new nuclear capacity which marked its end. The United States, and eventually the other great powers, had to grapple with deciphering the significance of nuclear weapons. The urgency of this task and the resources and energies devoted to it far overshadowed the minor residual interest in grand strategy of the time. Grand strategy, by numerous but not all definitions, had been eclipsed by nuclear strategy.

The conditions created by nuclear arsenals—specifically, the desire never to see them used again, especially against oneself—encouraged theorizing on limited war as a by-product. Limited war theory derived from, and competed against, certain (predominantly British) notions of grand strategy for its conceptual space. This lasted until the bitter experience of the Vietnam War, which largely discredited theories of limitation as well as, by implication, their sources in British grand strategic thought.

Theories of nuclear strategy and limited war may be matched against five major pre-Cold War interpretations of grand strategy to reveal the similarities, and reasons why the newer concepts prevailed. Of the five major interpretations, two were overshadowed by nuclear strategy, two by limited war theory, and one was partitioned by both new focuses in strategic thought. First, however, the hegemonic air power origins of nuclear strategy will establish why it was always likely to take conceptual priority over grand strategy in the circumstances of the early Cold War.

THE AIR POWER ORIGINS OF NUCLEAR STRATEGY

It has been well established that nuclear strategic thought began as an offshoot of strategic thought for air power, an argument made at least as early as 1948.[1] Rather than a transfer of strategic ideas from air power to the nuclear realm, the impetus was organizational. There was no transfer of ideas, but of personnel; the same set of men, such as Sir John Slessor and Curtis LeMay, wielded air power during the Second World War and would have had to practise atomic warfare from the late 1940s into the early 1960s.[2] They simply applied the air power ideas they knew to atomic warfare. This was not inappropriate, for atomic weapons were too large to fit on rockets, instead requiring heavy bombers for delivery. Air power attempted, in an organizationally hegemonic fashion, to claim for itself the atomic mission. The rest of the armed forces and government broadly, albeit temporarily, acquiesced to this annexation as there was no other alternative in the late 1940s and early 1950s.[3] Even the original classified think tank, RAND, was founded under the aegis of the United States Air Force.[4]

Air power theory, from its nascence, affected a hegemonic character which sidelined all other instruments. Nuclear strategic thought, drawing its underlying character from theories of air power, was similarly hegemonic. The fact that atomic armaments were from the very beginning considered the 'absolute weapon' naturally reinforced, if not confirmed, this founding bias, as did the advent of rocketry.[5]

Deterrence is considered the pivotal concept of the Cold War. 'The study of deterrence became synonymous with the study of the strategic conduct of the cold war.'[6] The hegemonic character of deterrence theory in strategic studies, combined with the hegemonic character of nuclear strategy within deterrence theory, encouraged one-dimensional strategic thinking, particularly during the early Cold War. John Lewis Gaddis has reflected on this theoretical limitation, which became most obvious after the largely unexpected surprise of the Soviet Union's collapse. 'Obviously both the historians and the theorists got it wrong. The error arose, I think, from the way we calculated power

---

[1] P. M. S. Blackett, *Military and Political Consequences of Atomic Energy* (London: Turnstile Press. 1948), 59; see also Bernard Brodie, *Strategy in the Missile Age* (Princeton: Princeton UP, 1959), part 1; George H. Quester, *Deterrence Before Hiroshima: The Airpower Background of Modern Strategy* (New Brunswick, NJ: Transaction Books, 1986); and Richard J. Overy, 'Air Power and the Origins of Deterrence Theory before 1939', *Journal of Strategic Studies* 15/1 (Mar. 1992), 73–101.

[2] David Alan Rosenberg, 'The Origins of Overkill: Nuclear Weapons and American Strategy, 1945–1960', *International Security* 7/4 (Spring 1983), 20.

[3] See David MacIsaac, 'The Evolution of Air Power', in Lawrence Freedman (ed.). *War* (Oxford: OUP, 1994), 289.

[4] See Alex Abella, *Soldiers of Reason: The RAND Corporation and the Rise of the American Empire* (Orlando, FL: Houghton Mifflin Harcourt, 2008), ch. 1.

[5] See Bernard Brodie (ed.), *The Absolute Weapon: Atomic Power and World Order* (New York: Harcourt, Brace & Co., 1946) on the meaning of atomic weapons; see William Liscum Borden, *There Will Be No Time: The Revolution in Strategy* (New York: Macmillan Co., 1946) on the meaning of rocketry.

[6] Lawrence Freedman, *Deterrence* (Cambridge: Polity, 2004), 116.

during the Cold War years. We did so almost entirely in monodimensional terms, focusing particularly on military indices, when a multidimensional perspective might have told us more.'[7]

The general eclipse of grand strategic thought by nuclear strategy was thus probably an inevitable occurrence, the confluence of a handful of intertwining factors. First, the air mission became the air-atomic mission by default, heavy bombers initially being the only machines capable of carrying atomic bombs across continental and intercontinental distances. The Air Force, or at least its RAND subsidiary, was the first to think critically, and with critical mass, about nuclear strategy. The invention of thermonuclear bombs, and the rockets which were capable of carrying them, only increased the immediacy of the nuclear power problem and threat. Although air power theory had implicitly striven to overshadow grand strategy, only nuclear strategy could actually do so.

NUCLEAR STRATEGY VERSUS GRAND STRATEGY ROUND 1 (H. H. FROST)

A considerable portion of grand strategic thought during, between, and about the two world wars emphasized the use of all instruments of national power to achieve victory in war. The national strategic thought of US Navy captain Holloway Halstead Frost may be singled out as broadly representative of American thinking on this subject. This interpretation of grand strategy had reached the epitome of successful praxis during the Second World War, to the extent that the American academic and policy maker William Kaufmann (1918–2008) lamented that '[a] less opportune moment at which to adapt to this new [nuclear] weapon is difficult to imagine. For more than a generation our military thinking had been dominated by the concept of world war.'[8] All minds had turned to total war, a fixation which continued into the nuclear age. Even Bernard Brodie, one of the original apostles of nuclear strategy, assumed that 'all war is total war' until he learned of the anticipated introduction of thermonuclear devices in 1952.[9]

It was widely assumed that atomic weaponry did not change the utility of the other instruments of power, and by implication that this specific notion of

---

[7] John Lewis Gaddis, *We Now Know: Rethinking Cold War History* (Oxford: OUP, 1998), 284.
[8] William W. Kaufmann, 'The Search for Security', William W. Kaufmann Papers, John F. Kennedy Presidential Library, Box 2, Folder 'The Search for Security (Four Lectures)', 9.
[9] Barry H. Steiner, *Bernard Brodie and the Foundations of American Nuclear Strategy* (Lawrence, KS: UP of Kansas, 1991), 13.

grand strategy retained utility.[10] Atomic armaments were originally just another weapon to use, and victory therefore still made sense. This attitude slowly changed, particularly after the Soviet acquisition of atomic weapons. Harbouring entire nuclear arsenals became more special even as the weapons themselves grew more common. War planners gradually assumed 'that any war would be a total nuclear conflict fought with weapons on hand at the start, and thus attention to mobilization declined'.[11] Time was the decisive factor for '[a]lthough the United States had greater resources available for industrial mobilization than any other nation in the world, military planners were convinced that there would not be time enough to mobilize in the event of war'.[12]

Previous wars in history had been total because the ends pursued by the participants drove them to employ every ounce of their power—military, economic, etc.—to struggle for victory. With the advent of superpower nuclear arsenals, this had changed. As Michael Howard observed, '[f]or the first time the Clausewitzian analysis is put in question: nuclear war, if it came, could be total, not because of the political objectives of the belligerents, but because of the military tools at their disposal'.[13] Total wars no longer required total mobilization. Indeed, total wars would now preclude *any* mobilization. The importance of non-military and, in fact, of non-nuclear military instruments in strategic theory had significantly diminished, until the advent of limited war theory after 1952–3. One half of the formulation of grand strategy, the mobilization and use of all forms of power for the pursuit of victory in war, had been discredited as not applicable to modern conditions of war.

Yet the overall nature of nuclear weapons, which overshadowed all other instruments of political power, also cast doubt on the plausibility of achieving victory. This distinctive nature had been mitigated by the initial small number of relatively weak atomic bombs, but by the mid-1950s the introduction of much more powerful thermonuclear armaments changed everything. NATO nearly immediately dropped the notion of victory in war and referred rather to bringing any war between the two superpowers to a conclusion. As the Cold War continued, 'the term "victory" was not part of the picture, nor the idea of "defeating" the enemy: at best, NATO could aim to persuade the enemy to

---

[10] Beatrice Heuser, 'Victory in a Nuclear War? A Comparison of NATO and WTO War Aims and Strategies', *Contemporary European History* 7/3 (Nov. 1998), 314; see also Maxwell D. Taylor, *The Uncertain Trumpet* (New York: Harper & Brothers, 1960), 3–4; James M. Gavin, *War and Peace in the Space Age* (New York: Harper & Brothers, 1958), 131.

[11] Steven Metz, 'Eisenhower and the Planning of American Grand Strategy', *Journal of Strategic Studies* 14/1 (1991), 58.

[12] David Alan Rosenberg, 'American Atomic Strategy and the Hydrogen Bomb Decision', *Journal of American History* 66/1 (June 1979), 64.

[13] Michael Howard, '*Temperamenta Belli*: Can War be Controlled?', in Michael Howard (ed.), *Restraints on War: Studies in the Limitation of Armed Conflict* (Oxford: OUP, 1979), 8.

desist from the course of aggression he had chosen'.[14] Only one concession to this new disavowal of victory was made. 'This is not to say that for that reason we have no interest in "win the war" capabilities and strategies. So long as there is a finite chance of war, we have to be interested in outcomes; and although practically all outcomes would be bad, some would be much worse than others.'[15] Victory in war, like the mobilization and employment of non-military (and military non-nuclear) forces in war, had been swept away by nuclear strategy.

NUCLEAR STRATEGY VERSUS GRAND STRATEGY ROUND 2 (EDWARD MEAD EARLE)

Much of American grand strategic thought prior to and during the Second World War blended peace and war under one overarching concept. Grand strategy was responsible not only for victory in war, to be achieved by all instruments of national power, as virtually every American thinker on grand strategy agreed. It was also responsible for the defence and security of the United States in peace, during which time it would control policy to deter the occurrence of war altogether through sufficient preparation. Edward Mead Earle is the best known proponent of such an interpretation of grand strategy; nuclear strategy, in its turn, developed a veritable stranglehold on peacetime policy and the deterrence of war.

Many commentators during the Cold War noted the expansion in meaning of strategy; 'there is no difference between what was once called a policy and what one now calls a strategy. The substitution of the latter can probably be explained by the new awareness of the confrontation or dialogue of the actors.'[16] Brodie connected this expansion directly to the impact of nuclear weapons, by stating that 'the new weapons force a shift in strategic thinking from a strictly military context to a wider one which is predominantly political and social'.[17] Nuclear strategy became the main influence on both armaments and foreign policies.

---

[14] Heuser, 'Victory in Nuclear War', 316, quote 319.

[15] Bernard Brodie, 'The Anatomy of Deterrence', *World Politics* 11/2 (Jan. 1959), 178.

[16] Raymond Aron, 'The Evolution of Modern Strategic Thought', in Alastair Buchan (ed.), *Problems of Modern Strategy: Part One*, Adelphi Paper 54 (London: IISS, 1969), 2; see also Ken Booth, 'The Evolution of Strategic Thinking', in John Baylis, Ken Booth, John Garnett, and Phil Williams, *Contemporary Strategy: Theories and Policies* (New York: Holmes & Meier Publishers, 1975), 28.

[17] Bernard Brodie, 'Nuclear Weapons and Changing Strategic Outlooks', Feb. 1957, Bernard Brodie Papers (Collection 1223), UCLA Library Special Collections, Charles E. Young Research Library, Box 10, Folder 23, 60-1.

That nuclear weapons had this effect on armaments policy stemmed from the assumed reality of the totality of any nuclear war emanating purely from the weapons themselves. Henry Kissinger (1923–) argued that 'an all-out war fought with modern weapons will be decided by the forces-in-being. We can no longer afford to count on a more or less prolonged period of mobilization. The only way we can derive an advantage from our industrial capacity is by utilizing it *before* the outbreak of a war.'[18] William Liscum Borden, one of the first to understand that there will be no time in nuclear war, slyly suggested that '[p]aradoxically, warfare remains a struggle between rival industrial systems. But the struggle takes place before hostilities begin, and industrial supremacy is measured in terms of stock piles available for immediate use.'[19] This was a new situation for Americans, 'who have been accustomed to expanding and reshaping our military power when the crisis was already upon us'.[20]

Not *all* industrial capacity was deemed equally valuable for the anticipated nuclear war. Shipyards, for instance, were to lose relevance because the slow effect of sea power was at odds with the immediate effect of an unrestrained bilateral nuclear war. The only aspects of sea power that mattered in nuclear conflict were submarines, once they became capable of launching ballistic missiles. The most important industries were those which could contribute directly to the nuclear war effort. As Brodie eloquently summarized, '[i]t is one of the profound consequences of nuclear weapons that all the strategic decisions of any importance are made before war begins, and most of them take the form of choices in [nuclear] weapons systems'.[21]

Readiness for general nuclear war formed the basis of nuclear strategy's influence on foreign policy, which revolved around the primary concern of deterring the Soviet Union. The Canadian diplomat Lester Pearson argued the correctness of this influence. 'Today foreign policy and defence policy cannot be separated. Why then should their planning and coordination be separated.'[22] Thomas Schelling (1921–), one of the major thinkers on nuclear strategy during the 1950s and 1960s, similarly insisted that it was natural for strategy to expand. 'Military strategy can no longer be thought of, as it could for some countries in some eras, as the science of military victory. It is now equally, if not more, the art of coercion, of intimidation and deterrence.

---

[18] Henry A. Kissinger, *Nuclear Weapons and Foreign Policy* (New York: Harper & Brothers, 1957), 93.

[19] Borden, *There Will Be No Time*, 73.

[20] Bernard Brodie, 'Scientific Progress and Political Science', 30 Nov. 1956, Brodie Papers, Box 14, Folder 9, 14.

[21] Bernard Brodie, 'Unlimited Weapons Choices and Limited Budgets', 18 Nov. 1958, Brodie Papers, Box 16, Folder 11, 22.

[22] Lester B. Pearson, *Diplomacy in the Nuclear Age* (Cambridge, MA: Harvard UP, 1959), 31.

The instruments of war are more punitive than acquisitive. Military strategy, whether we like it or not, has become the diplomacy of violence.'[23]

Strategic thought therefore turned to the utility of nuclear weapons in peace. As Kissinger suggested, '[s]trategy can assist policy only by developing a maximum number of stages between total peace (which may mean total surrender) and total war'.[24] Herman Kahn (1922–83) set himself to the task. He was a flamboyant thinker once described as 'Genghis Kahn, a monster who had written an insane, pornographic book, a moral tract of mass murder: how to plan it, how to commit it, how to get away with it, how to justify it'.[25] Kahn expostulated on an escalation ladder, 'a convenient list of the many options facing the strategist in a two-sided confrontation and that facilitates the examination of the growth and retardation of crises. Most important of all, the ladder indicates that there are many relatively continuous paths between a low-level crisis and an all-out war, none of which are necessarily or inexorably to be followed.'[26] Considerations of nuclear force and the relation of thermonuclear armaments to diplomacy never ceased throughout the forty-four rungs of escalation that Kahn had devised.

Ultimately, this expansion of strategy into diplomacy and foreign policy was unsustainable: 'deterrence cannot be an effective substitute for a sensible foreign policy or be utilized to cover up gross foreign policy errors'.[27] Nevertheless, the ideational landscape had been forever changed by this expansion of strategy into diplomacy, foreign policy, and international relations. In mainstream thought, strategy had become a concept of both peacetime and wartime, and nuclear strategy in particular had either usurped or precluded all of the responsibilities of grand strategy inherent in Earle's conception. Moreover, future conceptions of grand strategy were constructed within the newly modified environment where the concept to which it was meant to be superior, strategy, had itself expanded to grand strategy's scope under the aegis of nuclear strategy.

THE EMERGENCE OF LIMITED WAR THEORY

Theories of limited war are older than the Cold War or nuclear weapons, as the writings of Julian Corbett, J. F. C. Fuller, and Basil Liddell Hart attest.

---

[23] Thomas C. Schelling, *Arms and Influence* (New Haven: Yale UP, 1967), 34.
[24] Kissinger, *Nuclear Weapons and Foreign Policy*, 136.
[25] Quoted in John Garnett, 'Herman Kahn', in John Baylis and John Garnett, *Makers of Nuclear Strategy* (London: Pinter Publishers, 1991), 70.
[26] Herman Kahn, *On Escalation: Metaphors and Scenarios* (New York: Frederick A. Praeger, 1965), 37.
[27] Alexander L. George and Richard Smoke, *Deterrence in American Foreign Policy: Theory and Practice* (New York: Columbia UP, 1974), 190.

Indeed, thinking about limiting war is an ancient intellectual tradition which stems not only from strategic theory but also from just war theory, with its ideas of proportionality. Michael Howard notes that '[t]o control and limit the conduct of war is thus not inherently impossible; indeed without controls and limitations war cannot be conducted at all'.[28] Even the interwar United States produced some thoughts on the subject of finely controlling war, only to be dispelled by the experience of the Second World War.[29]

The apparent need for a theory of limited war emerged from two factors: the experience of the Korean War and the advent of thermonuclear weapons. The Korean War was one which policy makers in the United States believed had to be fought, but should not be escalated.[30] This war taught the American strategic studies community 'that great-power rivals occasionally prefer to test each other's strength and resolution with limited rather than unlimited commitments to violence, and it demonstrated also some of the major constraints necessary to keep a war limited'.[31] As General Maxwell Taylor put it, 'our massive retaliatory strategy may have prevented the Great War—a World War III—it has not maintained the Little Peace; that is, peace from disturbances which are little only in comparison with the disaster of general war'.[32]

Thermonuclear weapons, the second source of limited war theory, were judged so dangerous that there was no longer any choice: war *had* to be limited. 'Because the possibility of such destruction now exists, it becomes necessary to examine more closely the problems of limited war, for conflicts of this character do have a powerful rationale under present conditions.'[33] Brodie suggested that thermonuclear weapons, rather than mere atomic armaments, sparked this turn in strategic theory because the large number of atomic bombs and bomber aircraft required to deliver them allowed theorists 'to visualize a meaningful even if hardly satisfactory air defence both active and passive'.[34] As thermonuclear weapon stockpiles grew and second strike capabilities were assured, superpower relations were arguably stabilized through mutual deterrence. Schelling made the ironic but plausible observation that '[s]table deterrence might make limited wars more likely'.[35]

---

[28] Michael Howard, '*Temperamenta Belli*', in Howard, *Restraints on War*, 4.

[29] Bernd Greiner, '"The Study of the Distant Past is Futile": American Reflections on New Military Frontiers', in Roger Chickering and Stig Förster (eds), *The Shadows of Total War: Europe, East Asia, and the United States, 1919-1939* (Cambridge: CUP, 2003), 250.

[30] Kissinger, *Nuclear Weapons and Foreign Policy*, 48.

[31] Brodie, *Strategy in the Missile Age*, 308.

[32] Taylor, *Uncertain Trumpet*, 6.

[33] William W. Kaufmann, 'Limited Warfare', in William W. Kaufmann (ed.), *Military Policy and National Security* (Princeton: Princeton UP, 1956), 107.

[34] Bernard Brodie, 'More About Limited War', Oct. 1957, Brodie Papers, Box 15, Folder 3, 113.

[35] Robert Ayson, *Thomas Schelling and the Nuclear Age: Strategy as Social Science* (London: Frank Cass, 2004), 33.

Limited war theorists drew upon older literature on the limitation of war, particularly the strategic and grand strategic thought of Basil Liddell Hart. Brodie was quite explicit in acknowledging his debt. 'I was glad to mention that you had led all the rest of us in advocating the principle of limited war... I became in effect a follower of yours early in 1952, when I learned through my official connections that a thermonuclear weapon would be tested in the following autumn and would probably be successful.'[36] Thus the basics of British grand strategic thought leading up to the Second World War transformed into American limited war theory after the Korean War, although details differed, much as they had among Mahan, Corbett, Fuller, and Liddell Hart.

LIMITED WAR THEORY VERSUS GRAND STRATEGY ROUND 1 (JULIAN CORBETT)

Julian Corbett's notion of major strategy revolved around manipulating the boundaries of the war for one's own benefit, first to win in the distant theatre and then to escalate and force a peace on the European continent. It was an interpretation of grand strategy significantly at odds with two major elements of American limited war theory, as well as with American public opinion during the Vietnam War.

The first element of limited war theory stemmed from a consideration believed to be novel at the time—the deliberate restriction of available power.

> In using the term 'limited war,' we are not talking about a return to something. We are talking about something quite new. If wars were limited in ages past, the reasons why they were so have on the whole little relevance for us today. In the past, princes may have been inhibited militarily by moral and religious scruples, or by the feeling in any particular instance that the game simply was not worth the candle. Certainly the wars were kept limited by the relatively small margin of the national economic resources available for mobilization, as well as by the relatively small capabilities for destruction that could be purchased with those narrow margins... Today we speak of limited war in a sense that connotes a deliberate hobbling of a tremendous power that is already mobilized—for the sake only of inducing the enemy to hobble himself to a comparable degree.[37]

The major question arising from this was how to agree upon tacit limitations. In this regard Schelling acknowledged that qualitative differences were more

---

[36] Brodie to Liddell Hart, 26 Apr. 1957, Bernard Brodie Personal Papers, Department of Special Collections, Charles E. Young Library, UCLA, Box 1, Folder 'L Correspondence'.

[37] Bernard Brodie, 'Some Strategic Implications of the Nuclear Revolution', 14 May (?) 1957, Brodie Papers, Box 15, Folder 2, 9.

easily recognized than quantitative ones. For example, the use of no nuclear weapons was a clearer limitation and easier to maintain than limiting oneself to ten nuclear attacks. One popular suggestion was geographical; national borders or rivers are relatively unambiguous and so could be used to demarcate limits. 'Even parallels of latitude—arbitrary lines on a map reflecting an ancient number system based on the days in a year, applied to spherical geometry and conventionalized in Western cartography—become boundaries in diplomatic negotiations and conspicuous stopping places in war. They are merely lines on a map, but they are on *everybody's* map.'[38] The need for clear lines not to be crossed conflicted with the subtler Corbettian appreciation that borders can be manipulated. Schelling did nevertheless attempt to inject Corbettian subtlety into consideration of boundaries in limited war. 'Deliberately raising the risk of all-out war [through erosion of established limits] is thus a tactic that may fit in the context of limited war, particularly for the side most discontent with the progress of the war.'[39] It was, in theory, an attractive potential possibility in limited war. In practice, such potential could only be terrifying to policy makers and strategists.

The second element of limited war theory which opposes Corbett's conception of grand strategy, and actually precludes it, is that of sanctuary. 'The principle of sanctuary is a vital one in the whole concept of limited war.'[40] Whereas clearly defined boundaries prevented their manipulation altogether, sanctuaries were envisioned to protect the enemy from escalation in what were considered his most important territories. It was believed that the enemy might therefore reciprocate by also observing sanctuaries. Many theorists argued during the first half of the Cold War that granting sanctuary largely worked in Korea. The Chinese arguably understood and agreed with the tacit limitations of that war. The United States did not bomb Manchuria across the Yalu River, the Chinese never attacked US aircraft carriers. The unilateral granting of sanctuaries had significantly less benign effect in Vietnam. Sanctuaries precluded altogether Corbett's theorized second phase of war, which specifically involved escalation in the enemy's most important theatre of war to put pressure on him to sue for peace.

Much of limited war theory directly contradicted Corbettian notions of grand strategy. Yet the Nixon administration channelled, to some extent, Corbett's spirit during the last years of American involvement in the Vietnam War by ordering conventional incursions into what had previously been North Vietnamese sanctuaries and staging grounds in Cambodia (1970) and Laos (1971). Although arguably successful, such an expansion of the war outraged an increasingly dissenting American public, and led to renewed

---

[38] Schelling, *Arms and Influence*, 132–3.
[39] Ibid. 107.
[40] Bernard Brodie, *War and Politics* (New York: Macmillan, 1973), 67.

and enlarged anti-war demonstrations. Kissinger noted that 'Washington had convinced itself that the four Indochinese states were separate entities, even though the communists had been treating them as a single theatre for two decades and were conducting a coordinated strategy with respect to all of them.'[41] The public had thought the same way as Washington, and made its displeasure clear at what was actually a realignment to suit strategic reality. Regardless of whether limited war theory contradicted the Corbettian interpretation of grand strategy or how subtle that interpretation was, the Vietnam War demonstrated that the political viability of manipulating the boundary of the war could not be other than a politically contentious course of action.

LIMITED WAR THEORY VERSUS GRAND STRATEGY ROUND 2 (BASIL LIDDELL HART)

The explicit indebtedness of limited war theory to the work and theories of Basil Liddell Hart has already been indicated. Liddell Hart's conception of grand strategy emphasized limiting war for its own sake, through the employment of armour, sea power, or air power, as the case may be. He sought to limit great power war by limiting the means employed, as well as the ends to which they were to be applied. American limited war theory similarly sought to limit means, ends, and sometimes even ways, but also sought limitation in other dimensions, such as geography. Robert Osgood (1921–86), one of the major American authors writing on limited war, argued that

> a limited war actively involves only two (or very few) major belligerents in the fighting. The battle is confined to a local geographical area and directed against selected targets—primarily those of direct military importance. It demands of the belligerents only a fractional commitment of their human and physical resources. It permits their economic, social, and political patterns of existence to continue without serious disruption.[42]

The number of possible avenues of limitation resulted in a lack of focus within limited war theory. 'Even a casual reader...will already have been made aware, either implicitly or explicitly, that the term "limited war" is an ambiguous one.'[43] It was applied not only to superpower war, but also to the myriad brushfire conflicts ranging from large conventional wars such as the Korean War to minor interventions such as that in Lebanon in 1958. Despite limited

---

[41] Henry Kissinger, *Diplomacy* (New York: Simon & Schuster, 1994), 660.
[42] Robert E. Osgood, *Limited War: The Challenge to American Strategy* (Chicago: University of Chicago Press, 1957), 2.
[43] John Garnett, 'Limited "Conventional" War in the Nuclear Age', in Howard, *Restraints on War*, 79.

war theory's purported intellectual lineage back to Liddell Hart, it diverged significantly from Liddell Hart's own thinking on the limitation of war and even on which wars are worth limiting.

The aspect of limited war theory which most closely matches Liddell Hart's own emphasis on limiting great power war comprised continuous attempts to conceive of limited nuclear war in Europe. This required acceptance of limited goals, as 'it is clear that no major power will be forced to adopt a strategy of limited objectives because of insufficient resources. With modern weapons, a limited war becomes an act of policy, not of necessity.'[44] No theorist of nuclear strategy or of limited war ever developed a credible notion of limited nuclear war in the European context.

Ultimately, limited war theory went out of fashion after the experience of the Vietnam War. '[T]here has been a notable absence in the 1970s of new tactical or technical concerns or even of the revival or reappraisal of old strategic concerns with respect to limited-war strategy in the Third World. It is as though the trauma of Vietnam had suspended creative thought in this area.'[45] Because limited war theory did not seek to limit war by the same methods as did Liddell Hart, the latter's thoughts on strategy and operations survived, as did his definition of grand strategy. Yet limited war theory was, perhaps ironically, put to use in considering decisive conventional war in Central Europe. Liddell Hart was to be adopted by numerous scholars of grand strategy from the 1970s onwards. Academics, meanwhile, refuted his notion of the British way in warfare, one of the key methods he had identified for the limitation of war. But Liddell Hart's quest to limit war for its own sake was eschewed, replaced by the Weinberger (and later Weinberger-Powell) Doctrine of decisive and overwhelming force. Liddell Hart's holistic concept of grand strategy collapsed, while his successors treated his theory of strategy and grand strategy in a piecemeal fashion.

AMERICAN STRATEGIC THOUGHT VERSUS GRAND STRATEGY ROUND 1 (J. F. C. FULLER)

Writing about grand strategy during the interwar period, J. F. C. Fuller sought to limit war to preserve the global economic system and so maintain civilization. Concern for the future of civilization reached an understandable fever pitch during the Cold War, when the prospect of superpower nuclear war threatened not just national survival but the very survival of humanity itself.

---

[44] Kissinger, *Nuclear Weapons and Foreign Policy*, 139.
[45] Robert E. Osgood, *Limited War Revisited* (Boulder, CO: Westview Press, 1979), 67.

The future of civilization suddenly became a powerful mainstream impetus to strategic thought, and also a major component of nuclear strategy. Brodie, for instance, dramatically titled an article 'Strategy Hits a Dead End', where he noted that '[t]here is a stark simplicity about an unrestricted nuclear war that almost enables it to be summed up in one short statement: be quick on the draw and the trigger squeeze, and aim for the heart. One then has to add: but even if you shoot first, you will probably die too!'[46]

Superpower nuclear war was perhaps only ever an infinitesimal eventuality, but it was still possible. Nuclear strategists obsessed over this chance, thereby propelling the many considerations of limited nuclear war. 'While it is no exaggeration to say that we have failed to invent a war involving nuclear weapons that would fulfil traditional military and political ends, we cannot exclude the possibility that such an invention will occur. If it does, we may have to change our requirements for deterrence and for military operations in the event that deterrence should fail.'[47] Most of this effort revolved around trying to devise ways to limit nuclear war and to achieve reciprocal tacit agreement upon such limitations.

Kahn was one of the few to consider not just the conduct but also the aftermath of nuclear war. Which steps, from before the war through to recuperation afterward, would be necessary to ensure that civilization *does* survive a major nuclear exchange? He identified eight considerations and challenges. '1. Various time-phased programs for deterrence and defence and their possible impact on us, our allies, and others. 2. Wartime performance with different pre-attack and attack conditions. 3. Acute fallout problems. 4. Survival and patch-up. 5. Maintenance of economic momentum. 6. Long-term recuperation. 7. Post-war medical problems. 8. Genetic problems.'[48] He insisted that each stage was absolutely mandatory. None could be neglected. 'I repeat: To survive a war it is necessary to negotiate *all eight* stages. If there is a catastrophic failure in any one of them, there will be little value in being able to cope with the other seven.' Strategists had to get each stage right, since failure at any of them could or would be catastrophic. The realm of strategy thus increased significantly, as 'those waging a modern war are going to be as much concerned with bone cancer, leukaemia, and genetic malformations as they are with the range of a B-52 or the accuracy of an Atlas missile'.[49] In the face of nuclear assault civilization was fragile. It was the responsibility of nuclear strategy to ensure that such an attack did not happen and, if it did, to safeguard the future.

---

[46] Bernard Brodie, 'Strategy Hits a Dead End', *Harper's Magazine* 211/1265 (1955), 36.
[47] Kaufmann, 'The Search for Security', Kaufmann Papers, JFK Library, Box 2, Folder 'The Search for Security (Four Lectures)', 29.
[48] Herman Kahn, *On Thermonuclear War* (Westport: Greenwood Press, 1969), 22.
[49] Ibid. 23, 24.

Attempts to theorize on limiting the conduct of nuclear war foundered in the face of academic and public incredulity. With the end of the Cold War, concern for the future of civilization ceased to be associated with nuclear war, as most assumed that the danger of nuclear exchange had suddenly become a relic of the past.

CONCLUSION

The nuclear age began in 1945, and the thermonuclear age began in 1953. Many pre-existing concepts were immediately sidelined in favour of studying and understanding the new demands placed on strategists and policy makers. This effort culminated in the golden age of American strategic thought, which lasted from 1955 to 1960/65. 'The germination date was August, 1945; and the movement reached a kind of maturity, from which it never recovered, when it moved in 1961 into the Establishment, the Departments of State and Defence. The idea stage was about over then, although books reflecting earlier thought and work continued to appear in the early 1960s.'[50] This golden period happened to coincide with most of the great Cold War crises, giving much grist to the mill of strategic thought. As one historian has trenchantly noted, '[i]t is in the "crisis years" 1958–63 that the history of the Cold War perhaps comes closest to fitting Gibbon's famous definition of history itself as, "indeed, little more than the register of the crimes, follies, and misfortunes of mankind"'.[51] It is no wonder, therefore, that venerable old concepts such as grand strategy were sidelined, albeit not entirely extinguished.

The hegemonic aspect of these new ideas of nuclear strategy and, to a far lesser extent, of limited war theory indelibly altered the character and, in some instances, even the nature of strategic theory. The basic idea of pure strategy had expanded. This propelled grand strategy, when it re-emerged in the 1970s, to even further heights and even broader meanings to differentiate it from strategy itself.

---

[50] Thomas C. Schelling, 'Bernard Brodie (1910–1978)', *International Security* 3/3 (Winter 1978–9), 2.

[51] James G. Hershberg, 'Crisis Years, 1958–1963', in Odd Arne Westad, *Reviewing the Cold War: Approaches, Interpretations, Theory* (London: Frank Cass, 2001), 303.

6

Grand Strategic Thought Eclipsed

Scholars of the highly pragmatic field of strategic studies are naturally drawn to the pressing concerns of contemporary strategy. The great strategic issues of the early Cold War, upon which nearly all important strategic conclusions hinged, related to nuclear strategy and limited war theory. These concepts overtook grand strategy and occupied the various ideational spaces which different interpretations of grand strategy had filled prior to the nuclear age and the Cold War. Yet even during this twenty to thirty year overshadowing, grand strategy retained some currency, however notional, within strategic studies and policy-making circles.

Although little was said or written about grand strategy at the time, the usage of grand strategy which persisted formed the base upon which it later re-emerged into mainstream academe. A number of questions may be raised about grand strategy during this period. First, what was *national* strategy—was it a synonym of grand strategy and where did it come from? Second, who actually used the terms grand or national strategy? Third, what did these terms mean, and with whom or what were they associated in practice?

GRAND STRATEGY AND ITS SYNONYMS

New synonyms for grand strategy emerged and gained popularity during this period, although the creation of synonyms itself was not new. Julian Corbett had employed higher strategy, major strategy, and grand strategy as he developed his ideas throughout his career, all with approximately the same meaning. Holloway Halstead Frost had adopted the term national strategy from Colmar Von der Goltz, albeit Frost used it in a generic sense akin to grand strategy, rather than in Von der Goltz's original, culture-specific meaning.

During the first half of the Cold War, the term grand strategy fell out of favour relative to its cousin, national strategy. Essential equivalence between the two was easily established. 'The term "national strategy" is being used in the World War II sense of "grand strategy."[1] Herman Kahn, who wrote these words, also later on the same page implicitly equated national strategy with national policy, a frequent official usage of the term in the civilian branches of government. Other authors used the two terms, grand strategy and national strategy, almost interchangeably within the same work, on the rare occasions when they invoked either term.[2]

An author speculating about the rise in popularity of 'national strategy' suggested that '"[n]ational strategy" has been adopted in preference to "grand strategy" or "global strategy," for a nation's strategy may be neither grand nor global.'[3] The United States government has stayed with national strategy—or, more recently, national security strategy—even after the 1980s re-emergence of grand strategy as the main academic term. Bureaucratic processes and their language change but slowly. However, a recent British government report sheds some light on why nations may prefer national strategy to grand strategy. The House of Commons Public Administration Select Committee report concluded that grand strategy was a product of empire and empire-building, suggesting that 'its imperial, and potentially hubristic associations, may prove a hindrance'.[4] Grand strategy, despite its return to academic popularity, may simply no longer be politically correct. Also, because the main usage of national strategy stemmed from government, this specific term may be preferred because the government acts as a representative of its nation. Moreover, at the time national strategy became embedded into government documentation, the prime actors on the world stage *were* nations and states, before the proliferation of strategically significant sub-state or non-state actors.

GRAND STRATEGY IN OFFICIAL USE

Grand strategy, and particularly its synonym national strategy, were employed primarily by government during the first half of the Cold War, as the era's academics rarely saw utility in invoking the concept. The term 'grand strategy' had been used by government officials as early as the First World War but disappeared during the interwar period. President Franklin Delano Roosevelt then employed the term during the Second World War, at least in one letter

---

[1] Herman Kahn, *Thinking about the Unthinkable* (New York: Horizon Press 1962), 233.
[2] For one example, see E. J. Kingston McCloughry, *The Direction of War: A Critique of the Political Direction and High Command in War* (New York: Frederick A. Praeger, 1958).
[3] Stephen B. Jones, 'The Power Inventory and National Strategy', *World Politics* 6/4 (July 1954), 422-3.
[4] House of Commons Public Administration Select Committee, *Who Does UK National Strategy? First Report of Session 2010-11* (London: The Stationery Office, 2010), 3.

written to his Army Chief of Staff, George C. Marshall.[5] National strategy during the Second World War was a responsibility to which civilians also felt capable of contributing: Congressman Melvin J. Maas of Minnesota argued in 1943 that this was because national strategy was national policy.[6]

Throughout the early Cold War national strategy was occasionally invoked in official documents as well as by officials addressing Congress. In Congressional testimony of 1947 on the creation of an independent air force, Admiral Forrestal Sherman quoted Admiral Turner's own testimony of the previous year, which suggested that national strategy existed 'entirely outside the purview of normal military and naval strategy'.[7] One government document, *Mobilization Planning and National Security*, even went so far as to define what national strategy was, at least for that document. 'The national strategy includes far more than military strategy. It includes moral strength, physical strength, industrial strength and military strength.' Moreover, '[i]n their defensive roles, both psychological and economic warfare are inseparable from the total national strategy which has for its objective superiority in moral, economic and military armament'.[8]

Although national strategy was used as an official term, it was rarely invoked in federal documents or Congressional discussion, certainly compared to today. The institution which most frequently employed the notion of national strategy was the Naval War College. The Navy, of the three armed services of the United States, retained the greatest interest in concepts of strategy which were broader than the contemporary heavyweight ideas driving first nuclear strategy, which satisfied the Air Force, and second limited war theory, which gave the Army a unique strategic task. The Navy was left with a relative dearth of apparent purpose and utility, and so manifested its dissatisfaction with this state of affairs. Its most dramatic expression was the revolt of the admirals in 1949, but continuous usage of national strategy also fit the basic pattern of escaping the strategic no man's land in which they had landed early in the nuclear age. Chief of Naval Operations Robert B. Carney's testimony to Congress thus argued that '[a] strong Navy makes possible a flexible national strategy, and gives us added ability to retaliate at times and places of

---

[5] Franklin Delano Roosevelt to George C. Marshall, quoted in Maurice Matloff and Edwin M. Snell, *Strategic Planning for Coalition Warfare 1941–1942*. (Washington, DC: Office of the Chief of Military History, 1953), 214.

[6] US House of Representatives, *Extension of Lend-Lease Act: Hearings Before the Committee on Foreign Affairs, House of Representatives* (Washington, DC: Government Printing Office, 1943), 310.

[7] US Senate, *National Defense Establishment (Unification of the Armed Services), Hearings Before the Committee on Armed Services, United States Senate* (Washington, DC: Government Printing Office, 1947), 194.

[8] William Yandell Elliott, *Mobilization Planning and the National Security (1950–1960): Problems and Issues* (Washington, DC: Government Printing Office, 1959), 1, 37.

our choosing'.[9] The reasons behind the Navy's relative emphasis on national strategy were structural and inherent in sea power, and were similar to those which led Alfred Thayer Mahan and Julian Corbett to employ, respectively, broad concepts of naval strategy, and grand or major strategy.

The Naval War College published articles often on aspects of national strategy in its quarterly *Review*. Indeed, the majority of all articles expressly written on national strategy during the 1950s and 1960s were published in the *Naval War College Review*. During those two decades, the *Review* published seventeen articles on grand or national strategy.[10] These articles were frequently derived from lectures given to the students at the College by visiting scholars. The College also held annual national strategy seminars for reservists, which were frequently organized and sponsored by partner institutions. For example, the 1959 seminar was organized by the Foreign Policy Research Institute of the University of Pennsylvania and financed by the Richardson Foundation.[11] By the 1970s, the College had established a syllabus of *Required Readings in National Strategy*.[12]

The Army and Air Force had far less interest in national strategy. The Air Force did occasionally invoke it, but rarely in a meaningful way. The first 1954 semi-annual report of the Secretary of the Air Force noted that '[t]he Air Force must be prepared to carry out the national strategy wherever that strategy is applied and with whatever weapons are prescribed' and also that '[t]he Air Force is constantly increasing its capability to carry out the national strategy'.[13] None of the other Secretaries—of Defence, Army, or Navy—employed the term in their own reports during the early Cold War. The Army's interest in grand or national strategy was based primarily in its historical department, which was focused on writing detailed histories of the Second World War. Thus one of the Army's historians argued that 'Arcadia had produced only a concept, a "grand strategy"; the specific course of action best calculated to give

---

[9] US Department of Defense, *Statements by Secretaries and Chiefs of Staff before Congressional Committees, 1955* (Washington, DC: Government Printing Office, 1955), 50.

[10] For just a small selection of articles, see Harold D. Lasswell, 'Political Factors in the Formulation of Strategy', *Naval War College Review* 4/10 (June 1952), 49–64; Charles Wesley Lowry, 'Moral Factors of National Strategy', *Naval War College Review* 8/1 (Sept. 1955), 33–58; Bernard L. Austin, 'Military Considerations in National Strategy', *Naval War College Review* 16/4 (Dec. 1963), 1–15; and Stephen E. Ambrose, 'Grand Strategy of World War II', *Naval War College Review* 22/8 (Apr. 1970), 20–8.

[11] John Stennis and Special Preparedness Subcommittee, US Senate, *Military Cold War Education and Speech Review Policies* (Washington, DC: Government Printing Office, 1962), 174.

[12] Naval War College, *Required Readings in National Strategy* (Newport, RI: Naval War College, 1970).

[13] US Department of Defense, *Semiannual Report of the Secretary of Defense and the Semiannual Reports of the Secretary of the Army, Secretary of the Navy, Secretary of the Air Force, January 1 to June 31, 1954* (Washington, DC: Government Printing Office, 1955), 253, 311.

effect to this strategic concept, assuming the development of events so permitted, was a subject of lively debate' between the British and the Americans, as well as among the services of both countries.[14] This interpretation seems to be more akin to policy than strategy—setting the goal to be achieved rather than how to use the resources at hand to achieve said goal. Army historian Maurice Matloff similarly observed that military planners over the course of the Second World War slowly developed closer relations with the White House and State Department because of a growing realization that there were no strictly military problems in grand strategy.[15] Matloff further suggested, concerning the source material, that the most useful tomes were memoirs of the men who dealt with grand strategy, which was equivalent to high policy.[16] The Army's historians seemed to consider grand strategy to be akin to policy.

Grand or national strategy was thus invoked most frequently by government officials or Congressmen, or by the military. Nevertheless, some rare academic usage existed outside official government circles. Most notably, Henry Kissinger edited a tome of essays on myriad topics titled *Problems of National Strategy*.[17] Robert Osgood also employed the term in concluding limited war to be a true problem of national strategy because it combined military power with economic power, diplomacy, and other instruments.[18] A third well-known strategic theorist and air force officer, John Boyd, who advocated the tactical concept of the OODA loop, also employed grand strategy. Given the early Cold War context, he not surprisingly considered it in largely ideological terms. Grand strategy must '[s]hape pursuit of national goal so that we not only amplify our spirit and strength (while undermining and isolating our adversaries) but also influence the uncommitted or potential adversaries so that they are drawn toward our philosophy and are empathetic toward our success'.[19]

One political science textbook associated grand strategy with the President's responsibilities and powers as Commander-in-Chief.[20] Another textbook similarly suggests that '[b]y the very nature of the executive branch, only the President is in a position to reconcile the many factors that must go into a

---

[14] Kent Roberts Greenfield (ed.), *United States Army in World War II* (Washington, DC: Historical Division of the Army 1954), 200.
[15] Maurice Matloff, *Strategic Planning for Coalition Warfare 1943-1944* (Washington, DC: Office of the Chief of Military History, 1959), 41.
[16] Ibid. 561.
[17] Henry A. Kissinger (ed.), *Problems of National Strategy: A Book of Readings* (New York: Frederick A. Praeger, 1965).
[18] Robert E. Osgood, *Limited War: The Challenge to American Strategy* (Chicago: University of Chicago Press, 1957), 7.
[19] John Boyd, quoted in Frans P. B. Osinga, *Science, Strategy and War: The Strategic Theory of John Boyd* (London: Routledge, 2007), 179.
[20] Alfred de Grazia, *The Elements of Political Science* (New York: Alfred A. Knopf, 1952), 368.

truly integrated national strategy'. This was in part because devising national strategy was a task for generalists, but also because 'a truly national strategy is far more than the sum total of the various components that go into it, policy and strategy achieved through either addition or compromise are inadequate'. Only a President wielded the potential authority and power to push through a particular national strategy.[21] Other academics considered grand strategy as a trinity comprised of Army, Navy, and diplomatic corps, and simultaneously deplored historical American negligence of this trinity.[22] One of the most interesting academic studies which referenced grand strategy considered the strategic possibilities inherent in the geophysical sciences and included consideration of weather control, the political influence of earthquakes, and so on.[23]

Grand or national strategy also diffused even further, from strategic studies and governmental usage to non-military fields. Lawrence Freedman points to the agency of Alfred D. Chandler, Jr. in bringing the concept of strategy to the mainstream business world, after he had picked up national strategy while teaching at the US Naval War College in the 1950s.[24] However, this was only the pinnacle of a broader ongoing tendency to borrow military concepts, including grand strategy, since at least the latter half of the nineteenth century. The Church employed the term national strategy, much as Christian missionaries had employed grand strategy earlier in the twentieth century, and this usage continued to allude to geographic scope rather than to a particular level of decision-making.[25]

As strategy during this period of the Cold War came to consider and bear responsibility for the development of resources as well as for their employment to gain the desired ends, this conceptual expansion also affected the diffusion of strategy into other fields. Thus strategy as development was applied to the question of whether the United States had a shortage of scientific resources and what could be done about that.[26] National strategy was similarly applied to the provision of national health care.[27]

---

[21] William R. Kintner and Joseph Z. Kornfeder, *The New Frontier of War: Political Warfare, Present and Future* (Chicago: Henry Regnery Company, 1962), 308, 288, 297.

[22] C. Joseph Bernardo and Eugene H. Bacon, *American Military Policy: Its Development since 1775* (Harrisburg, PA: Military Service Publishing Co., 1955), 44.

[23] Helmut E. Landsberg, *Geophysics and Warfare* (Washington, DC: Research and Development Committee on General Sciences, 1954), 38.

[24] Lawrence Freedman, *Strategy: A History* (Oxford: OUP, 2013), 496.

[25] Owen E. Pence, *Present-Day Y.M.C.A.–Church Relations in the United States: A Diagnostic Report* (New York: Association Press, 1948), 95.

[26] James R. Killian, Jr., 'The Shortage Re-Examined: Some Elements of a Grand Strategy for Augmenting our Scientific and Engineering Manpower Resources', *American Scientist* 44/2 (Apr. 1956), 116.

[27] Harold O. Buzzell, 'A New National Strategy to Make Health Services Flexible and Responsive', *Health Services Reports* 88/10 (Dec. 1973), 895.

The British also contributed to sustaining grand strategy as a basic, if fairly neglected, term, primarily through two avenues. First was the work of Basil Liddell Hart, who remained a major figure in the British academic strategic studies community until his death in 1970. As Michael Howard noted, '[s]cores if not hundreds of students and disciples were bound to this implacable and loving master', and further that 'the depth and intensity which he brought to it over fifty years have transformed the nature of military thought itself'.[28] Liddell Hart propounded a particular interpretation of grand strategy, which was reason enough for many to accept the concept, although the effort he dedicated to developing the idea of grand strategy had exhausted itself in the late 1920s. His concept of grand strategy may have seeped into his correspondence and so reached other strategists by means other than his books, although he never shrank from self-promotion. The second main work which sustained the idea of grand strategy, although in a different interpretation from that of Liddell Hart, was the six-volume British Official History series *Grand Strategy* on the Second World War. These volumes, published between 1956 and 1976, kept the term grand strategy somewhat current, although only Michael Howard ever actually defined it in his volume of the series, published in 1970. As with US Army interest in grand strategy, however, the British academics used grand strategy in a historical sense to aid in understanding the Second World War for their government's official histories.

LACKING DEFINITION, PRACTICE, AND ACADEMIC NEED

The idea of grand strategy during the first half of the Cold War lacked three aspects which prevented it from entering mainstream strategic and political discussion. First, it lacked definition, as virtually no new or revised definitions of grand strategy relevant to the new era were developed during this period of time. Second, it lacked a distinct body of practice, or what scholars could point to as grand strategic practice discrete from the respective practices of strategy, politics, or policy. Third, there was no impetus or need on the part of academics and practitioners to employ the concept seriously or frequently in their writings.

During this period of sparse grand strategic thought, three different definitions permeated most extant academic or official use. First were those put forward by Basil Liddell Hart and Edward Mead Earle. Whenever an academic

---

[28] Michael Howard, 'Liddell Hart', in Michael Howard, *The Causes of War and Other Essays* (Cambridge, MA: Harvard UP, 1984), 198, 199.

104   *Evolution of Grand Strategic Thought*

actually defined grand strategy in his work, he might invoke either Liddell Hart or Earle's definitions. However, during this era the number of times either scholar was cited in this regard may together be counted on a single hand. The only new definition of national strategy to emerge out of this period was that provided to the military by the Joint Chiefs of Staff, at least as early as 1953 in the second revision of the *Dictionary of United States Military Terms for Joint Usage*: '[t]he art and science of developing and using the political, economic, and psychological powers of a nation, together with its armed forces, during peace and during war, to secure national objectives'.[29] This definition automatically entered the main dictionaries and glossaries of each individual armed service as well.

Unlike official usage in Congress, which effectively considered it a policy-level concept, the military considered national strategy to be a specific type of strategy, placed subordinate to, and supporting, policy: '*national strategy*—See *strategy*.'[30] Official definitions of strategy and national strategy were very similar, in their breadth of instruments and their continuous applicability during both peace and war. Military strategy had by now been demoted to a mere subset of the wider concept of strategy.[31] Although official definitions are significant, on the academic side no credible scholar posited a definition of grand strategy during this period of drought in grand strategic thought.

Without a serious academic definition, it was difficult to identify behaviour which one might credibly label as 'grand strategic'. Moreover, no one claimed to practise grand strategy. Even George F. Kennan (1904–2005), lauded as being among the greatest American grand strategists, never claimed to practise grand strategy. The historian John Lewis Gaddis suggests of his writings at the Policy Planning Staff that '[t]hey were an intellectual tour de force: an extraordinary attempt to devise a global grand strategy'.[32] Yet Kennan seems never to have considered himself a grand strategist, but instead simply a policy planner for foreign policy, or a diplomat.[33] Indeed, he seems to have outright avoided the term grand strategy—as well as its synonyms—even when coming into direct contact with them. In September 1946 Kennan gave a lecture titled 'Measures Short of War (Diplomatic)' at the National War College. During the questions afterward, one student asked 'Mr. Kennan, is it possible for a state such as the United States to have a grand strategy other than one of weakness?

---

[29] Quoted in Jones, 'The Power Inventory and National Strategy', 422 n.–3 n.

[30] US Department of the Air Force, *Air Force Manual 11-1: Glossary of Standardized Terms* (Washington, DC: US Dept of the Air Force. 1961), 98.

[31] Ibid. 136.

[32] John Lewis Gaddis, *George F. Kennan: An American Life* (New York: Penguin Press, 2011), 293.

[33] His books did not include grand strategy in the title, nor did they mention the term in the text. See e.g. George F. Kennan, *Realities of American Foreign Policy* (London: OUP, 1954); George F. Kennan, *American Diplomacy* (Chicago: University of Chicago Press, 1984).

In other words, we don't aspire to anything particularly except what we have; and what, mainly, can our grand strategy consist of?' This student's idea of grand strategy involved, as he developed his question after Kennan's initial answer, the use of economic power in other parts of the world, especially in a positive rather than negative role. Even when confronted with such a direct question on grand strategy, Kennan did not employ the term to reply, instead using military strategy as a surrogate concept to better explain his point.[34] It is unknown why he did not employ the term on this occasion, which may be the only instance 'grand strategy' appears anywhere in his personal papers. He may have believed it to be a superfluous concept. He may have considered it to be essentially military strategy, given how he replied to the inquisitive student. Any answer to this question can only be speculation.

One credible scholar who found the idea of grand strategy actually to be superfluous was Bernard Brodie. In a memorandum discussion to which Edward Mead Earle and a number of other strategists and scholars contributed, Brodie was the only one who argued against expanding strategy beyond its military connotations.

> I am aware that Mahan uses some such term as 'peacetime strategy', or 'strategy of peacetime', but notice that the term comprises several words and that as a unit it differs in meaning from any single one of its components (*the same might be said of 'grand strategy'*). The terms 'strategy' and 'peacetime strategy' bear very different meanings even in Mahan's usage—the former not being simply inclusive of the latter—and there is, moreover, no indication that the latter term has been commonly accepted in the relevant literature.[35]

Brodie also contributed an article on strategy to the 1965 edition of the *International Encyclopedia of Social Sciences* in which he marked his disapproval of grand strategy, because it represented a new level of strategic decision-making, and called efforts to introduce it into the wider literature 'abortive'.[36]

Curiously, at the same time that he disapproved of grand strategy, Brodie himself employed the term national strategy.[37] Being the official term used by

---

[34] 'Measures Short of War (Diplomatic)', 16 Sept. 1946, George F. Kennan Papers; 1861–2014 (mostly 1950–2000), Public Policy Papers, Department of Rare Books and Special Collections, Princeton University Library, Box 298, Folder 'Measures Short of War (Diplomatic), National War Colle...', 1–3.

[35] Bernard Brodie, 'Memorandum Regarding the Term "Strategy"', date unknown, Edward Mead Earle Papers; 1894–1954, Public Policy Papers, Department of Rare Books and Special Collections, Princeton University Library, Box 35, Folder 'Post-WW2: Strategy', 6.

[36] Bernard Brodie, 'Strategy', Bernard Brodie Papers (Collection 1223), UCLA Library Special Collections, Charles E. Young Research Library, Box 19, Folder 'Strategy', 2.

[37] Bernard Brodie, 'Strategy', Bernard Brodie Papers (Collection 1223), Box 19, Folder 'Strategy', 19. See also William P. Gerberding and Bernard Brodie, *The Political Dimension in National Strategy: Five Papers* (Los Angeles: UCLA Security Studies Project 1968).

the United States government, national strategy was naturally more attractive than grand strategy. Moreover, one might speculate that the meaning which Brodie attached to national strategy was that it was specific to the United States, rather than the new and unnecessary generic level of strategic consideration and decision-making which he saw as grand strategy. Brodie never explicitly defined national strategy, which may lend credence to the narrower cultural rather than generic meaning of national strategy. Just as with Kennan's avoidance of grand strategy, there will never be a definitive explanation for Brodie's dislike of grand strategy but simultaneous use of national strategy. On the few occasions when the term appeared in the broader strategic studies literature, other academics also occasionally treated grand strategy with disdain or excessive care. Two authors insisted always on writing 'grand strategy' in single quotes, as if it were not still an accepted term with currency, but rather a new and dubious item to be used with care, albeit one introduced by Edward Mead Earle.[38]

CONCLUSION

Grand strategy floundered during the first half of the Cold War, overshadowed by the concepts and pressing demands of considering nuclear strategy and limited war theory in practice. Few employed grand strategy, fewer employed it meaningfully and with definition, few associated themselves with it in practice, and few saw utility in the term. Those who were most engaged with grand or national strategy were the Navy and Congress. The Navy was interested because the theories of nuclear strategy and limited war theory of that time did not leave much for it to do. Further, the structural factors of sea power impelled the Navy much more than the Army or Air Force to consider its own utility, a trail Mahan and Corbett had blazed half a century earlier. Individual Congressmen were interested in grand or national strategy because interpreting it as policy could grant them greater influence in strategy making than they may otherwise have had. However, one of the most celebrated grand strategists in American history, George F. Kennan, apparently did not consider himself as such.

The treatment of grand or national strategy during this period of the Cold War showcases the vulnerability of even previously important concepts to intellectual fashion, and may even call into question its veracity as a general concept. It certainly highlights the difficulty of developing a definitive

---

[38] See Burton M. Sapin and Richard C. Snyder, *The Role of the Military in American Foreign Policy* (Garden City, NY: Doubleday & Co., 1954), 9, 24, 31, 37, 60.

definition. Nevertheless, despite the lack of explicitness, the range of possible meanings of the time was actually smaller than today, with its surfeit of multitudinous definitions. Ironically, the Cold War paucity of attention paid to grand strategy may well have spawned its later re-emergence as a popular strategic studies term.

7

The Re-emergence of Grand Strategic Thought

The re-emergence of grand strategy as a major idea in strategic studies was symptomatic of larger trends and the reopening of larger questions within the discipline. Thereafter, grand strategy was continually defined and redefined by those who used it, its ever shifting character and purpose a reflection of the individual backgrounds and research and policy interests of the authors employing it. This had, of course, always been the case, but in the late 1970s and 1980s the term started being appropriated and reappropriated with increasing frequency. The modern status of grand strategy as a nearly wholly amorphous idea is most strongly rooted in the final decade and a half of the Cold War.

Grand strategy re-emerged as an important concept in strategic studies within a particular intellectual context which influenced its four major interpretations. These interpretations had been developed throughout the debates on strategy, defence, and decline which took place after the Vietnam War and for the remainder of the Cold War. They reflected not only contemporary concerns but also the research and policy interests of their authors. First is the grand strategic thought of John Collins, who wrote the first American book on grand strategy and tied the idea to that of national security. Then Edward Luttwak contributed much towards the popularization of the term, defined as military statecraft. Barry Posen reconceived grand strategy as doctrine specifically for the achievement of security. Paul Kennedy uniquely approached the idea of grand strategy from a long-term perspective. The casual use of and some minor, idiosyncratic definitions of grand strategy are also surveyed.

THE INTELLECTUAL CONTEXT

The intellectual context of the 1970s significantly encouraged the re-emergence of grand strategy as a major concept within strategic studies.

The Re-emergence of Grand Strategic Thought

Henry Kissinger alluded to this new intellectual context while working for the Nixon administration. 'First of all, let me say that this Administration came to office at the end of a period of substantial collapse of foreign policy theory.'[1] The breakdown in foreign policy consensus over the 1970s enabled a new direction for academic strategic studies. Lawrence Freedman, reflecting on the very technical condition of contemporary strategic theory in the late 1970s, concluded that 'a healthy development in strategic studies would be a more searching inquiry into the political assumptions upon which so much of strategy rests'.[2]

By the time Freedman's observations were published, scholars had already begun moving in this direction along a small handful of different tacks. Old ideas were repurposed, or new concepts developed, to aid strategists in thinking about the bigger issues in strategy and policy, which suddenly needed consideration after the Vietnam War. One of these was grand strategy, re-emerging after being overshadowed by other, more apparently pressing or appropriate, concepts during the first half of the Cold War. A second, and new, concept was strategic culture. A third, also revived, idea was geopolitics. Another legacy of the Vietnam War which influenced the context and renewed evolution of grand strategy was the US Army's reaffirmed focus on questions of waging war in Central Europe. This led to an emphasis on doctrine, and later on the operational level of war, which injected a concern with practical military considerations into the development of the new or renewed concepts for big ideas. Fears of US decline also grew during this time, impelled by the apparent limits of US power in Vietnam and the economic rise of states such as Japan, which also influenced the re-emergence of grand strategy.

From its inception in 1977, the new idea of strategic culture was employed to explain why the Soviets did not think about nuclear strategy in the same manner as American strategists, and why this mattered.[3] Strategic culture was originally meant as an analytical tool of last resort, if none of the already existing concepts within strategic studies could adequately explain what strategists were observing.[4] Nevertheless, it caught on quickly. Ken Booth penned a treatise with lasting value on ethnocentrism and its dangers in 1979.[5] Colin Gray, among others, developed the concept further and applied it to American

---

[1] Henry Kissinger, 'Memorandum of Conversation', 12 Aug. 1971, Alexander M. Haig Papers, Richard M. Nixon Presidential Library, Box 49, Folder 'China Speech Material', 2.

[2] Lawrence Freedman, 'Has Strategy Reached a Dead-End?', *Futures* 11/2 (Apr. 1979), 130.

[3] Jack L. Snyder, *The Soviet Strategic Culture: Implications for Limited Nuclear Operations* (Santa Monica, CA: RAND, 1977).

[4] Jack Snyder, 'The Concept of Strategic Culture: Caveat Emptor', in Carl G. Jacobsen (ed.), *Strategic Power: USA/USSR*. (Houndmills: Macmillan, 1990), 4.

[5] Ken Booth, *Strategy and Ethnocentrism* (London: Croom Helm, 1979); see also Colin S. Gray. 'The Strategic Anthropologist', *International Affairs* 89/5 (2013), 1285–95.

nuclear strategy.[6] The strategic culture literature, which has only burgeoned since the late 1970s, has focused primarily on 'big picture' considerations such as the assumptions underpinning how individual polities think about war and strategy, how these assumptions affect the actual conduct of strategy through tactics and operations, and by which criteria individual polities consider victory and defeat in war.

Geopolitics similarly dealt with the question of fundamental assumptions, although from a perspective which emphasized geography. Despite the work of Halford Mackinder and Nicholas Spykman, among others, geopolitics fell out of favour as a concept after the Second World War. This was due in part to its supposed connection to Nazi Germany, as well as the relatively frozen geopolitical map of the first half of the Cold War. 'It needed signs of a real thaw in the Cold War before recovery began to take place, and this did not come until the end of the 1960s.'[7]

The opening of China by the Nixon administration contributed to this thaw, as did the Vietnam War's final discrediting of the domino theory and collapse of the foreign policy consensus. Geopolitics was recovered as a concept in France in the mid-1970s, and thereafter by the British and Americans.[8] Sometimes authors appeared to assume some sort of functional equivalence between geopolitics and grand strategy, and further between both concepts and national security policy. Colin Gray, for instance, remarked of his book *The Geopolitics of Super Power* that '[t]his is an old-fashioned book about U.S. national security policy. Had the long-hallowed British verbal formula of "grand strategy" not been expropriated to such a persuasive effect by Edward Luttwak, this book might have been called *The Grand Strategy of the United States*.'[9] The three concepts of geopolitics, grand strategy, and national security policy were considered sufficiently similar, due to their shared analytical purpose within strategic studies, to be used synonymously despite their somewhat varying approaches to addressing the assumptions of strategy.

The idea of grand strategy itself had been minimally sustained throughout its eclipse by other strategic concepts, primarily through official use in government and the military services, as well as by academics corralled by the government or military to work for them. By the late 1960s and the early 1970s, the idea of grand strategy began regaining popularity. Leading the

---

[6] Colin S. Gray, 'National Style in Strategy: The American Example', *International Security* 6/2 (Autumn 1981), 21–47; this article was followed by Colin S. Gray, *Nuclear Strategy and National Style* (London: Hamilton Press, 1986).

[7] Geoffrey Parker, *Geopolitics: Past, Present and Future* (London: Pinter, 1998), 43.

[8] Ibid., ch. 4; Colin S. Gray, *The Geopolitics of the Nuclear Era: Heartlands, Rimlands, and the Technological Revolution* (New York: Crane, Russak & Co., Inc., 1977); and Geoffrey R. Sloan, *Geopolitics in United States Strategic Policy, 1890–1987* (Brighton: Wheatsheaf Books, 1988).

[9] Colin S. Gray, *The Geopolitics of Superpower* (Lexington, KY: UP of Kentucky, 1988), 1.

charge was a tome dedicated to Anglo-French war planning prior to the First World War, *The Politics of Grand Strategy*, published in 1969, which assumed an understanding of grand strategy more similar to nineteenth-century grand strategic thought than that of the twentieth century.[10] A more notable indication of this sudden rise in popularity was the first American book dedicated solely to grand strategy in an expansive interpretation, *Grand Strategy: Principles and Practices*.[11] It was swiftly followed by Edward Luttwak's work on *The Grand Strategy of the Roman Empire*, which generated controversy that propelled grand strategy into renewed popularity.[12] The term grand strategy also became fashionable again for casual use, but serious academics such as Barry Posen and Paul Kennedy also employed developed interpretations of it in the subsequent decade. Moreover, other academics outside of strategic studies put forward concepts with similar functions at approximately the same time. The economic historian Alan Milward thus proposed the notion of strategic synthesis, which accounted for 'all the other factors which it is necessary to take into account, political, military, social and psychological'.[13]

It is apparent that the strategic studies community leapt at these new and renewed concepts with potential explanatory power for the new questions it faced after the Vietnam War. Doctrine and the operational level of war, and the declinism debate, were also part of this milieu which helped generate demand for the new concepts and influenced particular interpretations of grand strategy.

GRAND STRATEGY FOR SECURITY

Grand strategy as it first re-emerged in the United States revolved around national security. Unlike military strategy with its natural application within an analytical framework dominated by war and the pursuit of victory, grand strategy was interpreted as existing beyond war as well—as had largely been the case since the promulgation of Edward Mead Earle's definition. This fit the scholarship of Barry Posen and Edward Luttwak's initial forays into grand strategy, although Luttwak ultimately moved beyond security. Both these strategists were preceded by John M. Collins, who published the first American book on grand strategy in 1973.

---

[10] Samuel R. Williamson, Jr., *The Politics of Grand Strategy: Britain and France Prepare for War, 1904–1914* (Cambridge, MA: Harvard UP, 1969).

[11] John M. Collins, *Grand Strategy: Principles and Practices* (Annapolis, MD: Naval Institute Press, 1973).

[12] Edward N. Luttwak, *The Grand Strategy of the Roman Empire from the First Century A.D. to the Third* (Baltimore, MD: Johns Hopkins Press, 1976).

[13] Alan S. Milward, *War, Economy and Society, 1939–1945* (London: Allen Lane, 1977), 19.

Collins attempted thoroughly to contextualize grand strategy within the practice of strategy and policy, as well as within the structure of strategic theory. First, he believed that it was a concern largely unique to modern circumstances, the product of increasing complexity in safeguarding national security.[14] As polities grew more interdependent and as technology advanced, the scope for threatening another state's security by measures other than full-fledged invasion and conquest grew, requiring development of the idea of grand strategy to comprehend it all. Collins also interpreted such developments as providing a watershed in the evolution of strategic theory as well. Thus he considered grand strategy a post-Clausewitzian concept which 'debunks' Clausewitz's definition of strategy.[15]

The grand strategist's first task was 'to sort out those interests that relate specifically to national security'. This sorting was first because many interests—such as having a healthy and well-educated citizenry—impact significantly upon national security, but the government departments involved in ensuring them are not principally concerned with defence. Ultimately, Collins narrowed down the question of national security to the one vital concern of every polity: survival. Yet survival was a spectrum. 'At the upper end of the scale is Germany, whose national way of life, fundamental institutions, and values were destroyed during World War II, and whose territory was divided. The important thing, however, is that the nation survived, and West Germany today is the preeminent power in Free Europe. By way of contrast, some satellites behind the Iron Curtain survived as political, economic, and social zombies.'[16]

Collins considered grand strategy only one of a constellation of different types of strategy. At the top was national strategy, which 'fuses all the powers of a nation, during peace as well as war, to attain national interests and objectives' and which is comprised of the individual national economic, political, military, etc. strategies.[17] He, however, limited the scope of his endeavour by focusing on grand strategy, 'the art and science of employing national power under all circumstances to exert desired degrees and types of control over the opposition through threats, force, indirect pressure, diplomacy, subterfuge, and other imaginative means, thereby satisfying national security interests and objectives'.[18] However, because the ultimate security concern of grand strategy was national survival, grand strategy primarily concerned questions of military force and war—and of avoiding their use.

> 'Military strategy' and 'grand strategy' are interrelated, but are by no means synonymous. Military strategy is predicated on physical violence or the threat of violence. It seeks victory through force of arms. Grand strategy, if successful,

---

[14] Collins, *Grand Strategy*, p. xix. [15] Ibid. 15.
[16] Ibid. 1. [17] Ibid. 14. [18] Ibid.

alleviates any need for violence. Equally important, it looks beyond victory toward a lasting peace. Military strategy is mainly the province of generals. Grand strategy is mainly the purview of statesmen. Grand strategy *controls* military strategy, which is one of its elements.[19]

Collins's explanation of the relationship between grand and military strategy was effectively a synthesis of Liddell Hart's and Edward Mead Earle's interpretations of grand strategy, although heavily weighted towards that of Liddell Hart. Collins did not, however, cite Earle. It appears that he merely adapted Liddell Hart's interpretation by tying its main concern to national security, thereby bringing it into the conceptual territory occupied by Earle's definition.

GRAND STRATEGY AS MILITARY STATECRAFT

Edward N. Luttwak was one of the major figures involved in resurrecting grand strategy during the last decade and a half of the Cold War. His usage of grand strategy over his three most important books of that time treated grand strategy as statecraft, albeit narrowing its focus to consider primarily its military aspects. This approach resembled that of Edward Mead Earle. The resemblance was not exact, due in large part to the differing strategic and geopolitical contexts in which they lived. While Earle's interpretation was coloured by the Second World War, Luttwak's was dominated by Cold War concerns.

Luttwak's first, and most controversial, assay of grand strategy concerned the Roman Empire. This published work stemmed from his Ph.D. dissertation: 'Force and Diplomacy in Roman Strategies of Internal Security'.[20] Interestingly, it hardly mentioned grand strategy at all, save for a single casual use of the term. Instead, the focal concept was security, conceived as a system whose most important characteristic was economy of force.[21] The addition of grand strategy occurred between completion of the dissertation and its publication, perhaps due to the re-emergence of the concept into mainstream strategic studies.

Once Luttwak began employing the term 'grand strategy', he immediately established the synonymy of Roman grand strategy with its imperial statecraft. 'An investigation of the strategic statecraft of the Roman Empire scarcely requires justification. In the record of our civilization, the Roman achievement in the realm of grand strategy remains entirely unsurpassed, and even two

[19] Ibid. 15.
[20] Edward N. Luttwak, 'Force and Diplomacy in Roman Strategies of Imperial Security' (Ph.D. dissertation, Johns Hopkins University, 1975).
[21] Ibid., abstract.

millennia of technological change have not invalidated its lessons.'[22] Much like Earle's interpretation, which stressed the internal policies of a state, Luttwak did not restrict his interpretation of grand strategy or statecraft merely to external diplomacy, whether persuasive or coercive.

An important element of grand strategy was the integrated and coherent system which underpinned external diplomacy and the use of force. Luttwak, like Earle, also incorporated internal considerations into grand strategy, but their considerations differed. Earle, thinking and writing in an age of total war, envisioned the entire productive power of a state. Luttwak, immersed in imperial Rome, emphasized instead those factors which had enhanced the use of Roman military power, such as the roads that provided mobility and the signalling links which transmitted intelligence.[23]

Luttwak envisioned grand strategy as a system of infrastructure and capabilities, and applied this to Roman practice. The emphasis on diplomacy, military forces, road networks, and fortifications all point towards a concern about NATO and the front in Central Europe. Luttwak's main concern in the early 1980s was the operational level of war, which he and a handful of other theorists introduced into the Western strategic lexicon. Its purpose was to focus strategic thinking with regards actually to fighting the Soviet Union should events demand it.[24] One may perceive the seeds of this operational concern in his emphasis on the factors which enhanced the operational capabilities of the Roman army. Grand strategy and the operational level of war were intimate concepts within Luttwak's strategic thought, because most aspects of grand strategy were implemented through military practice at the operational level.

Luttwak also included alliances in his system of grand strategic thought, which is commentary on both contemporary events in Southeast Asia and on NATO. 'Efficient client states could provide for their own internal security and for their own perimeter defence against low-intensity threats, absolving the empire from that responsibility.'[25] Moreover, even though the Romans were sometimes forced to intervene in client states, 'the direct intervention of Rome in the affairs of a client state would not mean that every rebel band would have to be pursued into deep forest or remote desert as the Roman system of deterrence and Roman prestige required in provincial territory'.[26] His disapproval of the Vietnam War, at least as it had actually been fought, is clear. The South Vietnamese contribution to the free world's security was hardly even additive, let alone complementary. It may also be interpreted as an academic's warning shot (neither the first nor the last) at the European states

---

[22] Luttwak, *Grand Strategy of the Roman Empire*, p. xi.   [23] Ibid. 4.
[24] See e.g. Edward N. Luttwak, 'The Operational Level of War', *International Security* 5/3 (Winter 1980-1), 61–79.
[25] Luttwak, *Grand Strategy of the Roman Empire*, 24.   [26] Ibid. 25.

within NATO, who the United States constantly fretted were not pulling their just weight within the military alliance.

Luttwak's system of grand strategic thought thus focused on diplomacy, particularly through alliances, and force with emphasis on operational factors. Heavily influenced by the Roman subject matter of his first major historical investigation, he next employed his system to analyse the Soviet Union, whose control over other potential instruments of political power—economic, ideological, and so on—was far greater than that of the Romans. His force-centric system endured, however, because the Soviet Union's judged lack of potential regarding non-military instruments made the military its primary instrument.[27] This system of grand strategic thought considered alternative instruments to diplomacy and force only to eschew such factors as irrelevant to the grand strategy of the Soviet Union.

Luttwak's conception of grand strategy was preserved with only minor amendments in his major theoretical work on the paradoxical logic of war and peace. 'Now at last we are ready to encounter grand strategy, the highest level of final results. This is also the everyday form of strategy, because the dynamic workings of the paradoxical logic continue even in the absence of warfare. Peacetime international politics are conditioned by the same logic, insofar as the use of force is still a possible recourse.'[28] The use of force is the factor which distinguishes grand strategy from international relations as a whole. Luttwak clearly acknowledges that non-military instruments interact with grand strategy, but these other instruments were not part of grand strategy per se.[29] Only the plausible use of force engaged the adversarial logic of strategy, which no other instrument could.

Luttwak thus considered grand strategy to be effectively synonymous with military-focused statecraft, which likely stemmed from his concern with the operational level of war. This interpretation was supported by others as well, including the controversial air power theorist John Warden. As Warden explained, '[t]he *grand strategic level* of war is the place where the most basic but most consequential decisions are made. Here, a country determines whether it will participate in a war, who its allies and enemies will be, and what it wants for the peace.'[30] Warden had developed this interpretation as early as 1974-5 when he was working on his master's thesis.[31]

---

[27] Edward N. Luttwak, *The Grand Strategy of the Soviet Union* (London: Weidenfeld & Nicolson, 1983), 29.
[28] Edward N. Luttwak, *Strategy: The Logic of War and Peace* (Cambridge, MA: Belknap Press of Harvard UP, 1987), 177.
[29] Ibid. 179-80.
[30] John A. Warden III, *The Air Campaign: Planning for Combat* (Lincoln, NE: toExcel, 2000), 1.
[31] John Andreas Olsen, *John Warden and the Renaissance of American Air Power* (Washington, DC: Potomac Books, 2007), 28.

Luttwak's emphasis on the link between military force and statecraft led him to consider the political utility of force and deem modern grand strategy post-Clausewitzian. 'Only since 1945 has the emergence of new technologies of mass destruction invalidated the fundamental assumptions of the Clausewitzian approach to grand strategy.'[32] However, his preoccupation with the relationship between the military, with its operational concerns, and statecraft resembles that of Earle's second interpretation of grand strategy, as the link between military and political affairs. Earle's interpretation in turn may be placed in one tradition of grand strategic thought stretching back to the nineteenth century. As Luttwak suggested,

> [t]he firm subordination of tactical priorities, martial ideals, and warlike instincts to political goals was the essential condition of the strategic success of the empire. With rare exceptions, the misuse of force in pursuit of purely tactical goals, or for the psychic rewards of purposeless victories, was avoided by those who controlled the destinies of Rome. In the imperial period at least, military force was clearly recognized for what it is, an essentially limited instrument of power, costly and brittle.[33]

For Luttwak grand strategy was the political utility of the operational level of war, what is normally referred to in strategic studies as simply strategy, combined with diplomacy and alliances to achieve the military security of one's own polity. The other instruments of political power are necessarily relevant to grand strategy, but do not obey the fundamental logic of strategy as Luttwak identified it and so are not actually a part of grand strategy.

GRAND STRATEGY AS DOCTRINE FOR SECURITY

The early 1980s also saw Barry Posen experiment with the idea of grand strategy, which he tied to two additional concepts: military doctrine and security.[34] He accepted the security orientation of grand strategy which the renewed American interpretation emphasized, as propounded by Collins and then by Luttwak in his early writings on the topic. His doctrinal interest also reflected the broader debates on national security and defence which dominated the post-Vietnam period.

This era saw a handful of important revisions of the capstone American doctrinal publication FM 100-5 *Operations*, including the shifts to active defence and from that to the concept of AirLand Battle. Posen contributed

---

[32] Luttwak, *Grand Strategy of the Roman Empire*, p. xii.   [33] Ibid. 2.
[34] Barry R. Posen, *The Sources of Military Doctrine: France, Britain, and Germany between the World Wars* (Ithaca, NY: Cornell UP, 1984), 7.

to the debates surrounding these changes and particularly weighed in on the conventional balance within Europe.[35] His major work on doctrine and grand strategy was explicitly meant to contribute to this debate as well.[36]

Much like Luttwak, Posen originally used the term grand strategy only in a casual manner. It emerged in his writing later, when his work was published. His well-known definition of grand strategy is 'a political-military, means-end chain, a state's theory about how it can best "cause" security for itself'.[37] In his doctoral dissertation, which he completed three years prior to its final publication, he used instead the term strategic doctrine, rather than grand strategy.[38]

From the beginning, Posen was interested in the Clausewitzian relating of military means to political ends, also an element of Luttwak's and other previous interpretations of grand strategy. Strategic doctrine 'includes an explanation, implicit or explicit, of how and why the ends and means fit together, and how and why the entire chain leads to the security of the state'.[39] By the time his dissertation was published, Posen had expanded his idea of strategic doctrine into grand strategy. Whereas originally strategic doctrine integrated solely military and political concerns, grand strategy incorporated additional instruments of political power. 'A grand strategy must identify likely threats to the state's security and it must devise political, economic, military, and other remedies for those threats.'[40] He further inflated the idea of grand strategy, by giving it conceptual responsibility over multiple levels of policy consideration and implementation. 'It encompasses foreign policy, military doctrine, and even tactics.'[41]

Although Posen allowed grand strategy this greater breadth of responsibility, his own prime research interest remained the military-political integration which had defined his original interpretation of strategic doctrine.[42] He did approach the inflation of his core idea from strategic doctrine to grand strategy with some care and recognized that '[w]ithout some boundaries, the concept of grand strategy as a political-military means-ends chain can be expanded to unmanageable dimensions'.[43] Unfortunately, his concept attained these unmanageable dimensions by ultimately incorporating both breadth of instruments and depth of responsibility, from policy through to tactics. Marrying

---

[35] See Barry R. Posen, 'Measuring the European Conventional Balance: Coping with Complexity in Threat Assessment', *International Security* 9/3 (Winter 1984–5), 47–88; and Barry R. Posen, 'Is NATO Decisively Outnumbered?', *International Security* 12/4 (Spring 1988), 186–202.

[36] Posen, *Sources of Military Doctrine*, 241.   [37] Ibid. 13.

[38] Barry Posen, 'The Systemic, Organizational, and Technological Origins of Strategic Doctrine: France, Britain, and Germany between the World Wars' (Ph.D. dissertation, University of California, Berkeley, 1981), 6.

[39] Ibid. 17.   [40] Posen, *Sources of Military Doctrine*, 13.
[41] Ibid. 220.   [42] Ibid.   [43] Ibid.

this great theoretical expanse to security only guaranteed its unbounded nature, given the flexibility inherent in the idea of security.

Despite the virtually unlimited concept he had introduced, Posen's personal interest of relating military means to political ends limited his own exploration of the idea. His investigation of the sources of military doctrine suggested that doctrine which is well integrated with the political aims in question is more effective than doctrine which is not well integrated. It must also be socially and economically affordable. To be successful, doctrine must also be adaptable to changing political circumstances and advancing military technology. A successful doctrine might also have deterrent value. To fail at any of these factors would be to jeopardize the state's survival.[44] Posen thus loosely equated national security with survival, to which war was a danger. His interpretation of grand strategy resembled those of Edward Mead Earle, with a dual focus on war-relevant statecraft and on integrating military means and political ends. Earle largely kept these two interpretations separate. Posen merged them into one, with emphasis on the second.

GRAND STRATEGY AS LONG-TERM STRATEGY

Paul Kennedy, who at the dawn of the post-Cold War world would develop one of the most popular modern interpretations of grand strategy, approached the idea from a significantly different perspective than his contemporaries. A diplomatic historian, Kennedy swiftly expanded his interests into strategic history as well, with a dual focus on the interaction between economic and military bases and forms of power, and on history over the long term. These interests influenced his grand strategic thought in a manner unique to him, leading to an interpretation of grand strategy which, unlike most others of the time, did not focus on achieving security or in dwelling upon the political utility of force.

Kennedy's interpretation of grand strategy, like his histories, emphasized the long term and the relationship between military power and economic strength. As he explained in his discussion of grand strategy,

> a true grand strategy was now concerned with peace as much as (perhaps even more than) with war. It was about the evolution and integration of policies that should operate for decades, or even centuries. It did not cease at a war's end, nor commence at its beginning...
>
> Second, grand strategy was about the balancing of ends and means, both in peacetime and in wartime. It was not enough for statesmen to consider how to

[44] Ibid. 16, 24–5.

win a war, but what the *costs* (in the largest sense of the word) would be; not enough to order the dispatch of fleets and armies in this or that direction, but to ensure that they were adequately provided for, and sustained by a flourishing economic base; and not enough, in peacetime, to order a range of weapons systems without careful examination of the impacts of defence spending.[45]

While Kennedy acknowledged that military power and economic strength could be mutually improved through interactive use, he believed it was much easier for them to be antagonistic instead.[46] Indeed, military power and economic strength complementing each other usually led to the rise of new great powers, whereas their antagonism led to the fall of old great powers.[47] Kennedy's study of the rise and fall of great powers in (predominantly European) history ultimately led him to consider the position of the United States from a perspective which feared American decline due to inherited strategic commitments made decades earlier versus suddenly facing the limits of American power.[48] Moreover, Kennedy worried that even high-level policy officials or experienced strategic analysts in the United States were not able to think in a sustained manner about balancing demands on military power against the foundations of economic strength over the long term. Although the government attempted to imagine an integrated, long-term strategy, Kennedy judged the resulting document lacking the necessary breadth and depth, being instead a contemplation of military policy.[49]

Kennedy's idea of grand strategy, rather than aiming for achievement of a particular security condition or political goal, thus emphasized husbanding one's strength.[50] He did not address the question of a polity facing supreme national emergency and how such a challenge might distort the long-term demands which his concept of grand strategy imposed. In his history, such emergencies are generally indicative of previous policy failure in creating too many defence commitments without the necessary economic strength to support them. Yet long-term considerations have little appeal if short-term dangers threaten to erase the great power status of a powerful polity.

---

[45] Paul Kennedy, 'Grand Strategy in War and Peace: Toward a Broader Definition', in Paul M. Kennedy (ed.), *Grand Strategies in War and Peace* (New Haven: Yale UP, 1991), 4.
[46] See for instance Paul M. Kennedy, 'Strategy versus Finance in Twentieth-Century Great Britain', *International History Review* 3/1 (Jan. 1981), 44–61.
[47] Paul M. Kennedy, *The Rise and Fall of the Great Powers: Economic Change and Military Conflict from 1500 to 2000* (New York: Vintage Books, 1989), p. xxii.
[48] Ibid. 514–15.
[49] Paul Kennedy, 'Not So Grand Strategy', *New York Review of Books* 35/8 (12 May 1988), 5–8; Paul Kennedy, 'Grand Strategies and Less-than-Grand Strategies: A Twentieth-Century Critique', in Lawrence Freedman et al. (eds), *War, Strategy, and International Politics: Essays in Honour of Sir Michael Howard* (Oxford: Clarendon Press, 1992), 228.
[50] Kennedy, 'Toward a Broader Definition', 4.

Finally, Kennedy asserted that grand strategy 'rather naturally' concerned great rather than small or medium powers.[51] It was thus not a universal function or consideration in strategic theory or practice. Instead, grand strategy mattered only in the context of already being, or having the potential to be, a great world power.

Kennedy's summary of his interpretation emphasized its theoretical position, its balancing role, and its orientation towards the distant future. 'The crux of grand strategy lies therefore in *policy*, that is, in the capacity of the nation's leaders to bring together all the elements, both military and non-military, for the preservation and enhancement of the nation's long-term (that is, in wartime *and* in peacetime) best interests.'[52] It was a theoretical idea without universal application, due to its great power emphasis. It controlled policy rather than being controlled by it. Finally, it seemed to lose the instrumental logic of strategy, of using means to achieve ends, in favour of balancing different means and ways against each other in order not to upset the overall long-term strength of the polity. The status of any particular ends in question along the way thus remains unresolved, assumed to be never serious enough to threaten Kennedy's theoretical construct of grand strategy.

Superficial similarities with Earle's notion of grand strategy exist, particularly Earle's contention that France executed a single grand strategy over three hundred years. Kennedy's interpretation implies a Liddell Hartian willingness to compromise on ends to husband one's means. It is only through this compromise that a Kennedy-esque grand strategy may succeed in lasting for decades or centuries. Earle's example of a three-hundred-year French grand strategy stemmed instead from the constancy of France's objectives: keeping Central Europe weak, requiring continuous engagement; and maintaining its borders at natural geographical obstacles, requiring offence to reach and defence to maintain against those who feared an over-strong France. Kennedy-esque grand strategies hold distant time horizons by design and implicitly compromise interests to endure, whereas Earle's example just happened to be a three-century-long geopolitical effort. Kennedy's interpretation of grand strategy is instead the culmination of the British school of grand strategic thought, with its focus on economy and economical means and ways of waging war. It is Basil Liddell Hart's definition, applied equally to war and peace, over the very long term, implicitly predicated on compromising ends to preserve means.

Kennedy's interpretation was unique among the major theorists of grand strategy, but it did not arise from nowhere. There had been pressures within both the community of defence analysts and within government for a grand

---

[51] Ibid. 6.   [52] Ibid. 5.

strategy geared towards the distant future. One government-commissioned report, published prior to Kennedy's formulation of his own theoretical concept of grand strategy, argued that '[o]ur strategy must be designed for the long term, to guide force development, weapons procurement, and arms negotiations. Armaments the Pentagon chooses today will serve our forces well into the next century. Arms agreements take years to negotiate and remain in force for decades.'[53] Kennedy's concept fit well with prevailing inclinations in thinking about defence policy, which may have contributed to its continued popularity. As Hew Strachan notes, Kennedy's interpretation of grand strategy as a phenomenon geared towards the long term is the major conception accepted to this day.[54]

CASUAL USES AND MISCELLANEOUS INTERPRETATIONS OF GRAND STRATEGY

For every defined use of grand strategy during its re-emergence after the Vietnam War, numerous casual uses or minor definitions of the term were made. Through cumulative effect these minor references were part of the intellectual climate in which grand strategy made its return.

US naval historian and strategist John Hattendorf employed grand strategy as an analytical tool for examining the War of the Spanish Succession. He defined grand strategy simply: 'The conduct of grand strategy is the higher direction of warfare. It is the purposeful use of armed force to achieve broad objectives in international relations.'[55] This interpretation was in line with other historical and contemporaneous definitions of grand strategy emphasizing the question of the political utility of military force. He also dwelt on the limits of grand strategy as an analytical tool and noted that 'England's concept of grand strategy is an unsatisfactory explanation for all aspects of her conduct in war.'[56] Finally, contrary to a recent British initiative to retire the term grand strategy in favour of national strategy, Hattendorf noted that the implementation of a grand strategy might surpass the capabilities of the national polity conceiving it, yet remain sound. 'When English diplomatic efforts and goals are contrasted with England's actual use and employment of her own resources, it is apparent that the ministry in

---

[53] Fred Charles Iklé and Albert Wohlstetter, *Discriminate Deterrence: The Commission on Integrated Long-Term Strategy* (Washington, DC: US Government Printing Office, 1988), 1.
[54] Hew Strachan, 'Strategy and Contingency', *International Affairs* 87/6 (Nov. 2011), 1282.
[55] John B. Hattendorf, *England in the War of the Spanish Succession: A Study of the English View and Conduct of Grand Strategy, 1702–1712* (New York: Garland Publishing, 1987), 23.
[56] Ibid. 74–5.

London was fully aware that its grand strategy could not be carried out by one nation alone.'[57] This observation also gives Hattendorf's appreciation of grand strategy Corbettian undertones about manipulating the boundaries of the war.

John Lewis Gaddis, well known today for a broad definition of grand strategy as the calculated relationship of means to large ends, first tried his hand at defining grand strategy at the end of the Cold War. This early interpretation was propounded in a single article, and seems not to have been widely accepted. He suggested that

> [m]uch of the confusion over whether strategic 'logic' exists or not stems from the fact that we have never made the criteria for 'success' in strategy—and particularly in 'grand strategy'—very clear. The problem traditionally did not arise on the battlefield: one either won, lost, or produced a stalemate; strategies could then be evaluated in terms of those obvious results. But the realm of 'grand strategy' is much wider than that: it requires the integration of military strategy with such non-military considerations as politics, economics, psychology, law, and morality, and it involves doing so over indeterminate periods of time. Specifying what constitutes success under those conditions is indeed no easy task.[58]

This interpretation of grand strategy assumes that strategy itself resides in a vacuum with no relationships to other concepts or considerations, and is perhaps a reflection of broader American strategic thought during some periods of the Cold War. Gaddis makes a further assumption about strategic logic in his early interpretation of grand strategy by suggesting that grand strategy 'is simply the application of "strategy" as here defined, by states acting within the international state system, to secure their interests: it is what leads, if all goes well, to "statecraft."'[59] Grand strategy was *applied* strategy, an interpretation which contravened much of what other strategic authorities wrote on the basic practical nature of strategic studies as a discipline. As Bernard Brodie observed, '[a]bove all, strategic theory is a theory for action'.[60] Practicality is the bedrock of strategic concepts, and therefore separating the appreciation of a strategic situation from acting within that situation is superfluous.

A third author offering an idiosyncratic interpretation of grand strategy was Gregory Foster, who described grand strategy as he desired the United States to practise it. It was a concept born of the pressure of circumstance, growing

---

[57] Ibid. 166; for information on the British shift from grand strategy to national strategy see House of Commons Public Administration Select Committee, *Who Does UK National Strategy? First Report of Session 2010–11* (London: The Stationery Office, 2010), 8–9.

[58] John Lewis Gaddis, 'Containment and the Logic of Strategy', *The National Interest* (Winter 1987–8), 28.

[59] Ibid. 29.

[60] Bernard Brodie, *War and Politics* (New York: Macmillan, 1973), 452.

out of the old idea of military strategy. 'Strategy today can be thought of as grand strategy—the coordinated direction of all the resources, military and non-military, of a nation (or alliance) to accomplish its objectives.'[61] He believed considering strategy at any lower level to be unproductive, perhaps even counter-productive.[62] In part, this was because the recourse to military force represented an unfavourable situation to the strategist. 'In an ultimate sense, the use or threatened use of military force remains the most convincing form of power. But it is also the least creative, least controllable and most provocative manifestation of power. In fact, there is much to be said for the argument that the use of force represents an abdication of control, an admission of one's inability to engage in effective psychological manipulation.'[63] Ultimately, Foster placed grand strategy—and strategy generally—on a level above policy, from where policy was to be directed. 'The natural inclination is to view strategy as supporting policy, rather than the reverse...But strategy is more than this: it is the grand design, the overall mosaic into which the pieces of specific policy fit. It provides the key ingredients of clarity, coherence and consistency over time.'[64]

Besides Hattendorf, Gaddis, and Foster, who offered idiosyncratic interpretations or minor definitions of grand strategy, many others employed the term and concept in a casual, ill-, or undefined manner. The last decade of the Cold War produced much analysis of the Soviet Union through the lens of grand strategy. Besides Luttwak's work which rested on a previously developed understanding of grand strategy, books and articles casually using the term abounded.[65] It was also purposely turned towards the needs of the United States, or the West more generally, by those concerned by its apparent drift. As Luttwak mourned, after Vietnam '[i]t was the very notion of strategy that waned'.[66] Authors attempted to set right the United States' or West's course, relying on grand strategy as an engine for their analysis and prescriptions.[67]

---

[61] Gregory D. Foster, 'Missing and Wanted: A U.S. Grand Strategy', *Strategic Review* 13 (Autumn 1985), 15.

[62] Ibid. 22. [63] Ibid. 18. [64] Ibid. 14.

[65] See Brian MacDonald (ed.), *The Grand Strategy of the Soviet Union* (Toronto: Canadian Institute of Strategic Studies, 1984); Robert E. Osgood (ed.), *Containment, Soviet Behavior, and Grand Strategy* (Berkeley, CA: Institute of International Studies, 1981); and David Gibbs, 'Does the USSR Have a "Grand Strategy"? Reinterpreting the Invasion of Afghanistan', *Journal of Peace Research* 24/4 (Dec. 1987), 365–79.

[66] Edward N. Luttwak, 'On the Meaning of Strategy...For the United States in the 1980s', in W. Scott Thompson, *National Security in the 1980s: From Weakness to Strength* (San Francisco: Institute for Contemporary Studies, 1980), 262–3.

[67] See e.g. Seyom Brown, 'An End to Grand Strategy', *Foreign Policy* 32 (Autumn 1978), 22–46; Sherle R. Schwenninger and Jerry W. Sanders, 'The Democrats and a New Grand Strategy', *World Policy Journal* 3/3 (Summer 1986), 369–418; Jerry W. Sanders and Sherle R. Schwenninger, 'The Democrats and a New Grand Strategy, Part II', *World Policy Journal* 4/1 (Winter 1986-7), 1–50; James Chace, 'A New Grand Strategy', *Foreign Policy* 70 (Spring

The term, or the related term of national strategy, was also applied to other countries.[68]

Grand strategy was even adopted by literatures other than strategy and international relations. Business had already adopted the idea of strategy during the Cold War. It also later adopted grand strategy, usually defined 'as a corporation's major plan of action for achieving the sales and earnings' goals for the firm as a whole (rather than a product, division or market segment)', and synonyms such as master or primary strategy were also noted.[69] As an explicit plan of action, it was assumed to have an important relationship with planning formality.[70] Thus '[e]xplicit recognition by the firm of its grand strategy has often been supported as the basis of coordinated and sustained strategic management efforts'. Generic typologies of business grand strategy have been developed, such as 'stability (e.g. concentration), internal growth (innovation, market and product development), external acquisitive growth (vertical and horizontal integration, concentric and conglomerate diversification, joint venture), and retrenchment (turn-around, divestiture, liquidation)'.[71]

Grand strategy was also adapted for the direction and sustainability of higher education, which seemed to treat it much as did the business world. One commentator argued that '[i]f we must name this grand strategy, we should *not* call it strategic planning. As catchy as the term might be, it serves no useful purpose in higher education. If we must use the term "strategic" as a modifier, the only proper noun it can modify is management.'[72] As in business, grand strategy within higher education primarily concerned formalized plans and management.

1988), 3–25; and Stephen M. Walt, 'The Case for Finite Containment: Analyzing U.S. Grand Strategy', *International Security* 14/1 (Summer 1989), 5–49.

[68] See e.g. Samir Amin, 'Democracy and National Strategy in the Periphery', *Third World Quarterly* 9/4 (Oct. 1987), 1129–56; Fred Charles Iklé and Terumasa Nakanishi, 'Japan's Grand Strategy', *Foreign Affairs* 69/3 (Summer 1990), 81–95.

[69] Michael A. Hitt, R. Duane Ireland, and Gregory Stadter, 'Functional Importance and Company Performance: Moderating Effects of Grand Strategy and Industry Type', *Strategic Management Journal* 3/4 (Oct.–Dec. 1982), 315 n.; see also Michael A. Hitt, R. Duane Ireland, and K. A. Palia, 'Industrial Firms' Grand Strategy and Functional Importance: Moderating Effects of Technology and Uncertainty', *Academy of Management Journal* 25/2 (June 1982), 266.

[70] John A. Pearce II, D. Keith Robbins, and Richard B. Robinson, Jr., 'The Impact of Grand Strategy and Planning Formality on Financial Performance', *Strategic Management Journal* 8/2 (Mar.–Apr. 1987), 125–34.

[71] Ibid. 126.

[72] Cameron Fincher, 'The Return of Grand Strategy', *Research in Higher Education* 19/1 (1983), 127–8; see also Cameron Fincher, 'Grand Strategy and the Failure of Consensus', *Educational Record* 56 (1975), 10–20.

CONCLUSION

The idea of grand strategy entered a continuous cycle of definition and reappraisal after the Vietnam War when it was readopted by mainstream strategic studies and included in a wide variety of debates about the defence, or even the basic national health, of the United States. The constant reinvention of grand strategy prevented a single coherent idea from establishing conceptual hegemony during the debates, leading to grand strategy becoming amorphous as a concept. Despite this deleterious condition, certain themes may be identified in the grand strategic literature of the time, whose persistence may be measured back into nineteenth-century discussions of grand strategy.

Impelled by the traumatic experience of the Vietnam War, many strategists were concerned with the political utility of force—that is, whether force was actually still useful and, as a related question, whether strategists could control conflicts as propounded before the Vietnam War. Most of those who wrote on grand strategy related the concept to these questions, much as some nineteenth-century usages of grand strategy were concerned with the relationship between military force and political goals. If one includes the pursuit of security in this consideration, the range of authors whose work touches upon this theme includes Collins, Luttwak, Posen, and Hattendorf.

The familiar theme of grand strategy as manoeuvre returned as well, albeit in a metaphorical sense emphasizing the diplomatic aspect of grand strategy for the prevention of wars altogether. Thus Luttwak considered grand strategy to be military statecraft, and Foster deplored the use of force as an acknowledgement of the grand strategist's abdication of control, rather than as an exercise of control. Kennedy's ideas also fit partially within this theme due to his emphasis on balancing military commitments against available economic strength.

The theme of grand strategy as identifying the decisive point also re-emerges, through prescribing particular grand strategies for policy makers to follow. Prescription is an eternal product within strategic studies, but grand strategic prescriptions changed the nature of grand strategy away from the pragmatic instrumentality of strategy into policy, if not ideology.

The fourth historical theme within grand strategic thought, grand strategy as multi-theatre strategy, also makes an appearance, with Hattendorf's historical work on English grand strategy during the War of the Spanish Succession. This was, in many ways, one of the most familiar interpretations of grand strategy due to its natural resonance with the experience of the World Wars, particularly the Second.

Although the circumstances in which grand strategy is conceived and reconceived relentlessly change, many of the fundamental concerns which drive the development of both abstract theory and practical thought in strategic studies remain constant. These concerns were coloured but never transmuted by the events and contexts which surrounded the authors who developed grand strategy at the end of the Cold War. However, the parlous state of coherence within grand strategic thought only encouraged further dispersion of meaning by the new thinkers on grand strategy after the end of the Cold War.

8

Post-Cold War Grand Strategic Thought

Grand strategy re-emerged as a major strategic concept in the 1970s and during the 1980s gained momentum in mainstream awareness within, and beyond, strategic studies. Its popularity reached its apogee after the end of the Cold War, which greatly stimulated the literature on grand strategy—a body of work which dwarfs in scale, of ink on the page, the entire previous historical backlog of grand strategic thought. However, few authors sought to address the concept of grand strategy theoretically but preferred instead its non-rigorous employment to prescribe courses of action or to examine the course of historical events holistically.[1]

This deluge of grand strategic literature partially reflected a belief that basic political assumptions had to be studied. Some scholars encouraged strategic studies to extend beyond even grand strategy.[2] Many authors responded by expanding the concept of grand strategy even above national policy in the hierarchy of responsibility. The resulting debate concerned prescriptions for foreign policy which stemmed from ideological modes of viewing the world and the history of the United States. Historians also adopted the concept, and their usage frequently reflected the definitions developed in strategic studies by scholars such as Paul Kennedy or Barry Posen.

The two post-Cold War decades have brought a veritable avalanche of books and articles on grand strategy. It is both implausible and unnecessary to record exhaustively every minor current or eddy within this recent grand strategic thought. The fundamental insight, that the idea of grand strategy has little to no coherence due to its popular and widespread use and misuse, may be demonstrated well short of encyclopedic thoroughness.

Nevertheless, within this deluge of grand strategic prescriptions and historical studies, some authors must be highlighted for their attempts to grapple theoretically with the idea of grand strategy, for their resultant ideas, and for

---

[1] Avery Goldstein, *Rising to the Challenge: China's Grand Strategy and International Security* (Stanford, CA: Stanford UP, 2005), 17–18.

[2] John Chipman, 'The Future of Strategic Studies: Beyond Even Grand Strategy', *Survival* 34/1 (1992), 109–31.

their influence as scholars. John Lewis Gaddis develops an important and swiftly popular interpretation of grand strategy during this time. Robert Art proffers a definition of grand strategy which is akin to military strategy in the bounds it sets on the concept, save for one aspect in which it is as broad as policy itself. Edward Luttwak also continues developing his own grand strategic thought through study of the Byzantine Empire and the rise of China. Finally, a new trend in grand strategic thought has begun gaining ground in the past decade, although it was first posited in the 1980s. This is the idea that grand strategy is a universal concept which may be applied beyond even statecraft to become instrumental in daily life.

GRAND STRATEGY ABOVE POLICY

Many of the new interpretations of grand strategy to emerge in the 1970s and 1980s considered it to be a level of responsibility either synonymous with policy or hierarchically above it, for to coordinate non-military instruments of power it had to control all of those policy areas. Employing grand strategy as a synonym for policy is a fairly common and straightforward interpretation. Placing grand strategy higher than policy has its own particular logic, as grand strategy thus provides the bedrock assumptions and the fundamental ideology upon which policy is based.

Identification of grand strategy's proper role as higher than that of policy is not uncommon and only grew more popular as time marched on. Paul Kennedy and Gregory Foster both supported this interpretation. William Martel has suggested that 'grand strategy is a coherent statement of the concepts the state uses to deal with the full range of "threats to a nation's security" and "the military, political and economic means to meet them."' Furthermore, he posited that '[p]olicymakers cannot conduct an effective foreign policy unless they are equipped with a coherent grand strategy'.[3] As a third observer claimed, 'it should be clear to the reader that "grand strategy" and "foreign policy" are not synonymous. Grand strategy, the conceptual framework, is necessarily broader than foreign policy, the political actions of the state in international relations.'[4]

At this level, scholars are no longer discussing strategy, but rather ideologies or, within academia, schools of international relations. The grand strategy debate now revolves around the adequacy of realism compared to liberalism or any other theory of how international relations work, rather than ways and

---

[3] William C. Martel, 'Grand Strategy of "Restrainment"', *Orbis* 54/3 (Summer 2010), 357, 358.
[4] Braz Baracuhy, 'The Art of Grand Strategy', *Survival* 53/1 (Feb.–Mar. 2011), 151.

means of achieving particular objectives.[5] The neo-conservatives propose one grand strategy, the liberals another, the realists a third, and so on.[6] Political economists are also interested in applying their area of specialty to explain grand strategy.[7] Within this context, grand strategic thought comprises the exact same arguments as competing schools of international relations, only with a more prescriptive purpose. This interpretation of grand strategy has become synonymous with the assumptions underpinning policy. Assumptions are unavoidable; policy makers cannot *not* have assumptions. However, 'there is a practical requirement for those assumptions to be right, or to eliminate as much error in judgment as is possible'.[8] At this point grand strategy's synonymity with schools of international relations falters, as it becomes ideology.[9] True believers rarely compromise the integrity of their ideologies in the face of countervailing evidence, as they believe that they have identified the decisive point or policy for success. This current state of grand strategic thought is what led Marc Trachtenberg to write that 'one of the main problems with the idea of grand strategy is that it places a premium on a certain kind of intellectualizing'.[10]

Despite misgivings by some academics, for two decades the post-Cold War grand strategic literature has been inundated by international relations grand strategic prescriptions. Although the prescriptions themselves are of little interest to strategic studies and have been studied extensively elsewhere, they do contain certain interesting facets.

PRESCRIPTIONS, 1990S AND 2000S

The grand strategic prescriptions of the 1990s were arguably fuelled by uncertainty over what the purpose of the United States' foreign policy should be.

---

[5] See e.g. Colin Dueck, 'Ideas and Alternatives in American Grand Strategy, 2000–2004', *Review of International Studies* 30/4 (2004), 511–35; and Colin Dueck, 'Realism, Culture and Grand Strategy: Explaining America's Peculiar Path to World Power', *Security Studies* 14/2 (2005), 195–231.

[6] See examples such as Tom Farer, *Confronting Global Terrorism and American Neo-Conservatism: The Framework of a Liberal Grand Strategy* (Oxford: OUP, 2008); G. John Ikenberry, *Liberal Order and Imperial Ambition: Essays on American Power and World Politics* (Cambridge: Polity, 2006); and Colin Dueck, *Reluctant Crusaders: Power, Culture, and Change in American Grand Strategy* (Princeton: Princeton UP, 2006).

[7] Kevin Narizny, *The Political Economy of Grand Strategy* (Ithaca, NY: Cornell UP, 2007); Mark R. Brawley, *Political Economy and Grand Strategy: A Neoclassical Realist View* (London: Routledge, 2010).

[8] Ben Lombardi, 'Assumptions and Grand Strategy', *Parameters* 41/1 (Spring 2011), 29.

[9] See Adam Elkus, 'Must American Strategy Be Grand?', *Infinity Journal* 3/1 (Winter 2012), 24–8.

[10] Marc Trachtenberg, 'Making Grand Strategy: The Early Cold War Experience in Retrospect', *SAIS Review* 19/1 (Winter-Spring 1999), 36.

The Soviet Union, the traditional enemy, had collapsed, marking the success of nearly fifty years of containment. The world order had become unipolar. What was a hegemon to do? A number of different prescriptions or frameworks for foreign policy conception and action were developed and hotly debated.[11] Barry Posen and Andrew Ross examined and described these numerous prescriptions. 'Four grand strategies, relatively discrete and coherent arguments about the U.S. role in the world, now compete in our public discourse. They may be termed neo-isolationism; selective engagement; cooperative security; and primacy.'[12] As each of the four visions was based on a different tradition of thought in American foreign policy, the logic of strategy as they interpreted it also differed slightly.

The basic major difference among the four prescriptions revolved around the use of force, as that is the most consequential act of engagement, albeit adversarial, with another polity. What is perhaps striking is how little these prescriptions changed as the uncertainty of the 1990s transformed into the anti-terrorist certainties of the 2000s. As Posen notes in an article soon after the attacks on 9/11, '[a]lthough the outlines are not clear, advocates of alternative U.S. grand strategies during the last decade now seem inclined to superimpose these strategies on the campaign against terror'.[13] The ideologies do not change even when the circumstances do.

The differences in logic are most striking when proponents of the various grand strategies collaborate. One monograph published by the Center for a New American Security included chapters for each of the major grand strategic prescriptions, each by a well-known advocate. The editors proffered Edward Mead Earle's old definition of grand strategy, yet half of the contributors did not follow it but instead employed their own.[14] This implies that the various schools of international relations which fuel each grand strategic prescription are so disparate in their basic assumptions about the international environment that they are unlikely to accept a single definition of what grand strategy actually is, even a relatively neutral definition developed over sixty years previously.

The most unorthodox interpretation of strategic logic belonged to the neo-isolationists, particularly Eric Nordlinger. He preferred to label grand strategy as national strategy, as '[a] national strategy entails a near reversal of strategic

---

[11] Nicholas Kitchen, 'American Power: For What? Ideas, Unipolarity and America's Search for Purpose between the 'Wars', 1991–2001' (Ph.D. dissertation, London School of Economics, 2009), p. ii.

[12] Barry R. Posen and Andrew L. Ross, 'Competing Visions for U.S. Grand Strategy', *International Security* 21/3 (Winter 1996–7), 5.

[13] Barry R. Posen, 'The Struggle Against Terrorism: Grand Strategy, Strategy, and Tactics', *International Security* 26/3 (Winter 2001–2), 53.

[14] Michèle A. Flournoy and Shawn Brimley (eds), *Finding our Way: Debating American Grand Strategy* (Washington, DC: Center for a New American Security, 2008).

internationalism's great commonalities', in that it prescribed global non-engagement rather than engagement.[15] He thus interpreted strategy, including its basic military definitions, as fundamentally concerned with engaging with foreign powers.[16] Nordlinger is technically correct, given that military strategy may be defined as 'the art of the dialectic of force or, more precisely, *the art of the dialectic of two opposing wills using force to resolve their dispute*'.[17] Yet this adversarial engagement is inherent in military strategy and is a consequence of politics and policy, rather than being the driver of such engagement, as Nordlinger implies. The original decision to engage or not is not a strategic question, but a political one.

This short examination of the grand strategic prescriptions of the post-Cold War period excludes many books which were major works in their fields during this time.[18] It is particularly in the two fields of political science and international relational prescriptions that an exhaustive, encyclopedic mapping would be tedious, unnecessary, and unrelated to the wider purpose of this work. Nevertheless the differences in prescriptions may be traced back to differences in fundamental assumptions about the world and the logic of action therein.

GRAND STRATEGY IN HISTORY

The re-emergence of grand strategy as a concept in strategic studies in the 1970s and its use by eminent scholars also spurred its study within history.[19] Edward Luttwak, John Hattendorf, and Paul Kennedy were those who began its historical study, by their own individually preferred interpretations. As with all grand strategic thought, each individual historian has continued to define grand strategy to suit his own research interests, although frequently the definitions are drawn from or inspired by the major pre-existing conceptions of grand strategy.

Andrew Lambert, in treating the Crimean War, defined grand strategy as 'the development and implementation of strategy within the context of

---

[15] Eric A. Nordlinger, *Isolationism Reconfigured: American Foreign Policy for a New Century* (Princeton: Princeton UP, 1995), 3.

[16] Ibid. 8–9.

[17] André Beaufre, *An Introduction to Strategy*, tr. R. H. Barry (London: Faber & Faber, 1965), 22.

[18] Such as Dueck, *Reluctant Crusaders*; Charles A. Kupchan, *The Vulnerability of Empire* (Ithaca, NY: Cornell UP, 1994); and Christopher Layne, *The Peace of Illusions: American Grand Strategy from 1940 to the Present* (Ithaca, NY: Cornell UP, 2006).

[19] Examples of historical works on grand strategy not cited later include Paul C. Allen, *Phillip III and the Pax Hispanica, 1598–1621: The Failure of Grand Strategy* (New Haven: Yale UP, 2000) and Arther Ferrill, *Roman Imperial Grand Strategy* (Lanham, MD: UP of America, 1991).

national policy'.[20] This interpretation is in line with the long-standing relational military-political theme within grand strategic thought. Geoffrey Parker discussed 'the decisions of a given state about its overall security—the threats it perceives, the way it confronts them, and the steps it takes to match ends and means' during the reign of Philip II of Spain.[21] Such a definition of grand strategy seems to be inspired by the security focus of the American grand strategic literature of the late 1970s and early 1980s. Similarly, two Greek scholars have perceived in the writings of Thucydides 'an outline of a complete theory of grand strategy; a comprehensive theory of how states ensure their security. Thucydides' theory incorporates the economic, diplomatic, military, technological, demographic, psychological and other factors upon which a state's security depends.'[22]

In discussing the early relations between the United States and the People's Republic of China, Thomas Christensen defined grand strategy 'as the full package of domestic and international policies designed to increase national power and security'.[23] This definition borrows the logic of grand strategy as the coordinator of state policy. A similar definition has been used to examine Russian expansionism over the course of nearly two centuries between 1650 and 1831. 'Grand strategy required the mobilization of the political and military establishment, of the economy, and of the country's leading cultural and ecclesiastical figures, in order to realize a global vision, which in Russia's case was the establishment of its hegemony within the Heartland.'[24] This same emphasis on grand strategy as leading policy also looked at domestic policy. Aaron Friedberg conducted 'a study of the interior dimension of American grand strategy during the Cold War...to explain the shape and size of the domestic mechanisms through which, over the course of nearly half a century, the United States created the implements of its vast military power'.[25]

Some historians admit not being able to define grand strategy precisely. Williamson Murray suggests that '[t]here is, one must admit, considerable confusion of grand strategy with policy, military strategy, and strategies to achieve this or that specific goal. Grand strategy is none of these, but to one

---

[20] Andrew Lambert, *The Crimean War: British Grand Strategy Against Russia, 1853–56* (Farnham: Ashgate, 2011), 8.

[21] Geoffrey Parker, *The Grand Strategy of Philip II* (New Haven: Yale UP, 1998), 1.

[22] Athanassios G. Platias and Constantinos Koliopoulos, *Thucydides on Strategy: Grand Strategies in the Peloponnesian War and their Relevance Today* (New York: Columbia UP, 2010), 1.

[23] Thomas J. Christensen, *Useful Adversaries: Grand Strategy, Domestic Mobilization, and Sino-American Conflict, 1947–1958* (Princeton: Princeton UP, 1996), 7.

[24] John P. LeDonne, *The Grand Strategy of the Russian Empire, 1650–1831* (Oxford: OUP, 2004), 6.

[25] Aaron L. Friedberg, *In the Shadow of the Garrison State: America's Anti-Statism and its Cold War Grand Strategy* (Princeton: Princeton UP, 2000), 3; see also Richard Rosencrance and Arthur A. Stein (eds), *The Domestic Bases of Grand Strategy* (Ithaca, NY: Cornell UP, 1993).

extent or another, it consists of all of them.'[26] He even admits that '[n]o simple, clear definition of grand strategy can ever be fully satisfactory'.[27] Other historians have equated grand strategy with strategic culture, which is not surprising given the similar roles they have played in strategic studies since their introduction or reintroduction in the 1970s.[28]

Such usage of grand strategy by historians rarely contributes towards the theoretical debate on what grand strategy is, but rather acts as a reflection of that debate and how it influences other, albeit related, academic disciplines. It was perhaps inevitable that grand strategy would become a favoured concept with historians. Its breadth of meaning, by nearly any definition, provides significant versatility to explore the causal mechanisms of historical events.

GRAND STRATEGY, GEOGRAPHICALLY FRAMED

John Lewis Gaddis, who had proffered a minor interpretation of grand strategy in the final years of the Cold War, rethought grand strategy after his first essay on the topic and developed a new interpretation which defined the concept geographically. For the purposes of a course on grand strategy which he co-founded with Paul Kennedy and diplomat turned academic Charles Hill in the late 1990s, Gaddis produced a new and unique definition: 'grand strategy is the calculated relationship of means to large ends'.[29] This definition appears reasonable at first glance and has been adopted by other academics, including Colin Gray.[30] It does not immediately appear to be a definition based in one of the old geographically defined traditions of grand strategic thought. Gaddis's whole treatment of grand strategy, however, confirms that it is indeed a geographical understanding of the concept.

Gaddis explicitly noted that one of his personal reasons for founding a seminar on grand strategy at Yale was to counter what he called 'theateritis', 'the tendency of military commanders to look only at the needs of their own theatre of operation, and not at the requirements of fighting the war as a

---

[26] Williamson Murray, 'Thoughts on Grand Strategy', in Williamson Murray et al. (eds), *The Shaping of Grand Strategy: Policy, Diplomacy, and War* (Cambridge: CUP, 2011), 2–3.
[27] Ibid. 5.
[28] See Jeremy Black, 'Strategic Culture and the Seven Years' War', ibid. 63–78, and Alastair Iain Johnston, *Cultural Realism: Strategic Culture and Grand Strategy in Chinese History* (Princeton: Princeton UP, 1995).
[29] John Lewis Gaddis, 'What is Grand Strategy?', American Grand Strategy After War (26 Feb. 2009, Triangle Institute for Security Studies and Duke University Program on American Grand Strategy, unpublished), 7.
[30] See Colin S. Gray, *The Strategy Bridge: Theory for Practice*. (Oxford: OUP, 2010), 18.

whole'.[31] This may partly stem from an interest in systems theory and understanding how disparate and even purportedly independent elements interact in a complex system.[32] Strategically, a theatre is commonly understood to be an independent geographical entity.[33]

The historical example of 'theateritis' given by Gaddis tellingly focused on Douglas MacArthur's overriding interest in reining in China during the Korean War while ignoring the broader requirements of US foreign policy. Another example he employed from personal experience considered NATO eastward expansion after the end of the Cold War, how that might negatively impact the Russians and cause them to warm up relations with the Chinese, and the lack of thought given this possibility in Brussels.[34] Gaddis also reinforced the geographic character of his interpretation of grand strategy in a televised interview about the 2002 National Security Strategy in the United States. One of the reasons he considered it a grand strategy was 'that it is comprehensive. It does not simply break up the world into regions and say that we have an approach for this region and an approach for that region, but these don't necessarily interconnect.'[35]

Gaddis stresses the necessity of grand strategy because it is 'an *endangered* discipline, for in the absence of sufficiently grave threats to concentrate our minds, there are insufficient incentives to think in these terms'.[36] He concludes that grand strategies have been generally formed in periods of crisis, after major political or strategic shocks. Discussing the post-9/11 2002 NSS, he argued that '[f]irst of all, it responds to a crisis. And it is crises that generally generate grand strategies. So, just as the grand strategy that won World War II came out of the Pearl Harbour surprise attack, so this one did as well.' Contrary to the Second World War and the War on Terror, during the interwar period and the 1990s the United States did not have a grand strategy because nothing had sufficiently threatened it to demand such rigorous thinking.[37]

Gaddis's current conception of grand strategy, at least with reference to statecraft and war, emphasizes comprehension of the myriad disparate geographical demands of a superpower. It is a definition which seeks to frame grand strategy in a manner that may provide practical aid for US policy makers

---

[31] Gaddis, 'What is Grand Strategy?', 3.
[32] See Peter Layton, 'How to Change the World: Helping Policymakers Develop Better Grand Strategies' (Ph.D. dissertation, University of New South Wales, 2014), ch. 2.
[33] Carl von Clausewitz, *On War*, ed. and tr. Michael Howard and Peter Paret (Princeton: Princeton UP, 1984), 280.
[34] Gaddis, 'What is Grand Strategy?', 3.
[35] John Lewis Gaddis, 'Interview: John Lewis Gaddis', Public Broadcasting Service, *Frontline*, 13 Jan. 2003, <http://www.pbs.org/wgbh/pages/frontline/shows/iraq/interviews/gaddis.html>, accessed Aug. 2012.
[36] Gaddis, 'What is Grand Strategy?', 17.
[37] Gaddis, 'Interview'.

in understanding not just first-order effects of their policies, but also second-, third-, and so on, as they reverberate around the world. It also encourages such thinking even in the absence of shocks and calamities. Beyond aspirations for immediate public impact, its historical legacy is clear, as its popularity has marked the return of one of the old themes of grand strategic thought, of defining the concept with specific regard to geographical expanse.

GRAND STRATEGY AS MILITARY STRATEGY

Much as Gaddis's later interpretation of grand strategy falls seamlessly into one venerable tradition of grand strategic thought, Robert Art has proffered a conception of grand strategy which is clearly a modern interpretation of another recurring nineteenth-century theme: a focus on the relationship between force and policy. Unlike nearly every other major theorist of grand strategy after the beginning of the twentieth century, Art restricts his interpretation of grand strategy to consider only military force and its relation to policy goals. Much in line with contemporary theorists, however, he posits that grand strategy also has control over political objectives.[38] Its control of policy goals can be traced all the way to fundamental national political interests. 'Devising a grand strategy means hard thinking about basic interests and the proper role of military power in protecting them.'[39]

Art's interpretation of grand strategy stems from two sources. First, his aim was to maintain grand strategy as a useful concept distinct from foreign policy. 'Non-military instruments are as important to statecraft as the military one, but I do not treat them as part of grand strategy, because I wish to preserve the useful distinction between grand strategy and foreign policy, which includes all of the goals and all of the instruments of statecraft.'[40] However, he does recognize that the other instruments of statecraft may have decisive bearing on the efficacy of a chosen grand strategy relying on force.[41]

Second, Art developed his conception in a context of controversy and doubt surrounding the utility of force, from the humanitarian interventions of the 1990s to the counter-insurgency campaigns in Afghanistan and Iraq. His work fits another of the old themes of the nineteenth century: grand strategy as identifying the decisive point. Art has advocated adoption of a specific grand strategy, selective engagement. Such prescriptions are founded upon the

---

[38] Robert J. Art, *A Grand Strategy for America* (Ithaca, NY: Cornell UP, 2003), 1–2.
[39] Ibid. 2.
[40] Robert J. Art, 'A Defensible Defense: America's Grand Strategy After the Cold War', in Robert J. Art, *America's Grand Strategy and World Politics* (London: Routledge, 2009), 190.
[41] Robert J. Art, 'Looking Ahead—Near Term and Far', ibid. 373.

assumption that their authors have identified the decisive point—at this level of analysis, the most effective way to interact with the rest of the world. Thus, although definitionally Art's concept of grand strategy focuses on the relationship between force and policy, the underlying assumption is a prescriptive one about having identified the decisive point.

BYZANTINE AND CHINESE GRAND STRATEGY

Edward Luttwak, who began developing his own idea of grand strategy in the early 1970s and continued through the 1980s, returned to the topic in the late 2000s and early 2010s with two works on Byzantine and Chinese grand strategy. In doing so, he continued to refine his concept of grand strategy as military statecraft. Although the military aspect continued to predetermine the statecraft as grand strategic, this aspect's importance for achieving desired goals substantially diminished in later definitions. His work continues to fit into the theme of grand strategy as relating military means to political ends, but it now questions the plausibility of doing so without supporting force with non-military instruments of political power.

Luttwak refines the idea of grand strategy by reducing the number of major elements which he considers active parts of Byzantine grand strategy, and of grand strategy in general. '[G]rand strategy is simply the *level* at which knowledge and persuasion, or in modern terms intelligence and diplomacy, interact with military strength to determine outcomes in a world of other states, with their own "grand strategies."'[42] These three elements dominate any grand strategy; the others are relegated to a lower order of importance. This is a substantially pared down selection of major instruments to affect the aims of grand strategy compared to those listed in his expanded 2001 edition of *Strategy: The Logic of War and Peace*.[43]

As late as 2001 Luttwak seemed to consider all non-military elements to be of equal weight in theory, but not in practice. His more recent prioritization of certain instruments over others may stem from his study of Byzantine grand strategy, for which not all of these were necessarily relevant during its lifespan. Lower order elements remained potentially vital, however, and Luttwak recognized the crucial supporting functions the Byzantine economy and bureaucracy played for grand strategy.[44]

---

[42] Edward N. Luttwak, *The Grand Strategy of the Byzantine Empire* (Cambridge, MA: Belknap Press of Harvard UP, 2009), 409.

[43] Edward N. Luttwak, *Strategy: The Logic of War and Peace* (Cambridge, MA: Belknap Press of Harvard UP, 2001), 209.

[44] Luttwak, *Grand Strategy of the Byzantine Empire*, 5.

Luttwak already believed in the 1970s that military force was most potent when not used: 'For power born of *potential* force is not expended when used, nor is it a finite quantity. Force, on the other hand, is just that: if directed to one purpose, it cannot simultaneously be directed at another, and if used, it is *ipso facto* consumed.'[45] This perspective was strengthened by his study of Byzantine grand strategy. Byzantium survived for so long because it had 'a sustained ability, century after century, to generate disproportionate power from whatever military strength could be mustered, by combining it with all the arts of persuasion, guided by superior information'.[46]

How to employ means of second-order importance—as well as the major elements of knowledge and diplomacy—was central to this long-standing cultural and institutional skill which the Byzantines possessed. As Luttwak notes, '[i]n all their infinite variety, grand strategies can be compared by the extent of their reliance on costly force, as opposed to the leveraging of *potential* force by diplomacy ("armed suasion"), inducements (subsidies, gifts, honours), and deception and propaganda. The lesser the actual force content, the greater the possibility of transcending the material balance of strength, to achieve more with less.'[47] Instruments of second-order importance, such as economic inducements, deception, and propaganda, act as force multipliers, rather than as independent means in their own right. The Byzantines had to understand how these disparate first- and second-order means interacted with each other. 'It was by creative responses to new threats—by strategy, that is—that the empire survived century after century.'[48]

The decisive key to Luttwak's refined conception of grand strategy stems from the recognition that politics does not suffer definitive ends. '[W]hen they did fight, the Byzantines were less inclined to destroy enemies than to contain them, both to conserve their strength and because they knew that today's enemy could be tomorrow's ally.'[49] One could never clear the geopolitical board, as in a chess game, as there would always be another foe behind the present one, therefore there was little sense in attempting to do so.

This same key was emphasized in Luttwak's treatment of China as well. In addressing the frequent analogy of China with Imperial Germany, he notes of the latter that '[i]t was only much later that their utter incompetence at the level of grand strategy was universally recognized. The logic is the same at every level, but the grammar of combat requires sharp choices, whereas the grammar of grand strategy requires compromise.'[50] Definitive outcomes are

---

[45] Edward N. Luttwak, *The Grand Strategy of the Roman Empire from the First Century A.D. to the Third* (Baltimore, MD: Johns Hopkins Press, 1976), 33.
[46] Luttwak, *Grand Strategy of the Byzantine Empire*, 6.
[47] Ibid. 414–15.   [48] Ibid. 12.   [49] Ibid. 5.
[50] Edward N. Luttwak, *The Rise of China vs. the Logic of Strategy* (Cambridge, MA: Belknap Press of Harvard UP, 2012), 66.

not possible in politics, therefore should not be pursued; for Luttwak force is thus merely a means to a favourable compromise.

As with his writing during the late Cold War, Luttwak wrote his works for the present: 'America needs serious strategic counselling.'[51] He sought to explain why China cannot become a superpower, as it cannot escape the logic of strategy which would inevitably hinder its rise. His study of the Byzantine Empire aimed to influence policy makers in the United States to refrain from overusing force in favour of trusting to diplomacy a little more. He provided bite-sized prescriptions in *Foreign Policy* based on the Byzantine experience. These lessons include avoiding war whenever possible, prioritizing intelligence, choosing manoeuvre over attrition, not neglecting diplomacy in war, and subverting the enemy to gain cheap victory. Luttwak counselled the exact opposite of the American experience after 2001. As with nearly all authors on grand strategy after the end of the Cold War, Luttwak's writing on grand strategy also fit the tradition of grand strategy as identifying the decisive point, because of its prescriptive intent.

GRAND STRATEGIC UNIVERSALISM

One additional common aspect of Gaddis's and Luttwak's conceptions of grand strategy is the attempt to universalize their ideas to apply to more than war and statecraft. Of the two, Luttwak's grand strategic universalism is more consonant with his actual interpretation of grand strategy and has been present in his grand strategic thought since the late 1980s, whereas Gaddis's seems more likely to contradict his own theories. Luttwak argued that one could discern grand strategy 'even in a knife fight between two cutthroats in an alley...grand strategy may be present even on the smallest scale, insofar as individuals are acting as independent states, at least until the police arrive'.[52] Inasmuch as Luttwak defined grand strategy as the level at which the technical, tactical, and operational levels of strategy interact with non-military factors such as diplomacy, intelligence, propaganda, etc., his attempt to universalize the idea of grand strategy and, by implication, the whole logic of strategy does not necessarily contradict that logic or idea.

Gaddis, by contrast, argued that 'grand strategy need not apply only to war and statecraft: it's potentially applicable to any endeavour in which means

---

[51] Edward Luttwak, 'Take Me Back to Constantinople: How Byzantium, Not Rome, Can Help Preserve Pax Americana', *Foreign Policy* 19 Oct. 2009, <http://www.foreignpolicy.com/articles/2009/10/19/take_me_back_to_constantinople>, accessed Feb. 2014.

[52] Edward N. Luttwak, *Strategy: The Logic of War and Peace* (Cambridge, MA: Belknap Press of Harvard UP, 1987), 181.

must be deployed in the pursuit of important ends', these ends ranging from succeeding at university to falling in and out of love.[53] This attempt at universalizing his interpretation of grand strategy contradicts his concept, both because such ends are not 'large' and because, unlike Gaddis's core purpose with the idea of grand strategy, these other endeavours are not complex systems comprised of numerous theatres.

Both attempts to universalize grand strategy do call attention to the relationship between the logic of an idea and the phenomenon to which that logic is applied. As Luttwak admits, 'if the logic at work here is the same as in the setting of international politics, the phenomena it conditions are very different, not merely because of their trivial scale but because they are made of individual acts and individual thoughts'.[54] This is a fundamental question which bedevils much of modern grand strategic thought.

NEW SCHOLARSHIP

New scholars such as Hal Brands, whose work on grand strategy has become an important touchstone of the literature in the United States, and Peter Layton have recently begun investigating grand strategy in theory and have independently begun developing similar revised interpretations of the concept. Both scholars accept that grand strategy directs policy and gives policy a longer term coherence that it would otherwise lack. They represent an evolution of the mainstream conception of grand strategy rather than an altogether new interpretation of it.

Brands defines grand strategy as 'the highest form of statecraft, but it can also be the most perplexing. Reduced to its essence, grand strategy is the intellectual architecture that lends structure to foreign policy; it is the logic that helps states navigate a complex and dangerous world.'[55] As Brands explains in greater detail,

> grand strategy is not any one aspect of foreign policy, nor is it foreign policy as a whole. Foreign policy is the sum total of a government's interactions with the outside world, and it is expressed through initiatives ranging from diplomacy to foreign aid to humanitarian relief to the use of military force. Grand strategy, in contrast, is the conceptual logic that ensures that such instruments are employed in ways that maximize the benefits for a nation's core interests.[56]

---

[53] Gaddis, 'What is Grand Strategy?', 7.
[54] Luttwak, *Strategy* (1987), 181.
[55] Hal Brands, *What Good is Grand Strategy? Power and Purpose in American Statecraft from Harry S. Truman to George W. Bush* (Ithaca, NY: Cornell UP, 2014), 1.
[56] Ibid. 3–4.

This suggests that he envisages grand strategy as having a dual logic. The first is explanatory, as with many mainstream interpretations of grand strategy. Grand strategy is director of foreign policy. It explains why policies exist and which interests they are meant to serve. The second logic is instrumental, as Brands also gives grand strategy the responsibility for ensuring that implementation of chosen policies is tailored to the initial, explanatory logic of grand strategy. When these two logics combine, 'a grand strategy is a purposeful and coherent set of ideas about what a nation seeks to accomplish in the world, and how it should go about doing so'.[57] Layton similarly endorses George Foster's assessment that grand strategy direct policy, at least lower-level policy initiatives.[58]

The novelty of their approach, more explicitly described in Layton's work, is their belief that grand strategy is a specific type of decision-making process. Layton directly compares grand strategy to other processes or methods of decision-making, such as opportunism and risk management, which are approaches 'that await events; they respond to others' actions... Grand strategy is the opposite. A country uses a grand strategy to try to go where it wishes.'[59] Grand strategy is a far more proactive manner of interacting with the world and its events, even if its purposes may only be to sustain the present status quo. Brands does not base his analysis of grand strategy on such an explicit contrast between it and other modes of decision-making. Nevertheless, his writing conveys the impression that it is also a type of decision-making much as Layton sees it. '[G]rand strategy should originate not from mere reactions to day-to-day events, but from a judgment of those enduring interests and priorities that transcend any single crisis or controversy... grand strategy involves figuring out how to align today's initiatives with tomorrow's desired end-state'.[60] Unlike Layton, however, Brands does not see other decision-making processes as useful, or even potentially so. '*There is no good alternative to grand strategy.*'[61] Grand strategy may only be a particular type of decision-making related to identifying basic interests and designing policies to meet those interests, but it is the only type which matters or which produces advantageous results. This difference of opinion may be due to the two authors' differing backgrounds: Layton is an Australian, whereas Brands is an American. A smaller state such as Australia is much more likely to find opportunistic types of decision-making more amenable and more practical than a superpower.

---

[57] Ibid. 3.
[58] Peter Layton, 'The Idea of Grand Strategy', *RUSI Journal* 157/4 (Aug./Sept. 2012), 59.
[59] Peter Layton, 'Grand Strategy? What Does That Do for Me?' The Australia Strategic Policy Institute Blog, 23 July 2012, <http://www.aspistrategist.org.au/grand-strategy-what-does-that-do-for-me>, accessed Aug. 2012.
[60] Brands, *What Good is Grand Strategy?*, 4.   [61] Ibid. 194.

This interpretation of grand strategy as a specific type of policy making, which may be contrasted to other types of decision-making, appears to mark a new evolution in grand strategic thought by seemingly abandoning grand strategy as its own independent theoretical concept in favour of a focus on process. Yet making this change, both authors have striven to ground the idea of grand strategy in the basic notion that all strategy is relational—between goals and implementation for their achievement—and therefore have closed the distance between classical interpretations of strategy and modern grand strategic thought, the latter having grown increasingly remote from questions of practicability.

CONCLUSION

Grand strategy remains a standardless, incoherent concept, whose popularity surge after the end of the Cold War multiplied the lack of rigour with which it was employed. Utilized as the logic or framework which drives foreign policy, grand strategy and policy effectively switched theoretical roles: grand strategy laid down directions, and policy acted as the relational step to fulfil those goals with available means. Its focus now concerned how to interact with the rest of the world in a universe where it no longer had any peer or near peer competitor to act as a lodestone for policy initiatives. This led to a proliferation of prescriptions for a new grand strategy and a neglect of critical engagement with the theoretical function of grand strategy. As a result, one scholar has speculated that '[g]rand strategy may simply not be the sort of phenomenon that calls for a distinct theoretical literature; it may best be understood as one of many topics illuminated by theories about strategy in general'.[62] Historians have implicitly accepted this judgment by preferring to employ grand strategy as a tool to explore the past. Conversely, strategic theory cannot now explain many, if not most, modern ideas of grand strategy—which simply are no longer strategic.

A small handful of scholars nevertheless has still attempted to develop theoretical insights about grand strategy through the study of historical and contemporary events, including John Lewis Gaddis, Robert Art, and Edward Luttwak. Yet, as has been the case for the entirety of the history of grand strategic thought, their independent efforts are leading them in divergent directions. Their conclusions about what grand strategy is all about differ at a fundamental level. New scholars are also appearing who may hope to save the concept, seemingly by ridding it of theoretical overtones altogether.

[62] Goldstein, *Rising to the Challenge*, 18.

Conclusion

Or Thinking Theoretically about Grand Strategy

This history of grand strategic thought concludes at the present day. What significance does such a history hold? Why is it important? First, the history of grand strategic thought is a history of unexamined yet contextually reasonable assumptions, which resulted in continuous changes in meaning of the term and the concept. Second, the diverse use and meaning of grand strategy across multiple disciplines further confound the understanding of grand strategy. Third, the logic inherent in the concept of grand strategy has changed over time and among disparate contexts, despite the constancy of certain themes in application. Fourth, despite the ever-changing object of grand strategy (whether it be generalship, war, peace, both peace and war, policy, etc.), four themes have consistently recurred throughout its evolutions and have manifested themselves beyond concepts of grand strategy as well. Finally, one must address whether or not this inchoate concept is, or has the potential to be, useful. Can it clarify the phenomenon? Can those who employ it share its meaning? If not, it hinders rather than eases communication and understanding. If the concept is meant to be practical, it should be a realistic reflection of what is actually possible.

A HISTORY OF UNEXAMINED ASSUMPTIONS

The history of grand strategic thought is one of multiple evolutions driven by the desire to address immediate contingency. Context was a significant determinant for the shape and content of each individual interpretation of grand strategic thought. Each evolution in the meaning of the term is reasonable when judged by the context-based assumptions which gave rise to it. However, each of these assumptions may be effectively reduced to a particular observation that there is no concept that does x (such as limiting war) or encompasses y

(such as peacetime defence and security policy), but x or y is currently critically important for the future conduct of war or the future well-being of the country. Therefore, grand strategy should do x or encompass y. Grand strategy was continually reapplied to new problems, and its form and content as an analytical tool were changed to conform to the shape of the new problem. This process occurred and recurred largely without reference to wider strategic theory, although some authors did attempt to integrate their ideas of grand strategy into the cohesive discipline of general strategic theory.

These adaptations were also carried out with little critical engagement with previous ideas of grand strategy. The main historical engagement has generally been controlled by the individual author, who seeks examples in history of his own interpretation of grand strategy, if he draws upon history at all to illustrate it. The result is that grand strategic thought has been predominantly ahistorical. The major early thinkers did not even refer to contemporary notions of grand strategy in their work—it is as if Julian Corbett, J. F. C. Fuller, Basil Liddell Hart, or Edward Mead Earle derived their idiosyncratic definitions of grand strategy in isolation from the wider strategic literature of which their own works were a part. Only with the re-emergence of grand strategy from the 1970s onwards did scholars such as John Collins or Paul Kennedy refer to earlier definitions. Yet such reference has generally been limited to Liddell Hart and/or Earle, and with little real engagement with their ideas. Instead, the definitions of the past were merely invoked to lend credence to the new interpretations of grand strategy, which were designed to be specifically suited to relevant contemporary security and defence concerns.

It is one thing if certain ideas are developed purely as analytical tools for a specific contingency, to be abandoned as soon as they are no longer useful in the post-contingency context. It is, however, problematic if an idea is decisively shaped by the need to address a concrete problem yet is simultaneously assumed to be a general idea with enduring value. If ideas are to have general value, they must be generalizable to a subject (for example, but not necessarily, war), rather than be wholly specific to a particular time and place. Most authors of grand strategy have shaped concepts of grand strategy leaning more towards specific applicability in their immediate context, but which subsequently have masqueraded as ideas with general validity.

There is a difference between Liddell Hart's fully developed notion of grand strategy as a straightjacket on war and his pithy, more general single sentence definition of grand strategy. Most, if not all, later theorists of grand strategy have relied upon the latter without a full appreciation of the former. One may speculate that Corbett understood the tension between specific application and general idea. His references to grand or major strategy occurred primarily in teaching documents or lecture notes meant for delivery to future practitioners of strategy, whereas his scholarly historical works largely avoided using the term. Even his prime theoretical work, *Some Principles of Maritime*

Strategy, barely employed the term 'major strategy' and emphasized in its treatment of the ability to manipulate the boundaries of war that it was suitable primarily for modern imperial conditions, rather than being generally valid. Corbett seems to have taken care not to conflate specific applicability with general validity.

Grand strategy, as developed by individuals such as Corbett, Fuller, Liddell Hart, or Earle, or modern theorists such as Kennedy, Edward Luttwak, or John Lewis Gaddis, has universally been in reaction to, or influenced by, some new context. That context was necessarily multifarious: geopolitical and strategic events contemporary to, or past events personally experienced by, the author in question; the intellectual context which nourished the author's strategic thought; the personal context of how each author individually interpreted all other contextual dimensions. This is of course true of every human endeavour. Clausewitz's magnum opus began as a reaction to the intellectual challenge of understanding Napoleon and his way of warfare. Yet his work has endured, unlike every interpretation of grand strategy, because over the course of writing it evolved to encompass war as an entire phenomenon.

Most interpretations of grand strategy have favoured specific applicability to the particular context at hand rather than general validity. Corbett sought to teach practitioners; Liddell Hart desired (and achieved) policy influence; Barry Posen contributed to the debate about NATO and the hypothetical defence of Western Europe; Edward Luttwak argued, through Roman or Byzantine proxy, about American statecraft and the utility of force; and so on. The emphasis on applicability to context necessarily limits the shelf life of definitions of grand strategy, although as specific contexts come and go and sometimes return in similar form, one might quibble over which might make the difficult transition to general validity. Perhaps Liddell Hart became so popular during the initial re-emergence of grand strategy in the 1970s and 1980s, and again in the 2000s and 2010s, because the United States was suffering declinist doubts. Liddell Hart, writing at a time generally considered to be the 'locust years' of British defence, may have been seen as more practically relevant than Earle, whose context was that of a much greater and still rising industrial power. Nevertheless, although comparable contexts may return, many interpretations of grand strategy remain tied to particular conditions.

The evolution of grand strategy was thus almost haphazard. Characterized by a lack of historical perspective on what the idea had previously meant, it was dominated by unexamined and unspecified assumptions of what it *should* be. Visions of the concept derived primarily from what was going on around the authors in question. These in turn were fuelled by authorial biases and observations about global events both in history and in their present. The subjects which each new concept of grand strategy undertook to address, from generalship to war to peace to war and peace, etc., consequently changed to a greater or lesser extent with each new definition. Clausewitz's *On War* remains relevant because the nature of continually recurring war remains recognizably the same; definitions of grand strategy are transient because they reflect only their own particular geopolitical conditions. Strategy per se remains identifiable because it is tied to a subject; there is no agreement on what grand strategy is, per se, because its evolution has been one of subject as well as logic.

DEFINITIONS FROM MULTIPLE DISCIPLINES

One might question the significance of other disciplines appropriating the term 'grand strategy' and appending their own meaning to it. After all, good strategic studies is interdisciplinary and has itself borrowed many terms and concepts from alien fields, from the geometry-based strategic thought of the Enlightenment and Clausewitz's ideas and metaphors derived from physics and theology (e.g. friction and the trinity) to chaos and complexity theories in more recent strategic thought. But strategic studies has been losing this character. 'Thirty years ago strategic studies was a hybrid, a disciplinary mix of history, politics, law, some economics and even a little mathematics. Today the subject has been increasingly appropriated by departments of political science, its identity often subsumed under the amorphous title of "security studies".'[1]

The apparent disciplinary consolidation of strategic studies within political science implies a conceptual and methodological coherence which is not actually shared between strategic studies and most of the rest of international relations, much less the wider field of political science. Rare is the work in international relations, excluding strategic studies, which even touches upon war, and that which does tends to perceive war one dimensionally merely as an instrument of policy. International relations, again barring strategic studies, has no interest in the conduct of war but merely in its utility, but it is a fallacy to consider the utility of war without also examining the conduct which achieves utility. Only strategic studies considers war equally in terms of both conduct and utility. This difference leads to diverging assumptions about the foundations of the respective disciplines.

The evolution of grand strategic thought reflects this divergence between the whole of political science and its strategic studies subfield. Grand strategy has now evolved into a concept more suitable for political science, via the pathways of international relations, than for strategic studies. Originating in the desire to understand and make more effective the conduct of war, its initial

---

[1] Hew Strachan, *The Direction of War: Contemporary Strategy in Historical Perspective* (Cambridge: CUP, 2013), 253.

interpretations all revolved around generalship in one way or another. Only one of the original four interpretations appeared to emphasize the utility of war. The meaning of grand strategy expanded in different ways with each successive theorist, but even as late as Earle the concept of grand strategy balanced the conduct and the utility of war. With the re-emergence of grand strategy in the latter half of the Cold War, many interpretations belonged to international relations rather than strategic studies and, inasmuch as they paid any attention to war, focused on its utility without serious consideration of conduct. 'For after all allowances have been made for historical differences, wars still resemble each other more than they resemble any other human activity.'[2] Among instruments of political purpose, war is unique. Considering utility without conduct can only lead to a dangerously flawed appreciation of war as though it were a predictable, easily controlled instrument—an illusion with real and dangerous consequences.

Concept sharing among disciplines is to be expected, especially when they share a common purpose in contributing to political discourse and policy making. Yet the assumptions underpinning strategic studies differ from those of the rest of political science. Concepts which originated to examine the use of force indelibly change and lose their nuance during the transfer, even to sister disciplines such as international relations. For example, a core assumption of strategic studies is adversarial interaction: each strategic actor is actively attempting to impose his will upon his opponent. Realist schools of international relations downgrade interaction merely to competition where states seek to maximize their own power, but do not necessarily aim to vanquish other states. Liberal traditions decry competition, emphasize cooperation in international relations, and prefer altogether not to consider war.

As a residually interdisciplinary field, strategic studies still borrows from other disciplines, including concepts that were originally strategic but are no longer, such as most modern interpretations of grand strategy. Such borrowed concepts seem deceptively familiar, yet are underpinned by assumptions from related fields, which may wholly alter their meaning. William Martel's posthumously published 2015 work on grand strategy clearly illustrates the ultimate effects of approaching strategy from a new direction. '[S]trategy tells us *what* policies to pursue, whereas foreign policy is about the *how* to do so. Missing is the broad question of *why* the state pursues such policies using particular strategies, which is the precise function of grand strategy.'[3] Martel takes the strategy–policy relationship, one of the core concerns of strategic studies, and turns it on its head. Strategy, rather than being an instrumental concept, takes on one aspect of policy's directing role. Grand strategy in turn

---

[2] Michael Howard, 'The Use and Abuse of Military History', *Parameters* 11/1 (Mar. 1981), 13.
[3] William C. Martel, *Grand Strategy in Theory and Practice: The Need for an Effective American Foreign Policy* (New York: Cambridge UP, 2015), 4.

assumes a second responsibility of policy: the rationale for choice of objectives. Policy itself becomes the instrumental concept, yet lacks the tools necessary to achieve its newly imposed purpose, particularly in relation to war.

Such a reversal dilutes the long accepted valuable content of strategic studies and turns political science as an overarching field even further away from understanding war in its multiple dimensions. 'Strategy' is employed in multiple fields, but it is not the same as in its original strategic studies form. The meanings will differ because their underpinning assumptions diverge. Diverging assumptions hinder communication and preclude dialogue, especially when they remain unexamined—a state of affairs which is only encouraged by the structure and trends of modern academia.[4]

CHANGING SUBJECTS, SAME LOGIC?

Grand strategic thought in history has displayed an impressive breadth of conception in theoretical pieces, historical works, and prescriptive tracts. There is no generally accepted uniform meaning and new definitions continue to proliferate. It would seem reasonable to suggest that the theoretical function of grand strategy lies at the common juncture of all the myriad definitions proffered over the two centuries that grand strategy has persisted as a discrete term. This common ground is war—yet strategic studies treats war significantly differently than the rest of political science, which has intruded to the point that war is no longer the common element binding together every interpretation of grand strategy.

As a result, modern scholarship of grand strategy (as well as strategy) focuses primarily on the internal logic of strategy, of thinking about consequences with little regard for the subject of grand strategy. This even extends to practitioners of strategy. The US Joint Chiefs of Staff define strategy as '[a] prudent idea or set of ideas for employing the instruments of national power in a synchronized and integrated fashion to achieve theatre, national, and/or multinational objectives'.[5] Their definition of strategy is as broad as many definitions of grand strategy, but there is no entry in their dictionary for either grand or national strategy.

In treatments such as these strategy frequently stands alone, as logic bereft of subject. Potential or real use of force is usually cited as its defining aspect, but the lack of a more concrete subject has allowed other fields to dilute the meaning of strategy to eschew even any consideration of force whatsoever.

---

[4] See Jakub Grygiel, 'Educating for National Security', *Orbis* 57/2 (2013), 201–16.
[5] US Department of Defense, *Joint Publication 1-02: Department of Defense Dictionary of Military and Associated Terms* (Washington, DC: Department of Defense, 2015), 234.

Strategy was thus appropriated to refer to generalized instrumental and consequentialist thinking, rather than being a specialized subset of instrumental thinking suited for the non-linear, adversarial environment of war. To some degree, this was inevitable. '[S]trategy remains the best word we have for expressing attempts to think about actions in advance, in light of our goals and our capacities. It captures a process for which there are no obvious alternative words, although the meaning has become diluted through promiscuous and often inappropriate use.'[6] Strategy—and grand strategy—are thus made applicable to all situations in which some end must be sought in some way with the means at hand, whether it is in the realm of war or statecraft, or in university workloads or other more mundane challenges in life.

The universalization of strategy through an overemphasis on its internal logic alone may be a dubious prospect. Not all contexts are equivalent in significance, nor are all means similar in their nature. Strategic studies' assumptions differ radically from those of the rest of political science. Classical strategy developed to comprehend the conduct of war. Exceptional among all instruments of statecraft, war is the recourse of polities to the reciprocal adversarial use of force. The uniquely reciprocal and violent nature of war encourages escalation and may threaten to overtake the conduct of war from those unable or unwilling to control it, thereby imperilling its utility.

The texts of classical strategists such as Clausewitz and Jomini recognize this. For them, strategy not only has its own logic but is inextricably intertwined with the phenomenon of war, which strategy is meant to comprehend. War permeates not only their respective definitions of strategy but also the titles of their books. Classical strategy had to focus primarily on controlling violence—whether to limit it or to escalate it—so that it could then attempt to relate the threat and use of that violence to political purposes. The foundation of the utility of war is its conduct.

Classical strategy was inextricably linked to the phenomenon it described because war was in particular need of specific comprehension. The shift away from understanding strategy in the context of war to explore pure instrumental logic thus eschews the very thing which anchors and elucidates strategy. Grand strategy has been part of this shift away from phenomenon towards pure logic, and some scholars have taken it further by making the jump from instrumental to explanatory logic. The practical consequences of this evolution are a broad inability to understand war and thereby effectively to wage it. By detaching themselves from basic considerations of war, strategy and grand strategy have become theories of statecraft which sometimes happen to include military tools in their foreign policy calculus, if they are even considered to be relationships between means and ends at all. The basic subject has not

---

[6] Lawrence Freedman, *Strategy: A History* (Oxford: OUP, 2013), p. x.

only changed, it has become indeterminate. The unique difficulties inherent in the use of force are ignored because force is viewed as just another instrument, its dangerous caprice forgotten not only within political science but even within parts of strategic studies.

RECURRING THEMES IN GRAND STRATEGIC THOUGHT

The subject described by grand strategy has evolved from straightforward generalship to foreign policy assumptions and has touched many interim stages along the way. Despite the diverse and frequently non-congruous assumptions made by many scholars of grand strategy, this continual change of subject has also resulted in a shifting of the logic underpinning grand strategy. The actual nature of what has been considered grand strategy has expanded significantly between its first discovered use in English in the nineteenth century and today. Despite this fundamental change and despite a wide variety in personal, intellectual, and historical-strategic contexts within grand strategic thought, four themes recur time and again. These themes represent the greatest elements of continuity in a history of grand strategic thought otherwise fraught with nearly arbitrary change.

None of the four themes describes a unique theoretical function which grand strategy alone may fill. They characterize particular interpretations of grand strategy as manoeuvre, whether physical or diplomatic; as identifying the decisive point; as being geographically expansive; or as the relationship between military power and political purpose—or as a mixture of two or more of these. The first three are merely attributes. Specific strategies may feature or reflect any or all of these attributes. The fourth theme is fundamental to classical strategy itself as understood in strategic studies. Neither singly nor together do they give grand strategy a unique specific place in the general theory of strategy, as they all may also be attributed to military strategy and the three attributes to policy or military operations.

That recurring themes over the course of more than two hundred years are no more than mere attributes attests to the extent to which individual interpretations of grand strategy have been designed in response to specific contexts rather than as independent generalizable concepts. Where and when the problem of the day was considered to be (primarily) military, the concept remained limited to military strategy. Where and when the problem of the day was seen more as a question for policy, the meaning of grand strategy migrated accordingly. The evolution of grand strategic thought was, more than anything else, driven by the desire of individuals to apply their intellects to what they considered the major geopolitical and strategic issues of the day, regardless of whether they were thinking at the level of strategy or of policy. The main continuity within grand strategic thought lay in similarities of context over time rather than in anything inherent in grand strategy itself. This contrasts with classical strategy, which has always been anchored by its subject of war, unlike the conceptual nomad grand strategy. Yet by sharing the word 'strategy', the roving nature of grand strategy dilutes and shifts the otherwise properly fixed meaning of strategy itself.

CONSIDERING THE POTENTIAL OF GRAND STRATEGY

It is difficult to judge the actual or potential utility of grand strategy. Unable to contrive a formal definition, a US Supreme Court Justice once famously remarked of another phenomenon altogether 'I know it when I see it'.[7] In that case common sense identified its boundaries, which could not otherwise be encapsulated in a single academic definition. One fictional character of a light novel about the American Civil War also resorted to the invocation of common sense, by musing 'that common sense has its part to play in grand strategy, as in everything else'.[8] Might simple common sense perform the same role for grand strategy? Even though academic definitions fail entirely to agree upon the boundaries, purpose, and meaning of grand strategy, might one know it if one sees it?

This is doubtful. Given grand strategy's lack of a central core which holds fast, common sense pulls in different directions—each direction likely dependent on one's own biases towards both strategy and grand strategy. 'Definitions can be official and authoritative, but in truth they are arbitrary.'[9] Concepts are merely constructions we use to understand the world and its history. They cannot be right or wrong as such, only useful or not useful. Having defined grand strategy in any given way, one is likely to have success finding appropriate historical evidence in its support. Varying assumptions about what comprises grand strategy determine the choice of evidence sought to study its actual practice, and these varying assumptions sustain every interpretation. Common sense tells us that the current state of grand strategic

---

[7] Potter Stewart in *Jacobellis v. Ohio*, quoted in Paul Gewirtz, 'On "I Know It When I See it"', *Yale Law Journal* 105/4 (Jan. 1996), 1024.

[8] George Cary Eggleston, *The Master of Warlock: A Virginia War Story* (Boston: Lothrop Publishing Co., 1903), 165.

[9] Colin S. Gray, *Strategy and Defence Planning: Meeting the Challenge of Uncertainty* (Oxford: OUP, 2014), 3.

thinking is unhelpful. It fails to attain the necessary minimum standards for useful theory—clarification and commonality of meaning for the purposes of communication. Whether the term 'grand strategy' may be profitably applied at all is a question separate from its contemporary lack of utility.

Some scholars see potential in grand strategy despite its present inchoate condition. 'To scholars who are aware that there is far more to the reality of strategy than its military dimension, yet who reject the implicit demilitarization of their subject that menaces from the direction of security studies, the rediscovery of the concept of grand strategy may provide a satisfactory middle way.'[10] This middle way remains as riddled with unspecified assumptions as all the other interpretations of grand strategy. Nevertheless, it does point to an important service which grand strategy may yet do but to date has not, as scholars have instead sought to apply their own concept to a specific context. This potential service would be to contextualize military power within a landscape brimming with other forms of political power. The need for such contextualization in modern strategic theory was established at least as early as 1992. 'The view that strategy is bound up with the role of force in international life must be qualified, because if force is but one form of power then strategy must address the relationship between this form and others, including authority.'[11] These other forms of power include the non-military ones, which most modern grand strategic thought already encompasses. This task is particularly critical given to what degree violence and war differ from any other instrument of political power.

Although grand strategists frequently invoke the comprehensive approach of integrating military and non-military instruments into a single strategy, the task has yet to be done justice. There has yet to be any study of what such integration might look like, of what effect non-military instruments might impose on armed conflict, and of what effect the introduction of military power into political competition might have on the efficacy of non-military instruments. Ever since the rise of maritime strategic theory around the turn of the twentieth century, most grand strategists have espoused some sort of broadened notion of grand strategy which uses the full spectrum of political power. Ironically, to this day grand strategists have yet actually to consider the implications of this breadth. Such a study could be a first step to a potential rehabilitation of the concept of grand strategy.

Ultimately, a rehabilitation of grand strategy must reflect a more mature understanding of strategy, politics, and policy than may currently exist, one

---

[10] Colin S. Gray, 'Approaching the Study of Strategy', in Ralph Rotte and Christoph Schwarz, *International Security and War: Politics and Grand Strategy in the 21st Century* (New York: Nova, 2011), 17.

[11] Lawrence Freedman, 'Strategic Studies and the Problem of Power', in Lawrence Freedman et al., *War, Strategy, and International Politics: Essays in Honour of Sir Michael Howard* (Oxford: Clarendon Press, 1992), 290.

which both cements them in their respective places and recognizes their weaknesses and limitations. Such a rehabilitation must identify any gaps where a new concept may be suitable without unnecessarily weakening, overlapping, or replacing already existing concepts. Within the terra incognita on the conceptual map of strategic studies and its disciplinary environs may— or may not—reside a definite place for grand strategy. A rehabilitation would therefore be the end, not the beginning, of a scholarly journey of conceptual mapping, theory crafting, and consensus building to ensure intellectual and practical relevance for grand strategy.

Bibliography

Archives

Bernard Brodie Papers (Collection 1223), UCLA Library Special Collections, Charles E. Young Research Library.
McGeorge Bundy Papers, John F. Kennedy Presidential Library.
Julian Corbett Papers, National Maritime Museum.
Edward Mead Earle Papers; 1894–1954, Public Policy Papers, Department of Rare Books and Special Collections, Princeton University Library.
Alexander M. Haig Papers, Richard M. Nixon Presidential Library.
William Kaufmann Papers, John F. Kennedy Presidential Library.
George F. Kennan Papers; 1861–2014 (mostly 1950–2000), Public Policy Papers, Department of Rare Books and Special Collections, Princeton University Library.
Basil Liddell Hart Papers, Liddell Hart Centre for Military Archives, King's College London.
William Mitchell Papers, Manuscript Division, Library of Congress.
National Archives and Records Administration II: Series 282 'Pre-War War Plans Correspondence', RG165 NM84.
National Archives and Records Administration II: Series 284 'ABC File', RG165 NM84.

Unpublished Work

Gaddis, John Lewis. 'What is Grand Strategy?' American Grand Strategy After War (26 February 2009, Triangle Institute for Security Studies and Duke University Program on American Grand Strategy).
Kitchen, Nicholas. 'American Power: For What? Ideas, Unipolarity and America's Search for Purpose between the 'Wars', 1991–2001' (Ph.D. Dissertation, London School of Economics, 2009).
Luttwak, Edward N. 'Force and Diplomacy in Roman Strategies of Imperial Security' (Ph.D. Dissertation, Johns Hopkins University, 1975).
Posen, Barry. 'The Systemic, Organizational, and Technological Origins of Strategic Doctrine: France, Britain, and Germany between the World Wars' (Ph.D. Dissertation, University of California, Berkeley, 1981).

Books and Other Monographs

Abella, Alex. *Soldiers of Reason: The RAND Corporation and the Rise of the American Empire* (Orlando, FL: Houghton Mifflin Harcourt, 2008).
Allen, Paul C. *Phillip III and the Pax Hispanica, 1598–1621: The Failure of Grand Strategy* (New Haven: Yale UP, 2000).
Art, Robert J. *A Grand Strategy for America* (Ithaca, NY: Cornell UP, 2003).

Art, Robert J. *America's Grand Strategy and World Politics* (London: Routledge, 2009).
Ayson, Robert. *Thomas Schelling and the Nuclear Age: Strategy as Social Science* (London: Frank Cass, 2004).
Beaufre, André. *An Introduction to Strategy*, tr. R. H. Barry (London: Faber & Faber, 1965).
Bernardo, C. Joseph, and Eugene H. Bacon. *American Military Policy: Its Development since 1775* (Harrisburg, PA: Military Service Publishing Co., 1955).
Bigelow, John. *The Principles of Strategy, Illustrated Mainly from American Campaigns* (Philadelphia: J.B. Lippincott Co. 1894).
Blackett, P. M. S. *Military and Political Consequences of Atomic Energy* (London: Turnstile Press, 1948).
Bond, Brian. *Liddell Hart: A Study of his Military Thought* (London: Cassell, 1977).
Bond, Brian. *War and Society in Europe, 1870–1970* (Leicester: Leicester UP, 1983).
Booth, Ken. *Strategy and Ethnocentrism* (London: Croom Helm, 1979).
Borden, William Liscum. *There Will Be No Time: The Revolution in Strategy* (New York: Macmillan Co., 1946).
Bradford, James C. *Guide to the Microfilm Edition of the Papers of John Paul Jones, 1747–1792* (Cambridge: Chadwyck-Healey, 1986).
Brands, Hal. *The Promise and Pitfalls of Grand Strategy* (Carlisle: Strategic Studies Institute, 2012).
Brands, Hal. *What Good is Grand Strategy? Power and Purpose in American Statecraft from Harry S. Truman to George W. Bush* (Ithaca, NY: Cornell UP, 2014).
Buchan, Alastair. *War in Modern Society: An Introduction* (London: C. A. Watts & Co., 1966).
Brodie, Bernard. *Seapower in the Machine Age* (Princeton: Princeton UP, 1944).
Brodie, Bernard (ed.). *The Absolute Weapon: Atomic Power and World Order* (New York: Harcourt, Brace & Co., 1946).
Brodie, Bernard. *Strategy in the Missile Age* (Princeton: Princeton UP, 1959).
Brodie, Bernard. *War and Politics* (New York: Macmillan, 1973).
Buell, Augustus C. *Paul Jones: Founder of the American Navy*. 2 vols (New York: Charles Scribner's Sons, 1900).
Carrington, Henry B. *Battle Maps and Charts of the American Revolution with Explanatory Notes and School History References* (New York: A. S. Barnes & Co., 1881).
Carrington, Henry B. *Battles of the American Revolution 1775–1781* (New York: A. S. Barnes & Co., 1904).
Castex, Raoul. *Strategic Theories*, tr. and ed. Eugenia C. Kiesling (Annapolis: Naval Institute Press, 1994).
Christensen, Thomas J. *Useful Adversaries: Grand Strategy, Domestic Mobilization, and Sino-American Conflict, 1947–1958* (Princeton: Princeton UP, 1996).
Clausewitz, Carl von. *On War*, ed. and tr. Michael Howard and Peter Paret (Princeton: Princeton UP, 1984).
Collins, John M. *Grand Strategy: Principles and Practices* (Annapolis: Naval Institute Press, 1973).
Corbett, Julian S. *England in the Seven Years War*. 2 vols (London: Longmans, Green, & Co., 1907).

Corbett, Julian S. *The Successors of Drake* (London: Longmans, Green & Co., 1916).
Corbett, Julian S. *England in the Mediterranean*. 2 vols (London: Longmans, Green, & Co., 1917).
Corbett, Julian S. *Some Principles of Maritime Strategy* (Annapolis: Naval Institute Press, 1988).
Danchev, Alex. *Alchemist of War: The Life of Basil Liddell Hart* (London: Weidenfeld & Nicolson, 1998).
Dueck, Colin. *Reluctant Crusaders: Power, Culture, and Change in American Grand Strategy* (Princeton: Princeton UP, 2006).
Eggleston, George Cary. *The Master of Warlock: A Virginia War Story* (Boston: Lothrop Publishing Co., 1903).
Elliott, William Yandell. *Mobilization Planning and the National Security (1950-1960): Problems and Issues* (Washington, DC: Government Printing Office, 1959).
Farer, Tom. *Confronting Global Terrorism and American Neo-Conservatism: The Framework of a Liberal Grand Strategy* (Oxford: Oxford University Press, 2008).
Ferrill, Arther. *Roman Imperial Grand Strategy* (Lanham, MD: UP of America, 1991).
Flournoy, Michèle A., and Shawn Brimley (eds). *Finding our Way: Debating American Grand Strategy* (Washington, DC: Center for a New American Security 2008).
Freedman, Lawrence. *Deterrence* (Cambridge: Polity, 2004).
Freedman, Lawrence. *Strategy: A History* (Oxford: OUP, 2013).
Friedberg, Aaron L. *In the Shadow of the Garrison State: America's Anti-Statism and its Cold War Grand Strategy* (Princeton: Princeton UP, 2000).
Friedberg, Aaron L. *The Weary Titan: Britain and the Experience of Relative Decline, 1895-1905* (Princeton: Princeton UP, 2010).
Fuller, J. F. C. *The Reformation of War* (London: Hutchinson & Co., 1923).
Fuller, J. F. C. *The Foundations of the Science of War* (London: Hutchinson & Co., 1926).
Fuller, J. F. C. *On Future Warfare* (London: Sifton Praed & Co., 1928).
Fuller, J. F. C. *The Generalship of Ulysses S. Grant* (London: John Murray, 1929).
Fuller, J. F. C. *Lectures on F.S.R. II.* (London: Sifton Praed & Co., 1931).
Fuller, J. F. C. *The Dragon's Teeth: A Study of War and Peace* (London: Constable & Co., 1932).
Fuller, J. F. C. *Lectures on F.S.R. III* (London: Sifton Praed & Co., 1932).
Fuller, J. F. C. *War and Western Civilization 1832-1932: A Study of War as a Political Instrument and the Expression of Mass Democracy* (London: Duckworth, 1932).
Fuller, J. F. C. *Grant and Lee: A Study in Personality and Generalship* (London: Eyre & Spottiswoode, 1933).
Fuller, J. F. C. *Memoirs of an Unconventional Soldier* (London: Ivor Nicholson & Watson, 1936).
Gaddis, John Lewis. *We Now Know: Rethinking Cold War History* (Oxford: OUP, 1998).
Gaddis, John Lewis. *George F. Kennan: An American Life* (New York: Penguin Press, 2011).
Gat, Azar. *A History of Military Thought* (Oxford: OUP, 2001).
Gavin, James M. *War and Peace in the Space Age* (New York: Harper & Brothers, 1958).

George, Alexander L., and Richard Smoke. *Deterrence in American Foreign Policy: Theory and Practice* (New York: Columbia UP, 1974).
Gerberding, William P., and Bernard Brodie. *The Political Dimension in National Strategy: Five Papers* (Los Angeles: UCLA Security Studies Project, 1968).
Goldrick, James, and John B. Hattendorf (eds). *Mahan is Not Enough: The Proceedings of a Conference on the Works of Sir Julian Corbett and Admiral Sir Herbert Richmond* (Newport, RI: Naval War College Press, 1993).
Goldstein, Avery. *Rising to the Challenge: China's Grand Strategy and International Security* (Stanford, CA: Stanford UP, 2005).
Gray, Colin S. *The Geopolitics of the Nuclear Era: Heartlands, Rimlands, and the Technological Revolution* (New York: Crane, Russak & Co., Inc., 1977).
Gray, Colin S. *Nuclear Strategy and National Style* (London: Hamilton Press, 1986).
Gray, Colin S. *The Geopolitics of Superpower* (Lexington, KY: UP of Kentucky, 1988).
Gray, Colin S. *Modern Strategy* (Oxford: OUP, 1999).
Gray, Colin S. *The Strategy Bridge: Theory for Practice* (Oxford: OUP, 2010).
Gray, Colin S. *Strategy and Defence Planning: Meeting the Challenge of Uncertainty* (Oxford: OUP, 2014).
Grazia, Alfred de. *The Elements of Political Science* (New York: Alfred A. Knopf, 1952).
Greenfield, Kent Roberts (ed.). *United States Army in World War II* (Washington, DC: Historical Division of the Army, 1954).
Hattendorf, John B. (ed.). *The Influence of History on Mahan* (Newport, RI: Naval War College Press, 1991).
Herzog, Siegfried. *The Iron Circle: The Future of German Industrial Exports: Practical Suggestions for Safeguarding the Growth of German Export Activity in the Field of Manufactures After the War*, tr. M. L. Turrentine (London: Hodder & Stoughton, 1918).
Heuser, Beatrice. *The Evolution of Strategy: Thinking War from Antiquity to the Present* (Cambridge: CUP, 2010).
Hattendorf, John B. *England in the War of the Spanish Succession: A Study of the English View and Conduct of Grand Strategy, 1702–1712* (New York: Garland Publishing, 1987).
Horne, Thomas Budd Van. *The Life of Major-General George H. Thomas* (New York: Charles Scribner's Sons, 1882).
House of Commons Public Administration Select Committee. *Who Does UK National Strategy? First Report of Session 2010–11* (London: The Stationery Office, 2010).
Howard, Michael. *Grand Strategy, iv. August 1942–September 1943* (London, Her Majesty's Stationery Office, 1972).
Howard, Michael. *The Causes of War and Other Essays* (Cambridge, MA: Harvard UP, 1983).
Hurley, Alfred F. *Billy Mitchell: Crusader for Air Power* (Bloomington, IN: Indiana UP, 1975).
Ikenberry, G. John. *Liberal Order and Imperial Ambition: Essays on American Power and World Politics* (Cambridge: Polity, 2006).
Iklé, Fred Charles, and Albert Wohlstetter. *Discriminate Deterrence: The Commission on Integrated Long-Term Strategy* (Washington DC: US Government Printing Office, 1988).

James, Charles. *A New and Enlarged Military Dictionary, or, Alphabetical Explanation of Technical Terms* (London: The Military Library, 1805).
Johnston, Alastair Iain. *Cultural Realism: Strategic Culture and Grand Strategy in Chinese History* (Princeton: Princeton UP, 1995).
Jomini, Baron de. *The Art of War*, tr. G. H. Mendell and W. P. Craighill (Westport, CT: Greenwood Press, 1862).
Kahn, Herman. *Thinking about the Unthinkable* (New York: Horizon Press, 1962).
Kahn, Herman. *On Escalation: Metaphors and Scenarios* (New York: Frederick A. Praeger, 1965).
Kahn, Herman. *On Thermonuclear War* (Westport, CT: Greenwood Press, 1969).
Karsten, Peter. *The Naval Aristocracy: The Golden Age of Annapolis and the Emergence of Modern American Navalism* (New York: Free Press, 1972).
Kennan, George F. *Realities of American Foreign Policy* (London: OUP, 1954).
Kennan, George F. *American Diplomacy* (Chicago: University of Chicago Press, 1984).
Kennedy, Paul M. *The Rise and Fall of the Great Powers: Economic Change and Military Conflict from 1500 to 2000* (New York: Vintage Books, 1989).
Kintner, William R., and Joseph Z. Kornfeder. *The New Frontier of War: Political Warfare, Present and Future* (Chicago: Henry Regnery Co., 1962).
Kissinger, Henry. *Diplomacy* (New York: Simon & Schuster, 1994).
Kissinger, Henry A. *Nuclear Weapons and Foreign Policy* (New York: Harper & Brothers, 1957).
Kissinger, Henry A. (ed.). *Problems of National Strategy: A Book of Readings* (New York: Frederick A. Praeger, 1965).
Koselleck, Reinhart. *The Practice of Conceptual History: Timing History, Spacing Concepts*, tr. Todd Samuel Presner (Stanford, CA: Stanford UP, 2002).
Kupchan, Charles A. *The Vulnerability of Empire* (Ithaca, NY: Cornell UP, 1994).
Lambert, Andrew. *The Crimean War: British Grand Strategy Against Russia, 1853–56* (Farnham: Ashgate, 2011).
Landsberg, Helmut E. *Geophysics and Warfare* (Washington, DC: Research and Development Committee on General Sciences, 1954).
Layne, Christopher. *The Peace of Illusions: American Grand Strategy from 1940 to the Present* (Ithaca, NY: Cornell UP, 2006).
LeDonne, John P. *The Grand Strategy of the Russian Empire, 1650–1831* (Oxford: OUP, 2004).
Liddell Hart, Basil. *Paris, or the Future of War* (London: Kegan Paul, Trench, Trubner & Co., 1925).
Liddell Hart, Basil. *A Greater than Napoleon: Scipio Africanus* (London: William Blackwood & Sons, 1926).
Liddell Hart, Basil. *The Decisive Wars of History: A Study in Strategy* (London: G. Bell & Sons, 1929).
Liddell Hart, Basil. *The British Way in Warfare* (London: Faber & Faber, 1932).
Liddell Hart, Basil. *The Strategy of Indirect Approach* (London: Faber & Faber, 1941).
Liddell Hart, Basil. *Thoughts on War* (London: Faber & Faber, 1944).
Liddell Hart, Basil. *Strategy* (New York: Meridian, 1991).
Lippmann, Walter. *The Stakes of Diplomacy* (New York: Henry Holt & Co., 1917).

Luttwak, Edward N. *The Grand Strategy of the Roman Empire from the First Century A.D. to the Third* (Baltimore, MD: Johns Hopkins Press, 1976).

Luttwak, Edward N. *The Grand Strategy of the Soviet Union* (London: Weidenfeld & Nicolson, 1983).

Luttwak, Edward N. *Strategy: The Logic of War and Peace* (Cambridge, MA: Belknap Press of Harvard UP, 1987).

Luttwak, Edward N. *Strategy: The Logic of War and Peace* (Cambridge, MA: Belknap Press of Harvard UP, 2001).

Luttwak, Edward N. *The Grand Strategy of the Byzantine Empire* (Cambridge, MA: Belknap Press of Harvard UP, 2009).

Luttwak, Edward N. *The Rise of China vs. the Logic of Strategy* (Cambridge, MA: Belknap Press of Harvard UP, 2012).

McCloughry, E. J. Kingston. *The Direction of War: A Critique of the Political Direction and High Command in War* (New York: Frederick A. Praeger, 1958).

MacDonald, Brian (ed.). *The Grand Strategy of the Soviet Union* (Toronto: Canadian Institute of Strategic Studies, 1984).

McPherson, James M. *Battle Cry of Freedom: The Civil War Era* (Oxford: OUP 1988).

Mahan, Alfred Thayer. *The Influence of Sea Power upon the French Revolution and Empire 1793–1812*. 2 vols (London: Sampson Low, Marston & Co., 1892).

Mahan, Alfred Thayer. *The Interest of America in Sea Power Present and Future* (London: Sampson Low, Marston & Co., 1897).

Mahan, Alfred Thayer. *Naval Strategy Compared and Contrasted with the Principles and Practice of Military Operations on Land* (London: Sampson Low, Marston & Co., 1911).

Mahan, Alfred Thayer. *The Influence of Sea Power upon History 1660–1783* (New York: Hill & Wang, 1957).

Martel, William C. *Grand Strategy in Theory and Practice: The Need for an Effective American Foreign Policy* (New York: Cambridge UP, 2015).

Matloff, Maurice, and Edwin M. Snell. *Strategic Planning for Coalition Warfare 1941–1942* (Washington, DC: Office of the Chief of Military History, 1953).

Matloff, Maurice. *Strategic Planning for Coalition Warfare 1943–1944* (Washington, DC: Office of the Chief of Military History, 1959).

Meade, George Gordon. *The Life and Letters of George Gordon Meade*. 2 vols (New York: Charles Scribner's Sons, 1913).

Mearsheimer, John J. *Liddell Hart and the Weight of History* (Ithaca, NY: Cornell UP, 1988).

Meyers, George J. *Strategy* (Washington, DC: Byron S. Adams, 1928).

Miller, Edward S. *War Plan Orange* (Annapolis: Naval Institute Press, 1991).

Milward, Alan S. *War, Economy and Society, 1939–1945* (London: Allen Lane, 1977).

Mitchell, William. *Winged Defense: The Development and Possibilities of Modern Air Power—Economic and Military* (New York: G. P. Putnam's Sons, 1925).

Narizny, Kevin. *The Political Economy of Grand Strategy* (Ithaca, NY: Cornell UP, 2007).

Naval War College, *Required Readings in National Strategy* (Newport, RI: Naval War College, 1970).

Nichols, George Ward. *The Story of the Great March: From the Diary of a Staff Officer* (New York: Harper & Brothers, 1865).

Nordlinger, Eric A. *Isolationism Reconfigured: American Foreign Policy for a New Century* (Princeton: Princeton UP, 1995).
Olsen, John Andreas. *John Warden and the Renaissance of American Air Power* (Washington, DC: Potomac Books, 2007).
Oman, Charles. *A History of the Art of War in the Middle Ages* (London: Meuthen & Co., 1978).
Osgood, Robert E. *Limited War: The Challenge to American Strategy* (Chicago: University of Chicago Press, 1957).
Osgood, Robert E. *Limited War Revisited* (Boulder, CO: Westview Press, 1979).
Osinga, Frans P. B. *Science, Strategy and War: The Strategic Theory of John Boyd* (London: Routledge, 2007).
Parker, Geoffrey. *Geopolitics: Past, Present and Future* (London: Pinter, 1998).
Parker, Geoffrey. *The Grand Strategy of Philip II* (New Haven: Yale UP, 1998).
Patton, Cornelius H. *The Lure of Africa* (New York: Missionary Education Movement of the United States and Canada, 1917).
Patten, William. *The Grand Strategy of Evolution: The Social Philosophy of a Biologist* (Boston: Gorham Press, 1920).
Pearson, Lester B. *Diplomacy in the Nuclear Age* (Cambridge, MA: Harvard UP, 1959).
Pence, Owen E. *Present-Day Y.M.C.A.–Church Relations in the United States: A Diagnostic Report* (New York: Association Press, 1948).
Pettit, James S. *Elements of Military Science: For the Use of Students in Colleges and Universities* (New Haven: The Tuttle, Morehouse & Taylor Press, 1895).
Platias, Athanassios G., and Constantinos Koliopoulos. *Thucydides on Strategy: Grand Strategies in the Peloponnesian War and their Relevance Today* (New York: Columbia UP, 2010).
Pollard, Edward A. *Southern History of the War: The Third Year of the War* (New York: Charles B. Richardson, 1865).
Posen, Barry R. *The Sources of Military Doctrine: France, Britain, and Germany between the World Wars* (Ithaca, NY: Cornell UP, 1984).
Quester, George H. *Deterrence Before Hiroshima: The Airpower Background of Modern Strategy* (New Brunswick, NJ: Transaction Books, 1986).
Reid, Brian Holden. *J. F. C. Fuller: Military Thinker* (London: Macmillan, 1987).
Reid, Brian Holden. *Studies in British Military Thought: Debates with Fuller and Liddell Hart* (Lincoln, NE: University of Nebraska Press, 1998).
Robinson, Oliver Prescott. *The Fundamentals of Military Strategy* (Washington, DC: United States Infantry Association, 1928).
Røksund, Arne. *The Jeune École: The Strategy of the Weak* (Leiden: Brill, 2007).
Rosencrance, Richard, and Arthur A. Stein (eds). *The Domestic Bases of Grand Strategy* (Ithaca, NY: Cornell UP, 1993).
Sapin, Burton M., and Richard C. Snyder. *The Role of the Military in American Foreign Policy* (Garden City, NY: Doubleday & Co., 1954).
Sargeaunt, Henry Antony, and Geoffrey West. *Grand Strategy* (New York: Thomas Y. Crowell Co., 1941).
Schelling, Thomas C. *The Strategy of Conflict* (New York: OUP, 1963).
Schelling, Thomas C. *Arms and Influence* (New Haven: Yale UP, 1967).

Schurman, Donald M. *The Education of a Navy: The Development of British Naval Strategic Thought, 1867–1914* (London: Cassell, 1965).

Schurman, Donald M. *Julian S. Corbett, 1854–1922: Historian of British Maritime Policy from Drake to Jellicoe* (London: Royal Historical Society, 1981).

Seager II, Robert, and Doris D. Maguire (eds). *Letters and Papers of Alfred Thayer Mahan*. 3 vols (Annapolis: Naval Institute Press, 1975).

Seversky, Alexander P. de. *Victory through Air Power* (New York: Simon & Schuster, 1942).

Sloan, Geoffrey R. *Geopolitics in United States Strategic Policy, 1890–1987* (Brighton: Wheatsheaf Books, 1988).

Snyder, Jack L. *The Soviet Strategic Culture: Implications for Limited Nuclear Operations* (Santa Monica, CA: RAND, 1977).

Spykman, Nicholas J. *America's Strategy in World Politics: The United States and the Balance of Power* (New Brunswick, NJ: Transaction Publishers, 2008).

Steiner, Barry H. *Bernard Brodie and the Foundations of American Nuclear Strategy* (Lawrence, KS: UP of Kansas, 1991).

Stennis, John, and Special Preparedness Subcommittee, United States Senate. *Military Cold War Education and Speech Review Policies* (Washington, DC: Government Printing Office, 1962).

Strachan, Hew. *The Direction of War: Contemporary Strategy in Historical Perspective* (Cambridge: CUP, 2013).

Sumida, Jon Tetsuro. *Inventing Grand Strategy and Teaching Command: The Classic Works of Alfred Thayer Mahan Reconsidered* (Washington, DC: Woodrow Wilson Center Press, 1997).

Supplemental Report of the Joint Committee on the Conduct of the War, in Two Volumes (Washington, DC: Government Printing Office, 1866).

Swinton, William. *The Twelve Decisive Battles of the War: A History of the Eastern and Western Campaigns, in Relation to the Actions that Decided their Issue* (New York: Dick & Fitzgerald, 1867).

Taylor, Maxwell D. *The Uncertain Trumpet* (New York: Harper & Brothers, 1960).

Thursfield, James R. *Nelson and Other Naval Studies* (New York: E. P. Dutton & Co., 1920).

Trythall, Anthony John. *'Boney' Fuller: The Intellectual General 1878–1966* (London: Cassell, 1977).

United States Congress. *Investigation of the War Department: Hearings before the Committee on Military Affairs, United States Senate, Sixty-Fifth Congress, Second Session…1918* (Washington, DC: Government Printing Office 1918).

United States Department of Defense. *Semiannual Report of the Secretary of Defense and the Semiannual Reports of the Secretary of the Army, Secretary of the Navy, Secretary of the Air Force, January 1 to June 31, 1954* (Washington, DC: Government Printing Office, 1955).

United States Department of Defense. *Statements by Secretaries and Chiefs of Staff before Congressional Committees, 1955* (Washington, DC: Government Printing Office, 1955).

United States Department of Defense. *Joint Publication 1-02: Department of Defense Dictionary of Military and Associated Terms* (Washington, DC: Department of Defense, 2015).

United States Department of the Air Force. *Air Force Manual 11-1: Glossary of Standardized Terms* (Washington, DC: Department of the Air Force 1961).

United States House of Representatives. *Extension of Lend-Lease Act: Hearings Before the Committee on Foreign Affairs, House of Representatives* (Washington, DC: Government Printing Office, 1943).

United States House of Representatives. *Hearings Before the Committee on Naval Affairs of the House of Representatives on Estimates Submitted by the Secretary of the Navy, 1915* (Washington, DC: Government Printing Office, 1915).

United States Senate. *National Defense Establishment (Unification of the Armed Services), Hearings before the Committee on Armed Services, United States Senate* (Washington, DC: Government Printing Office, 1947).

Ward, James H. *A Manual of Naval Tactics: Together with a Brief Critical Analysis of the Principal Modern Naval Battles* (New York: D. Appleton & Co., 1859).

Warden III, John A. *The Air Campaign: Planning for Combat* (Lincoln, NE: toExcel, 2000).

Wedemeyer, Albert C. *Wedemeyer Reports!* (New York: Henry Holt & Co., 1958).

Weigley, Russell F. *The American Way of War: A History of United States Military Strategy and Policy* (Bloomington, IN: Indiana UP, 1973).

Widén, J. J. *Theorist of Maritime Strategy: Sir Julian Corbett and his Contribution to Military and Naval Thought* (London: Ashgate, 2012).

Williamson, Jr, Samuel R. *The Politics of Grand Strategy: Britain and France Prepare for War, 1904-1914* (Cambridge, MA: Harvard UP, 1969).

Wright, Quincy. *A Study of War*. 2 vols (Chicago: University of Chicago Press, 1942).

Wyeth, John Allan. *That Devil Forrest: Life of General Nathan Bedford Forrest* (New York: Harper & Brothers, 1959).

Articles & Chapters

Ambrose, Stephen E. 'Grand Strategy of World War II', *Naval War College Review* 22/8 (Apr. 1970), 20-8.

Amin, Samir. 'Democracy and National Strategy in the Periphery', *Third World Quarterly* 9/4 (Oct. 1987), 1129-56.

Apt, Benjamin L. 'Mahan's Forebears: The Debate over Maritime Strategy, 1868-1883', *Naval War College Review* 50/3 (Summer 1997), 86-111.

Aron, Raymond. 'The Evolution of Modern Strategic Thought', in Alastair Buchan (ed.), *Problems of Modern Strategy: Part One*, Adelphi Paper 54 (London: IISS, 1969), 1-17.

Austin, Bernard L. 'Military Considerations in National Strategy', *Naval War College Review* 16/4 (Dec. 1963), 1-15.

Baker, Ray Stannard. 'The Valley that Found itself', *The World's Work* 31/6 (Apr. 1916), 681-5.

Baracuhy, Braz. 'The Art of Grand Strategy', *Survival* 53/1 (Feb.—Mar. 2011), 147-52.

Bellows, Henry Adams. 'Notes of an Amateur Strategist', *The Bellman* 23 (1917), 578-80.

Black, Jeremy. 'Strategic Culture and the Seven Years' War', in Williamson Murray, Richard Hart Sinnreich, and James Lacey (eds), *The Shaping of Grand Strategy: Policy, Diplomacy, and War* (Cambridge: CUP, 2011), 63-78.

Booth, Ken. 'The Evolution of Strategic Thinking', in John Baylis, Ken Booth, John Garnett, and Phil Williams. *Contemporary Strategy: Theories and Policies* (New York: Holmes & Meier Publishers, 1975), 22–49.

Brodie, Bernard. 'Strategy Hits a Dead End', *Harper's Magazine* 211/1265 (1955), 33–7.

Brodie, Bernard. 'The Anatomy of Deterrence', *World Politics* 11/2 (Jan. 1959), 173–91.

Brown, Seyom. 'An End to Grand Strategy', *Foreign Policy* 32 (Autumn 1978), 22–46.

Buzzell, Harold O. 'A New National Strategy to Make Health Services Flexible and Responsive', *Health Services Reports* 88/10 (Dec. 1973), 894–7.

Campbell, John C. 'Review of *Grand Strategy*', *Military Affairs* 6/1 (Spring 1942), 40–1.

Chace, James. 'A New Grand Strategy', *Foreign Policy* 70 (Spring 1988), 3–25.

Chipman, John. 'The Future of Strategic Studies: Beyond Even Grand Strategy', *Survival* 34/1 (1992), 109–31.

Crowl, Philip A. 'Alfred Thayer Mahan: The Naval Historian', in Peter Paret (ed.), *Makers of Modern Strategy: From Machiavelli to the Nuclear Age* (Oxford: Clarendon Press, 1986), 444–77.

Daniel, John W. 'The Great March', *Debow's Review, Agricultural, Commercial, Industrial Progress and Resources* 5/4 (Apr. 1868), 337–46.

Dapont, Durant. 'New Orleans and Ship Island Ship Canal', *Debow's Review, Agricultural, Commercial, Industrial Progress and Resources* 6/1 (Jan. 1869), 21–9.

Drezner, Daniel W. 'Does Obama Have a Grand Strategy? Why We Need Doctrines in Uncertain Times', *Foreign Affairs* 90/4 (July/Aug. 2011), 57–68.

Dueck, Colin. 'Ideas and Alternatives in American Grand Strategy, 2000–2004', *Review of International Studies* 30/4 (2004), 511–35.

Dueck, Colin. 'Realism, Culture and Grand Strategy: Explaining America's Peculiar Path to World Power', *Security Studies* 14/2 (2005), 195–231.

Earle, Edward Mead. 'American Military Policy and National Security', *Political Science Quarterly* 53/1 (Mar. 1938), 1–13.

Earle, Edward Mead. 'Political and Military Strategy for the United States', *Proceedings of the Academy of Political Science* 19/2, The Defense of the United States (Jan. 1941), 2–9.

Earle, Edward Mead. 'Introduction', in Edward Mead Earle (ed.), *Makers of Modern Strategy: Military Thought from Machiavelli to Hitler* (New York: Atheneum, 1966), pp. vii–xi.

Ekbladh, David. 'Present at the Creation: Edward Mead Earle and the Depression-Era Origins of Security Studies', *International Security* 36/3 (Winter 2011–12), 107–41.

Elkus, Adam. 'Must American Strategy Be Grand?', *Infinity Journal* 3/1 (Winter 2012), 24–8.

Fincher, Cameron. 'Grand Strategy and the Failure of Consensus', *Educational Record* 56 (1975), 10–20.

Fincher, Cameron. 'The Return of Grand Strategy', *Research in Higher Education* 19/1 (1983), 125–8.

Forbes, Archibald. 'Abraham Lincoln as a Strategist, Part 1', *North American Review* 155/428 (July 1892), 53–69.

Foster, Gregory D. 'Missing and Wanted: A U.S. Grand Strategy', *Strategic Review* 13 (Autumn 1985), 13–23.

Freedman, Lawrence. 'Has Strategy Reached a Dead-End?', *Futures* 11/2 (Apr. 1979), 122–31.
Freedman, Lawrence. 'Strategic Studies and the Problem of Power', in Lawrence Freedman, Paul Hayes, and Robert O'Neill. *War, Strategy, and International Politics: Essays in Honour of Sir Michael Howard* (Oxford: Clarendon Press 1992), 279–94.
Frost, Holloway Halstead. 'Our Heritage from Paul Jones', *Naval Institute Proceedings* 44/188 (Oct. 1918), 2275–96.
Frost, Holloway Halstead. 'National Strategy', *Proceedings* 51/8 (Aug. 1925), 1343–90.
Gaddis, John Lewis. 'Containment and the Logic of Strategy', *The National Interest* (Winter 1987–8), 27–38.
Gaddis, John Lewis. 'Interview: John Lewis Gaddis', Public Broadcasting Service *Frontline*, 13 Jan. 2003, <http://www.pbs.org/wgbh/pages/frontline/shows/iraq/interviews/gaddis.html>, accessed Aug. 2012.
Garnett, John. 'Limited "Conventional" War in the Nuclear Age', in Michael Howard (ed.), *Restraints on War: Studies in the Limitation of Armed Conflict* (Oxford: OUP, 1979), 79–102.
Garnett, John. 'Herman Kahn', in John Baylis and John Garnett. *Makers of Nuclear Strategy* (London: Pinter Publishers, 1991), 70–97.
Gewirtz, Paul. 'On "I Know It When I See it"', *Yale Law Journal* 105/4 (Jan. 1996), 1023–47.
Gibbs, David. 'Does the USSR Have a "Grand Strategy"? Reinterpreting the Invasion of Afghanistan', *Journal of Peace Research* 24/4 (Dec. 1987), 365–79.
Glaser, Elisabeth. 'Better Late than Never: The American Economic War Effort, 1917–1918', in Roger Chickering and Stig Förster (eds), *Great War, Total War: Combat and Mobilization on the Western Front, 1914–1918* (Cambridge: CUP, 2000), 389–407.
Gooch, John. 'The Weary Titan: Strategy and Policy in Great Britain, 1890–1918', in Williamson Murray, MacGregor Knox, and Alvin Bernstein (eds), *The Making of Strategy: Rulers, States, and War* (Cambridge: CUP, 1994), 278–306.
Gray, Colin S. 'National Style in Strategy: The American Example', *International Security* 6/2 (Autumn 1981), 21–47.
Gray, Colin S. 'Approaching the Study of Strategy', in Ralph Rotte and Christoph Schwarz (eds), *International Security and War: Politics and Grand Strategy in the 21st Century* (New York: Nova, 2011), 11–22.
Gray, Colin S. 'The Strategic Anthropologist', *International Affairs* 89/5 (2013), 1285–95.
Greiner, Bernd. '"The Study of the Distant Past is Futile": American Reflections on New Military Frontiers', in Roger Chickering and Stig Förster (eds), *The Shadows of Total War: Europe, East Asia, and the United States, 1919–1939* (Cambridge: CUP 2003), 239–51.
Grenville, J. A. S. 'Diplomacy and War Plans in the United States, 1890–1917', in Paul M. Kennedy (ed.). *The War Plans of the Great Powers, 1880–1914* (London: George Allen & Unwin, 1979), 23–38.
Grygiel, Jakub. 'Educating for National Security', *Orbis* 57/2 (2013), 201–16.
Hamilton, John. 'Reviews and Exchanges: History of the Mexican War', *Journal of the Military Service Institution of the United States*, 14 (1893), 198–200.

Hamilton, John. 'Reviews and Exchanges: The Story of the Civil War', *Journal of the Military Service Institution of the United States*, 17 (July–Dec. 1895), 189–95.

Herriot, F. J. 'The Germans of Iowa and the "Two-Year" Amendment of Massachusetts', *Deutsch-Amerikanische Geschichtsblätter (German-American Historical Review)* 13 (1913), 202–308.

Hershberg, James G. 'Crisis Years, 1958–1963', in Odd Arne Westad. *Reviewing the Cold War: Approaches, Interpretations, Theory* (London: Frank Cass, 2001), 303–25.

Heuser, Beatrice. 'Victory in a Nuclear War? A Comparison of NATO and WTO War Aims and Strategies', *Contemporary European History* 7/3 (Nov. 1998), 311–27.

Heuser, Beatrice. 'Strategy Before the Word: Ancient Wisdom for the Modern World', *RUSI Journal* 155/1 (Feb./Mar. 2010), 36–42.

Hitt, Michael A., R. Duane Ireland, and K. A. Palia. 'Industrial Firms' Grand Strategy and Functional Importance: Moderating Effects of Technology and Uncertainty', *Academy of Management Journal* 25/2 (June 1982), 265–98.

Hitt, Michael A., R. Duane Ireland, and Gregory Stadter. 'Functional Importance and Company Performance: Moderating Effects of Grand Strategy and Industry Type', *Strategic Management Journal* 3/4 (Oct.–Dec. 1982), 315–30.

Hood, John. 'Naval Policy; as it Relates to the Shore Establishment, and the Maintenance of the Fleet', *Naval Institute Proceedings* 40/2 (Mar.—Apr. 1914), 319–44.

Howard, Michael. '*Temperamenta Belli*: Can War be Controlled?', in Michael Howard (ed.), *Restraints on War: Studies in the Limitation of Armed Conflict* (Oxford: OUP, 1979), 1–16.

Howard, Michael. 'The Use and Abuse of Military History', *Parameters* 11/1 (Mar. 1981), 9–14.

Howard, Michael. 'Grand Strategy in the Twentieth Century', *Defence Studies* 1/1 (Spring 2001), 1–10.

Iklé, Fred Charles, and Terumasa Nakanishi. 'Japan's Grand Strategy', *Foreign Affairs* 69/3 (Summer 1990), 81–95.

Johnson, Richard Mentor. 'Statement of the History and Importance of the Military Academy at West Point, New York, and Reasons Why it Should Not Be Abolished', *American State Papers, 1789–1838*, Military Affairs vol. 5. 1832–1836, 347–55.

Jones, Stephen B. 'The Power Inventory and National Strategy', *World Politics* 6/4 (July 1954), 421–52.

Kaufmann, William W. 'Limited Warfare', in William W. Kaufmann (ed.), *Military Policy and National Security* (Princeton: Princeton UP, 1956), 102–36.

Kennedy, Paul. 'Not So Grand Strategy', *New York Review of Books* 35/8 (12 May 1988), 5–8.

Kennedy, Paul. 'Grand Strategy in War and Peace: Toward a Broader Definition', in Paul M. Kennedy (ed.), *Grand Strategies in War and Peace* (New Haven: Yale UP, 1991), 1–7.

Kennedy, Paul. 'Grand Strategies and Less-than-Grand Strategies: A Twentieth-Century Critique', in Lawrence Freedman, Paul Hayes, and Robert O'Neill, *War, Strategy, and International Politics: Essays in Honour of Sir Michael Howard* (Oxford: Clarendon Press, 1992), 227–42.

Kennedy, Paul M. 'Strategy versus Finance in Twentieth-Century Great Britain', *International History Review* 3/1 (Jan. 1981), 44–61.

Killian, Jr, James R. 'The Shortage Re-Examined: Some Elements of a Grand Strategy for Augmenting our Scientific and Engineering Manpower Resources', *American Scientist* 44/2 (Apr. 1956), 115–29.

Lambert, Andrew. 'The Naval War Course, *Some Principles of Maritime Strategy* and the Origins of the "British Way in Warfare"', in Keith Neilson and Greg Kennedy (eds), *The British Way in Warfare: Power and the International System, 1856–1956: Essays in Honour of David French* (Farnham: Ashgate 2010), 219–56.

Lasswell, Harold D. 'Political Factors in the Formulation of Strategy', *Naval War College Review* 4/10 (June 1952), 49–64.

Layton, Peter. 'Grand Strategy? What does that do for me?' The Australia Strategic Policy Institute Blog, 23 July 2012, <http://www.aspistrategist.org.au/grand-strategy-what-does-that-do-for-me>, accessed Aug. 2012.

Layton, Peter. 'The Idea of Grand Strategy', *RUSI Journal* 157/4 (Aug./Sept. 2012), 56–61.

Liddell Hart, Basil. 'Economic Pressure or Continental Victories', *RUSI Journal* 76/503 (Aug. 1931), 486–510.

Lombardi, Ben. 'Assumptions and Grand Strategy', *Parameters* 41/1 (Spring 2011), 29–40.

Lowry, Charles Wesley. 'Moral Factors of National Strategy', *Naval War College Review* 8/1 (Sept. 1955), 33–58.

Luttwak, Edward. 'Take Me Back to Constantinople: How Byzantium, Not Rome, Can Help Preserve Pax Americana', *Foreign Policy*, 19 Oct. 2009, <http://www.foreignpolicy.com/articles/2009/10/19/take_me_back_to_constantinople>, accessed Feb. 2014.

Luttwak, Edward N. 'On the Meaning of Strategy...For the United States in the 1980s', in W. Scott Thompson (ed.), *National Security in the 1980s: From Weakness to Strength* (San Francisco: Institute for Contemporary Studies, 1980), 259–73.

Luttwak, Edward N. 'The Operational Level of War', *International Security* 5/3 (Winter 1980–1), 61–79.

McConnell, Frank J. 'The Function of the University in the Present Intellectual Conflict', *Bostonia* 3/2 (July 1902), 11–15.

MacIsaac, David. 'The Evolution of Air Power', in Lawrence Freedman (ed.), *War* (Oxford: OUP, 1994), 288–91.

Mackinder, Halford J. 'The Round World and the Winning of the Peace', *Foreign Affairs* 21/4 (July 1943), 595–605.

Martel, William C. 'Grand Strategy of "Restrainment"', *Orbis* 54/3 (Summer 2010), 356–73.

Meilinger, Phillip S. 'Proselytiser and Prophet: Alexander P. de Seversky and American Airpower', in John Gooch (ed.), *Airpower: Theory and Practice* (London: Frank Cass, 1995), 7–35.

Metz, Steven. 'Eisenhower and the Planning of American Grand Strategy', *Journal of Strategic Studies* 14/1 (1991), 49–71.

Mitchell, Wesley, C., et al. 'Academy at West Point', *American Quarterly Review* 16/32 (December 1834), 358–75.

Molineux, General E. L. 'Riots in Cities and their Suppression', *Journal of the Military Service Institution of the United States*, 4 (Mar.–Dec. 1883), 335–70.

Mott, John R. 'Response to the Address of Welcome', *Christian Work in Latin America*, 3 (New York: The Missionary Education Movement, 1917), 273–7.

Murray, Williamson. 'Thoughts on Grand Strategy', in Williamson Murray, Richard Hart Sinnreich, and James Lacey (eds). *The Shaping of Grand Strategy: Policy, Diplomacy, and War* (Cambridge: CUP, 2011), 1–33.

Nichols, George Ward. 'How Fort M'Allister was Taken', *Harper's New Monthly Magazine* 37/219 (Aug. 1868), 368–70.

Nourse, Henry S. 'The Burning of Columbia, S.C., February 17, 1865', *Papers of the Military Historical Society of Massachussets* 9 (1912), 417–47.

Overy, Richard J. 'Air Power and the Origins of Deterrence Theory before 1939', *Journal of Strategic Studies* 15/1 (Mar. 1992), 73–101.

Pearce II, John A., D. Keith Robbins, and Richard B. Robinson, Jr. 'The Impact of Grand Strategy and Planning Formality on Financial Performance', *Strategic Management Journal* 8/2 (Mar.–Apr. 1987), 125–34.

Porter, Patrick. 'Beyond the American Century: Walter Lippmann and American Grand Strategy, 1943–1950', *Diplomacy and Statecraft* 22/4 (2011), 557–77.

Posen, Barry R. 'Measuring the European Conventional Balance: Coping with Complexity in Threat Assessment', *International Security* 9/3 (Winter 1984–5), 47–88.

Posen, Barry R. 'Is NATO Decisively Outnumbered?', *International Security* 12/4 (Spring 1988), 186–202.

Posen, Barry R. 'The Struggle Against Terrorism: Grand Strategy, Strategy, and Tactics', *International Security* 26/3 (Winter 2001–2), 39–55.

Posen, Barry R., and Andrew L. Ross. 'Competing Visions for U.S. Grand Strategy'. *International Security* 21/3 (Winter 1996–7), 5–53.

Quick, Herbert. 'Inland Waterways', *The Reader: An Illustrated Monthly Magazine* 11/2 (Jan. 1908), 119–34.

Richmond, Herbert W. 'Considerations of the War at Sea', *Naval Review* 5 (1917), 7–41.

Robinett, Paul M. 'Grand Strategy and the American People', *Military Affairs* 16/1 (Spring 1952), 30–4.

Rosenberg, David Alan. 'American Atomic Strategy and the Hydrogen Bomb Decision', *Journal of American History* 66/1 (June 1979), 62–87.

Rosenberg, David Alan. 'The Origins of Overkill: Nuclear Weapons and American Strategy, 1945–1960', *International Security* 7/4 (Spring 1983), 3–71.

Sanders, Jerry W., and Sherle R. Schwenninger. 'The Democrats and a New Grand Strategy, Part II', *World Policy Journal* 4/1 (Winter 1986–7), 1–50.

Schelling, Thomas C. 'Bernard Brodie (1910–1978)', *International Security* 3/3 (Winter 1978–9), 2–3.

Schreiner, T. L. 'Some Ideas of a South African about the War', *RUSI Journal* 45/282 (1901), 1075–1119.

Schwenninger, Sherle R., and Jerry W. Sanders. 'The Democrats and a New Grand Strategy', *World Policy Journal* 3/3 (Summer 1986), 369–418.

Sherman, William T. 'Address to the Graduating Class of the Michigan Military Academy', Michigan Military Academy, Orchard Lake, Michigan, 19 June 1879.

Sherman, William T. 'Address of General W. T. Sherman to the Society of the Army of the Tennessee', in *Report of the Proceedings of the Society of the Army of the*

Tennessee at the Twentieth Meeting, held at Detroit, Mich., September 14th and 15th, 1887 (Cincinnati: Press of F.W. Freeman, 1888).

Sherman, William T. 'The Grand Strategy of the War of the Rebellion', *The Century* 35/4 (Feb. 1888), 582-98.

Sinnreich, Richard Hart. 'About Turn: British Strategic Transformation from Salisbury to Grey' in Williamson Murray, Richard Hart Sinnreich, and James Lacey (eds), *The Shaping of Grand Strategy: Policy, Diplomacy, and War* (Cambridge: CUP, 2011), 111-46.

Snyder, Jack. 'The Concept of Strategic Culture: Caveat Emptor', in Carl G. Jacobsen (ed.), *Strategic Power: USA/USSR* (Houndmills: Macmillan, 1990), 3-9.

Strachan, Hew. '"The Real War": Liddell Hart, Cruttwell, and Falls', in Brian Bond (ed.), *The First World War and British Military History* (Oxford: Clarendon Press, 1991), 41-68.

Strachan, Hew. 'The Lost Meaning of Strategy', *Survival* 47/3 (July 2005), 33-54.

Strachan, Hew. 'Strategy and Contingency', *International Affairs* 87/6 (Nov. 2011), 1281-96.

Trachtenberg, Marc. 'Making Grand Strategy: The Early Cold War Experience in Retrospect', *SAIS Review* 19/1 (Winter/Spring 1999), 33-40.

United States Congress, Joint Committee on the Conduct of the War. 'Discussion: The Bases of an American Defense Policy: Armed Forces', *Proceedings of the Academy of Political Science* 19/2: The Defense of the United States (January 1941), 49-57.

Walt, Stephen M. 'The Case for Finite Containment: Analyzing U.S. Grand Strategy', *International Security* 14/1 (Summer 1989), 5-49.

Weinberg, Gerhard L. 'The Politics of War and Peace in the 1920s and 1930s', in Roger Chickering and Stig Förster (eds), *The Shadows of Total War: Europe, East Asia, and the United States, 1919-1939* (Cambridge: CUP, 2003), 23-34.

Wolseley, K. P. 'An English View of the Civil War, VI', *North American Review* 149/396 (Nov. 1889), 594-607.

Zalinski, E. L. 'The Army Organization, Best Adapted to a Republican Form of Government, Which Will Insure an Effective Force', *Journal of the Military Service Institution of the United States*, 14 (1893), 926-77.

Index

air power
 impact on grand strategy theories 76–7
 importance in Cold War strategies 83–4
alliances 114–15
American Civil War 17–19, 21–3, 24, 25, 48, 62, 64, 151
American Political Science Association (APSA) 78–9
American War of Independence 62
Art, Robert 1, 128, 135–6, 141
Australia, strategic thinking in 140

Baldwin, Hanson 78–9
Belisarius (Byzantine general) 55
Bigelow, John 23
blockade, use of 49–50
Boer War 46
Booth, Ken 109
Borden, William Liscum 88
Boyd, John 101
Brands, Hal 139–40
Brodie, Bernard 7, 79, 85, 87, 88, 90, 95, 105–6, 122
 Seapower in the Machine Age 79
Buell, Augustus C. 17
business, strategy of 124
Byzantine Empire 15, 55, 136–8, 145

Canada
 English/French over 38–9
 US plans for hostilities with 64
Carney, Robert B, Admiral 99
Casablanca Conference (1943) 68
Castex, Raoul, Admiral 28, 70
Center for a New American Security 130
Central Europe, as (potential) locus of conflicts
 French focus on 72, 120
 US focus on 94, 109, 114
Chamberlain, Joseph 42
Chamberlain, Neville 52
Chandler, Alfred D., Jr. 102
China
 historical commentaries 137–8
 US relations with 92, 110, 132, 134
Christensen, Thomas J. 132
Christianity *see* missionaries
Clausewitz, Carl von 17, 19, 21, 145–6, 149
 influence on later writers 22–3, 38, 43, 48, 77–8, 117, 146
 objections to 20, 112, 116
 twentieth-century commentaries 70, 71, 86
Cold War 2, 10, 36, 58, 80, 81, 83–5, 92, 97–107
 aftermath 126, 127–8, 129–31, 141
 crisis points 96
 deterrence theory 84–5
 end 81, 84–5, 96, 122, 126
 fears of mutual destruction 94–5
 impact on grand strategy theory/ terminology 97–8, 103, 106–7
Collins, John M. 108, 116, 125, 144
 Grand Strategy: Principles and Practices 111–12
Colomb, Sir John 37
Colomb, Phillip, Vice-Admiral 37
colonies, naval attacks on 33
commerce, relationship with war/ strategy 32–4, 32–5
conceptual history 8
Corbett, Sir Julian Stafford 5–6, 9, 13, 27, 29–30, 37–43, 89, 97, 100, 106
 England in the Mediterranean 37–8, 41
 Some Principles of Maritime Strategy 37, 43, 144–5
 The Successors of Drake 37
 on British geopolitical/strategic situation 41–3
 compared with American theorists 91–3
 influence on later writers 43–4, 45, 54, 60, 122
 integration of naval with other strategies 39–41
Crimean War 131–2
Crusades 25
Cuba, US plans for hostilities with 64, 74

determinism 31
deterrence 54–5, 57
 Cold War 84–5
 hegemony in strategic studies 84–5
diplomacy, interaction with grand strategy 40, 70, 114–16, 137

Earle, Edward Mead 6, 7, 13, 61, 71–3, 78–9, 80, 89, 105, 144, 145, 147
 The Makers of Modern Strategy 30, 78

Earle, Edward Mead (*cont.*)
  'Memorandum Regarding the Term "Strategy"' 71
  central place in strategic studies 4–5, 10, 65, 68–9
  definition of grand strategy 4–5, 69, 87, 103–4, 106, 111, 113–14, 116, 118, 120, 130
education, strategy of 124
Eggleston, George Cary, *The Master of Warlock* 151
evolutionary theory, grand strategy related to 64

First World War 49–50, 55
  impact on strategic thinking 46–7, 60, 67, 69–70
foreign policy
  distinguished from grand strategy 72
  influence of war on 72–3
Foster, George 140
Foster, Gregory D. 122–3, 125, 128
France
  (alleged) policy in Central Europe 72, 120
  international conflicts 33–4, 38–9
  strategy theory in 25, 28
Freedman, Lawrence 8, 102, 109
French (language), importance in strategic writings 16–17
French Revolution 67
Frederick II 'the Great' of Prussia 40
Friedberg, Aaron L. 132
Frost, Holloway Halstead 66–8, 80, 97
  flaws in theory 67
Fuller, John Frederick Charles, Maj.-Gen. 4, 5–6, 10, 13, 45, 47–52, 66, 67, 89, 91, 144, 145
  The Foundations of the Science of War 47, 50
  'Projected Bases for the Tactical Employment of Tanks in 1918' 46
  The Reformation of War 47, 52
  'Unstrategic Bombing and World Ruin' 50
  contrasted with later writers 59, 94–5
  influence on contemporaries/later writers 52–3, 54, 58
  influences on 43–4, 60
  summary of system 51–2

Gaddis, John Lewis 1–2, 11, 84–5, 104, 122, 123, 128, 133–5, 138–9, 141, 145
Gat, Azar 20, 52
geography, relationship with strategy 24, 28–9, 31, 134–5, 150
geopolitics 109, 110

Germany
  industrial/economic expansion 42–3, 63–4
  postwar survival/development 112
Gibbon, Edward 96
grand strategy
  appropriation of term by other disciplines 124, 143–4, 146–8
  broadening of concept 28–9, 32, 48, 68, 117, 150
  constant themes 143, 150–1
  declining interest in (Cold War) 84, 97–8, 103, 106–7, 110
  definitions 16, 18–24, 25–6, 38, 47–8, 51–4, 61, 65–6, 68, 103–4, 116, 117, 118–19, 121, 122–3, 134–5, 138–40 (*see also* Earle, Edward Meade; Liddell Hart, Basil)
  differing interpretations 3–4, 5, 28–9, 91, 125, 132–3, 143, 148–50, 151–3
  distinguished from foreign policy 72
  distinguished from military strategy 112–13
  early uses of term 15–16, 17–19, 45–6
  future directions 151–3
  impact of Cold War/nuclear issues 97–8, 103, 106–7
  interaction with diplomacy 40, 70, 114–16, 137
  interaction with minor strategy 39
  limited to world powers 120
  maritime 27–44
  modern trends 1–3
  national trends in thought *see* France; United Kingdom; United States
  objections to term/theory 25, 73–7, 104–6
  objectives 38, 52–3, 56–8, 143
  official use of term 98–103
  peacetime 5, 32–3, 35–6, 47–8, 63, 70–1, 87
  re-emergence (1970s/80s) 108–11, 131
  relationship with IR theories 128–9
  relationship with political science 79
  synonyms 97–8
  unexamined problems 6–7, 143–6
grand tactics 51
Grant, Ulysses S., General 19, 20, 21, 22, 66
Gray, Colin S. 5, 77–8, 109–10, 113
  The Geopolitics of Super Power 110
Guadeloupe 33
Guibert, Jacques-Antoine-Hippolyte, comte de 15

Hamilton, Colonel 18
Hattendorf, John B. 121–2, 123, 125, 131
Heraclitus 57
Heuser, Beatrice 8
Hiroshima, bombing of 81
history, theories of 48–9

Index

Hobbes, Thomas 6
Howard, Michael 65–6, 71, 86, 90, 103

IR (international relations) theory 128–9

James, Charles, *A New and Enlarged Military Dictionary* 15–16
Japan
  economic rise 109
  US plans for hostilities with 64, 74–6
Johnson, Richard Mentor 16–17
Joly de Maïzeroy, Paul-Gédéon 15
Jomini, Antoine-Henri de, baron 17, 19–20, 21, 23, 43, 149
  influence on later thinkers 30–1, 36
Jones, John Paul, Capt. 17

Kahn, Herman 89, 95, 97–8
Kant, Immanuel 6
Kaufmann, William 85
Kennan, George F. 104–5, 106
Kennedy, Paul 1–2, 5, 11, 108, 111, 118–21, 125, 127, 128, 131, 133, 144, 145
Kersaint, Armand-Guy-Simon de Coetnempren, comte de 17
Kissinger, Henry 88, 89, 93, 109
  Problems of National Strategy 101
Korean War 90, 91, 93, 134
  sanctuaries 92
Koselleck, Reinhart 8

Lambert, Andrew 131–2
Laughton, Sir John Knox 37
Layton, Peter 139–40
LeMay, Curtis, General 84
Leo VI, Byzantine Emperor 15
Liddell Hart, Basil, Capt. 13, 20, 42, 45, 46–7, 50–1, 52–7, 67, 89
  Paris, or the Future of War 52–4
  The Strategy of Indirect Approach (The Decisive Wars of History) 54–5
  central place in strategic studies 4–5, 6–7, 10, 60, 68–9, 145
  contrasted with later writers 59, 93–4
  definition of grand strategy 4–5, 52–4, 60, 66, 103–4, 113
  influence on later writers 58, 91, 93, 103–4, 113, 120, 144–5
  influences on 43–4, 46, 52–3, 60
  theory of deterrence 54–5, 57
  wartime experiences 52, 55
limited war theory 89–94
  agreement on limitations 91–2
  impact of nuclear weaponry 90–1, 94
  naval basis 40–1
  and sanctuary 92–3

  as strategic priority 45, 51–2, 54–5, 56
Lippmann, Walter 63, 78–9
Locke, John 6
Luce, Stephen B., Admiral 31
Luttwak, Edward 1–2, 11, 108, 110, 113–16, 117, 123, 125, 131, 136–9, 141
  'Force and Diplomacy in Roman Strategies of Internal Security' 113
  The Grand Strategy of the Byzantine Empire 128, 136–8, 145
  The Grand Strategy of the Roman Empire 111, 113–15, 145
  The Grand Strategy of the Soviet Union 115
  The Rise of China vs. the Logic of Strategy 128, 137–8
  Strategy: The Logic of War and Peace 136

Maas, Melvin J., Congressman 99
Mackinder, Halford 4, 110
Mahan, Alfred Thayer 9, 27, 28, 29–37, 91, 105, 106
  The Influence of Sea Power upon History, 1660–1783 30–1
  compared with British thinkers 39, 42, 43, 45, 50
  influence on later writers 43–4, 60, 66, 69, 70, 79–80
  objectives in writing 31
  philosophical stance 31
  treatment of peacetime strategy 35–6
  treatment of war/commerce 32–6
Marshall, George C., General 98–9
Martel, William 128, 147–8
Martinique 33
Matloff, Maurice 101
Meade, George Gordon, General 19
Mearsheimer, John 55
Mexico, US plans for hostilities with 64, 74–5
Meyers, George, Capt. 69–71, 73, 80
military strategy, distinguished from grand strategy 112–13
Milward, Alan S. 111
minor strategy, links with grand 39, 150
missionaries 63, 102
Mitchell, William 'Billy,' General 76–7
mobilization, redundancy of 86
Moltke, Helmuth von 40
Montecuculi, Raimondo de 15
Murray, Williamson 132–3

Nagasaki, bombing of 81
Napoleon I, Emperor 9, 15, 17, 19, 20, 21, 34, 145
Napoleonic Wars 33–4
national strategy
  commentators' use of term 105–6

national strategy (*cont.*)
  official use of term 98–103
  as synonym for grand strategy 97–8
NATO (North Atlantic Treaty
    Organization) 86–7, 114–15
naval strategy 27–44, 60, 70–1
  breadth of definition 36
  contrasted with military 28
  core elements 32
  interaction with military 38–40
  peacetime 32–3, 35–6
  relationship with commerce 32–5
  (supposed) obsolescence 77
  see also sea power
Naval War College, Newport, RI 99–100
Navigation Acts 1660–1673 (UK) 35
Nelson, Horatio, Lord 33
Nixon, Richard M. 92, 109, 110
Nordlinger, Eric 130–1
nuclear power/strategy 77, 80, 81–96
  aftermath of use 95
  and deterrence 84–5
  domination of strategic thinking 84, 96, 97
  evolution from air power 83–4
  feared consequences of use 94–5
  impact on peacetime policies 87–9
  proposed limits on use 91–2, 96
  wholesale reconceptualization of
    strategy 86–7

Oman, Sir Charles 25, 46
Osgood, Robert E. 93, 101
Oxford English Dictionary 15

Paret, Peter 30
Parker, Geoffrey 132
peace
  as aim of war/strategy 49, 53, 56
  continuation of strategy in 69–70, 71–2, 87
  under nuclear umbrella 87–9
Pearl Harbor 134
Pearson, Lester 88
Pemberton, John C., General 21
Pitt, William 'the Elder' 39, 43
Pitt, William 'the Younger' 43
political science, relationship with military/
    grand strategy 79, 146–7
Poole, DeWitt Clinton 72
Posen, Barry 1–2, 11, 108, 111, 116–18, 125,
    127, 130, 145
Potter, Stewart, Judge 151
Puységur, Jacques de Chastenet, marquis
    de 15

RAND (Research And Development)
    Corporation 84, 85

Richmond, Herbert 46
Roberts, 1st Earl, Field-Marshal 46
Robinett, Paul 79
Roman Empire 113–15, 145
Roosevelt, Franklin D. 98–9
Roosevelt, Theodore 35
Ross, Andrew 130

sanctuary 92–3
Sargeaunt, Henry Antony 45, 47, 57–9, 60
Saxe, Maurice, Maréchal de 15
Schelling, Thomas C. 88–9, 90, 91–2
sea power
  coinage of term 29
  relationship with commerce 32–5
  relationship with politics 35–6
  role in grand strategy 30–1, 38–9
  see also naval strategy
Second World War 36, 50, 56, 65, 78, 80, 134
Seven Years War 38–9
Seversky, Alexander de 76–7
Sherman, Forrest, Admiral 99
Sherman, William T., General 18, 20, 21, 22,
    25, 45–6, 62
  'The Grand Strategy of the War of the
    Rebellion' 18–19, 24
Slessor, Sir John 84
Soady, France J., Lt.-Col. 18
social philosophy, grand strategy related to 64
Soviet Union
  collapse (1989) 84–5, 130
  plans for combat with 114
  theoretical analyses 109–10, 115
Special Plan Blue 74
Spykman, Nicholas 65, 110
Stimson, Henry L., Col. 73
Stokes, Harold 78
Strachan, Hew 2, 52, 121
strategic culture, theories of/relationship with
    grand strategy 109–10, 133
strategy, etymology of 15
Sumida, Jon Tetsuro 32

tanks, military use of 50–1, 67
Taylor, Maxwell, General 90
'theateritis' 133–4
Thomas, George, General 22–3
Thucydides 132
Thursfield, James R. 46
Trachtenberg, Marc 3, 129
Turner, Richmond Kelly, Admiral 99

United Kingdom
  approach to war 42–3, 54
  geopolitical/strategic situation 41–3, 54, 60
  historical strategies/practices 121–2, 125

Index

impact of First World War 46–7, 49, 55, 60
international conflicts 33–4, 38–9, 121–2, 125
strategic vocabulary 98
trends in strategic thought 3–4, 10, 103
US plans for hostilities with 64, 74, 76

United States
  Air Force 83–5, 100–1
  colour-coded war plans 74–6
  geopolitical supremacy 36–7, 65
  growth as world power 42–3
  impact of First World War 61, 64, 70–1
  military planning 64–5, 67–8, 74–6
  National Security Strategy (2002) 134
  nuclear strategies 81–96
  role of President 101–2
  as single superpower 129–30
  strategic vocabulary 97–8
  trends in strategic thought 2–3, 4, 10–11, 61–80, 108–13, 121–4, 131–6

Vietnam War 10–11, 83, 108, 109, 110, 111, 121, 123, 125
  expansion into Cambodia/Laos 92–3
  impact on limited war theory 91, 93, 94
  objections to 92–3, 114–15
Von der Goltz, Colmar, General 66, 97

war
  classifications 38–9
  economic implications 32–4, 46–7, 49–50
  historical theories of 48–9
  influence on foreign policy 72–3
  necessity for 51–2
  (projected) limitation *see* limited war theory
  relationship with society 57–8
  (risk of) escalation 40, 41
  role of/significance for non-participant nations 69–70
War of the Spanish Succession 121–2, 125
'War on Terror' 134
War Plan Green 74–5
War Plan Orange 74–6
War Plan Red 74, 76
War Plan Tan 74
Ward, James H., *A Manual of Naval Tactics* 17–18
Warden, John 115
Warner, Edward 78
Wedemeyer, Albert Coady 68
Weigley, Russell 23
Weinberger(-Powell) Doctrine 94
West, Geoffrey 45, 47, 57–9, 60
West Point Military Academy 16
Williamson, Samuel R., Jr., *The Politics of Grand Strategy* 110–11
Wolseley, K.P. 45–6
Wright, Quincy, *A Study of War* 78
Wyeth, John Allan 21–2, 23, 24, 77